Julien Sidney Devereux
and his
Monte Verdi
Plantation

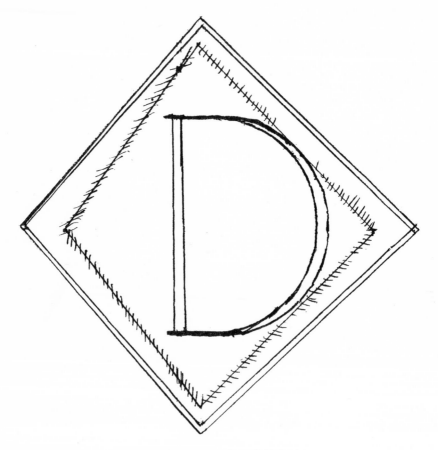

THE DEVEREUX BRAND

Recorded for Julien Sidney Devereux
on March 18, 1845,
by William H. Fowler, County Clerk
Montgomery County, Republic of Texas

Julien Sidney Devereux

and his

Monte Verdi

Plantation

by

Dorman H. Winfrey

Foreword   Introduction

by   by

H. Bailey Carroll   O. Douglas Weeks

TEXIAN PRESS ★ WACO, TEXAS

Published 1964 by

P. O. Box 1684
Waco, Texas

To Professor and Mrs. Oliver Douglas Weeks I am indebted for the use of the Devereux Papers. Mrs. Weeks, named Julien Devereux for her grandfather, and her husband were made custodians of the Devereux Family Papers when her father, William Penn Devereux, died in 1928 in Minden, Louisiana. The Weeks knew and appreciated the historical value of primary source materials, and they brought the papers to Austin and cared for and preserved the documents. For more than a decade the Weeks let me keep the Devereux Papers in my possession, and never once did they question the work I was doing or ask me to speed up my research. The Weeks were always available when I needed questions answered, and I am appreciative of the trust, faith, and patient understanding they have had during the time I have been engaged in research and writing.

Outside the Devereux Papers the only source material of major significance has been the Record of the Devereux Family and Memoirs of John William Devereux, now in the possession of Colonel Homer Garrison, Jr., of Austin. Colonel Garrison was especially kind to my wife and me and provided us with pleasant conditions in which to work while transcribing the diary.

The friendship of Mr. and Mrs. Emmett Lowry, who began restoration of the Monte Verdi Mansion House in 1959, has meant much to the Winfreys. Mrs. Lowry, whose ancestors have been closely identified with the history and development of East Texas, called me long distance when she bought the dilapidated Devereux Mansion House, and we have been in rather close contact since that time. The Winfreys have watched and admired the progress the Lowrys have made in their restoration.

During the years the writing has been underway Miss Myrtis Watkins, my former history teacher, has always been consulted for advice and suggestions. Along with her sister and brother-in-law, Mr. and Mrs. Jimmie Harris, I have "talked Devereux" for a great many hours. Miss Watkins read each chapter and made valuable suggestions. Pax and Jimmie Harris provided a good many tanks of Humble "Esso Extra" gasoline so that some necessary traveling could be done.

Mrs. Abigail Curlee Holbrook, an authority on Texas plantations, has given help and made suggestions from time to time. From her master's thesis on The History of a Texas Slave Plantation, 1831-1863, and her doctoral dissertation, A Study of Texas Slave Plantations, 1822-1865, I secured many ideas which helped me while working on Monte Verdi Plantation.

The University of Oklahoma Press and Harvard University Press granted permission for the use of the map "Principal Communities and Roads in Settled Area of Republic of Texas Based on a Map by Richard S. Hunt and Jesse F. Randel, 1845." Deep appreciation is expressed to Mr. Gail Rasco for his drawing of the "Map of Rusk County, 1850's."

A special note of thanks is extended to Mr. Jack B. Giberson and Mr. Herman H. Forbes in the General Land Office for tremendously valuable assistance in making available the information concerning Devereux's land holdings in Rusk County.

Mr. William Beare, Jr., produced the Devereux genealogical chart, and Mr. William A. Berry did the two drawings of Monte Verdi.

Mr. Fred Pentecost, Jr., and Mr. Randolph Harris took most of the photographs of the Monte Verdi Mansion House before and after restoration.

Mrs. Dick Taylor, granddaughter of Julien Sidney Devereux, graciously supplied the pictures of Sarah Ann and Julien Sidney Devereux.

The Newberry Library, Chicago, and the University of Oklahoma Press granted permission to reproduce the William Bollaert drawing of "A Texan Farm in Montgomery County."

Minister Plenipotentiaire Jean Delalande of the Ministry of Foreign Affairs of France supplied some information from French sources on the Devereux family in France and the cathedral Notre Dame d'Evreux of Evreux.

Mrs. Bessie Owen of Montgomery, Texas, has been most helpful for a number of years, for she has spent considerable time searching in the early records to gather information on Julien Devereux in Montgomery County.

Mrs. Velma Pool Capps supplied many valuable notes for the early history of the Devereux family, and Mrs. Capps copied many census records and supplied other data which saved me from going into many sources.

Mr. David Gracy, Mr. Joe Smyer, and Mr. Gail Rasco, Mr. Alwyn Barr, Mr. William K. Peace, and Mr. Paul Loftin, spent many valuable hours of their own time in helping read proof on the manuscript.

The following persons also contributed to the completion of the dissertation: Miss Winnie Allen, Professor James C. Bonner, Mr. Peter A. Brannon of the Alabama Department of Archives and History, Mrs. Mary Givens Bryan of the Georgia

Department of Archives and History, Mr. and Mrs. Archie Buckner, Ruth Lapham Butler of the Newberry Library in Chicago, Mrs. Nita Byrd, Mrs. C. E. Carlock, Mr. Homer E. Davis, Mr. James M. Day, Dr. Llerena Friend, Mrs. Mary Flynn, Mrs. B. W. Gandrud, Mrs. Lilla M. Hawes of the Georgia Historical Society in Savannah, Mr. Chester V. Kielman, Miss Millicent Huff, Miss Willa Allene Robinson, Miss Bess Richardson, Miss Virginia Richardson, Mrs. B. F. Thompson, and Mr. Luke Winfrey.

My wife, Ruth Carolyn, has paid the greatest price to see Devereux finished. She has traveled most of the miles with me to gather the information. Besides spending long hours in dusty Georgia courthouses taking notes, eating cheese sandwiches on the back roads of Georgia and Alabama while we were doing research, and helping me take measurements of the Monte Verdi Mansion House on the coldest Thanksgiving Day I can remember, she has made many sacrifices too numerous to list. The only compensation she has asked is that the green filing cabinet containing Devereux notes be taken from the bedroom to the garage. She has done so splendid a job typing the manuscript that I am going to move that filing cabinet to the garage this week. I, too, am also tired of having Devereux in the bedroom.

Dorman H. Winfrey

September 4, 1961

INTRODUCTORY NOTE

The principal source for this study of *Julien Sidney Devereux and his Monte Verdi Plantation* is a voluminous collection of personal papers which belonged to two East Texas pioneers, a father and a son, John William Devereux (1769-1847) and Julien Sidney Devereux (1805-1856). The former was born in Virginia and the latter in Georgia. Both afterwards were long-time residents of Alabama. In the early 1840's they came to the Republic of Texas settling first in Montgomery County and finally in 1846 in Rusk County. By this time the father was elderly and soon died. The son, however, before his untimely death in 1856 was able to build up a plantation of 10,721 acres worked by some eighty slaves. He thus was one of the leading citizens of Rusk County and East Texas in their early years. At the time of his death, he was a member of the Texas House of Representatives. He had previously served in the Alabama legislature. His father had served in both the Georgia and Alabama lawmaking bodies. Julien Sidney Devereux was survived by his second wife, Sarah Landrum Devereux, many years his junior, whom he had married in Texas. She was left with four very young sons who lived to maturity. She was able to keep the plantation going throughout the Civil War, but thereafter it became increasingly difficult. She lived until 1900, dying in Jacksonville, Texas, at the home of her son, William P. Devereux.

The Devereux papers were for many years the property of William P. Devereux. Not long before his death in 1928, he assigned them to the joint custody of his daughter, Mrs. Julien Devereux Weeks, and me, her husband. We carefully preserved the papers from that time until October 24, 1961, when they were transmitted to the Archives of The University of Texas. This was under the terms of the will of the late Mrs. Mary Perkins Devereux, widow of William P. Devereux. She died in 1960, and he had bequeathed the papers to her.

Mrs. Devereux's will (February 5, 1954) provided:

I hereby give, devise, and bequeath:
(e) Unto the University of Texas all the papers of Julien S. Devereux, known as the "Devereux Papers" now in the custody of my son-in-law, Douglas Weeks, and stored in his office in Garrison Hall at the University of Texas provided, however, that the said Douglas Weeks shall be permitted to retain custody of such papers so long as he may desire and provided, further, that any member of my family shall be

permitted full and free access to all of such papers, including the right to photostat and copy.

Mrs. Devereux's desire that the papers become the property of The University of Texas was motivated by a life-long interest in and many connections with the University. She herself was a student here in the long session of 1884-1885 at a time when her brother-in-law, the late Professor George P. Garrison was a member of the faculty. Her two children, my wife and Dr. William P. Devereux of Dallas, and two of her grandchildren, Sarah Jane Weeks Hills and Julien Devereux Weeks, as well as a number of her nieces and nephews, were graduates of the University. My long service on the faculty was also of influence.

The Devereux papers consist of several thousand items and are made up of letters, diaries, day books, bills and receipts, broadsides, and other memoranda belonging to John W. Devereux, and other members of the Devereux family. The collection is without doubt one of the most complete records of any antebellum Texas slave plantation. It is rich with primary source material on early Georgia, Alabama, and Texas. Some items date from the eighteenth century. The items are most numerous for the period from 1840 to 1856 when Julien S. Devereux lived in Texas in Montgomery and Rusk Counties. In Rusk County, where he last resided, the records of his Monte Verdi plantation are especially voluminous. In his last years he erected an imposing mansion on this plantation, which has recently been carefully restored by Mr. and Mrs. Emmett Lowry of Texas City, Texas. They use it as their country home, but they have been very generous in making it available to the public.

Dr. Dorman H. Winfrey, now Director and Librarian of the Texas State Library, has done a most painstaking job in what was his doctoral dissertation at The University of Texas. His doctoral committee were agreed on its superior quality. My wife and I as well as all other members of the Devereux family are quite grateful to Dr. Winfrey for restoring to proper prominence an important figure in the early development of Texas.

O. Douglas Weeks
Professor of Government,
The University of Texas

July 10, 1964

TABLE OF CONTENTS

ILLUSTRATIONS AND MAPS
OPPOSITE PAGE 78

FOREWORD

The account of Julien Sidney Devereux is indeed a challenging one in that, on the one hand, it is in substance as far away from current life and social problems as the Stone Age, while on the other, the experiences related therein are necessarily basic to the tumultuous modern world.

Devereux was a frontiersman who lived close to the land—close in the way that his generation and era had learned to use land functionally. In his time the best utilization of land was the result of division of labor, and it was the proper handling of that division which made things work on Devereux land and brought into being the necessities of life. The relationship of man to land was never closer or more intimate. Land itself then was intrinsically meaningful proportionately to a far greater segment of the population than at the midpoint of the twentieth century which was concerned with the soil and its productivity.

The study reveals the true drama of life as a century or more ago East Texas was being settled by Anglo-Americans. Significantly and properly, there has been no attempt to include any of the manufactured melodrama of the frontier as portrayed by Hollywood. This is a genuine account. It offers opportunity to read and relive American culture as it in the nineteenth century finally reached the eastern portion of Texas. The study depicts a part of the Texan and the American heritage. This is a genuine reconstruction of the past and that, after all, is the essence of history.

The book is the product of careful and scholarly research, but it also has something more. The facts are brought to light with an understanding of the land and of its inhabitants that results not only from the author's East Texas background but also from his long standing devotion to history and to the highest standards of historical interpretation.

> H. Bailey Carroll
> Professor of History, The University of Texas
> Director, Texas State Historical Association

July 4, 1964

For

Ruth Carolyn, Laura, and Jennifer

PREFACE

My attention was called to Julien Sidney Devereux and his Monte Verdi Plantation, located in southwestern Rusk County, during the early 1940's when I was a student in the Texas history class of Miss Myrtis Dean Watkins in Henderson High School and a member of Junior Historian Chapter 22 of the Texas State Historical Association. As a high school student I was never able to uncover much on Devereux in my own locality, except his will on file in the courthouse.

After military service I entered the University of Texas and was employed by the Texas State Historical Association as a student writer for the Association's projected two-volume *Handbook of Texas*. Two subjects assigned to me were Julien Sidney Devereux and Monte Verdi. A total of three references were to be had on the subjects—two brief mentions were to be found in the Index to Biographical Studies of Texans in the Texas Collection of the University of Texas Library and one citation was found in the United States Census for 1850 in the Archives Collection. After considerable searching for additional sources without any success, I asked the Archivist, Miss Winnie Allen, for possible material on Devereux. She replied, "There is nothing here. Professor Weeks in the government department has everything."

I called on Professor O. Douglas Weeks and he did indeed have "everything." Since I was working under Professor H. Bailey Carroll at the time, and after seeing the wealth of primary source material Dr. Weeks had, I suggested to Dr. Carroll the Devereux topic for a thesis. Dr. Carroll approved the subject, and Dr. Weeks granted me permission to use the papers.

After completing the articles on Julien Sidney Devereux and Monte Verdi for the *Handbook of Texas*, I then started taking notes for my thesis. It soon became obvious to me that the wealth of material on Devereux and Monte Verdi made the subject one worthy of a doctoral dissertation. Dr. Carroll approved the idea and made the suggestion for a master's thesis that I do a history of Rusk County to get the necessary background for the locality where Devereux lived and operated his plantation. This suggestion made by Dr. Carroll was, for me, wise counsel. The thesis on Rusk County was completed in January of 1951.

During the past decade, while working on the Devereux Papers, I took graduate work in the University of Texas and held full time employment as a Research Associate with the Research in Texas History Division of the Texas State Historical Association, University of Texas; Archivist of the Texas State Library; and Archivist of the University of Texas Library. For me, working in these areas of Texas history has been invaluable in securing ideas and source material on the Devereux subject.

The Devereux family lived for a number of years in Georgia and Alabama, and it was essential that archival sources in these states be examined. The Daughters of the Republic of Texas made this research possible through their Clara Driscoll Scholarship for Research in Texas History for 1952-1953 and 1953-1954. Deep appreciation is expressed here to the Daughters, for the early chapters could not have been written without their support.

To Professor H. Bailey Carroll goes my greatest debt. He brought me to the University of Texas to work in the field of history. While I worked on the Devereux dissertation, Dr. Carroll always guided me wisely, and, at the same time, he allowed me to do the study in my own way. Dr. Carroll knew the work load I was carrying at the University and the demands upon the State Archivist, and he never rushed me so that I have never had ulcers or had to take tranquilizers. Dr. Carroll urged me to "walk over the ground" where the Devereuxs lived—in distant Milledgeville, Georgia, and especially in Montgomery County and Rusk County, Texas. I have done the walking and the searching—strictly according to his methods and suggestions— and I hope the writing will convey adequately the type person Julien Devereux was, the times in which he lived, and picture for the reader what Monte Verdi Plantation may have been like.

With some training in archives I may have developed too great a respect for primary source materials with the result that portions of the Devereux Papers have been quoted at perhaps greater length than some persons may think necessary. My feeling came to be that a more vivid description of the people, the events, and the times could be had by reading the words of the participants than by attempting to summarize in my own words what had been written by the contemporaries on the scene. My thoughts were similar to those of my good friend Herbert Gambrell who made the following statement concerning extensive quotations in his biography of Mirabeau B. Lamar: "The reader gains . . . a more vivid sense of contemporaneousness by reading the words of the actors than he could get from summaries of their talk, however skillfully done."

CHAPTER I

The Early Background

The Devereuxs, whose ancestral seat was Evereux [sic] in France, were driven out of France in 1685 by the revocation of the Edict of Nantes.[1]—John William Devereux

My father was a decendant [sic] from one of the ancient Hugenot [sic] families that had left France from persecution after the revocation of the edict of Nantz and has been long established in Brittain England and Wales.[2]—John William Devereux

AMONG the small number of persons of French Huguenot ancestry who came to Texas during the periods of Anglo-American colonization and the Republic were such well-known

---

[1] John William Devereux's writings on the fly leaf of Louis Pierre Anquetil (trans.), **A Summary of Universal History.** This book is now in the private library of Professor and Mrs. Oliver Douglas Weeks.

The Devereux Family Papers, now deposited in the Archives Collection of the University of Texas Library in Austin, Texas, were for many years the property of William P. Devereux, son of Julien S. Devereux. Not long before his death in 1928, William P. Devereux assigned the papers to the custody of his daughter, Julien Devereux Weeks, and her husband, O. Douglas Weeks, of Austin. By the will of William P. Devereux the papers became the property of his widow, Mary Perkins Devereux, who died in 1960. By her will they passed to The University of Texas under conditions prescribed by her son-in-law, O. Douglas Weeks.

Without the Devereux Family Papers this monograph could never have been written, and deep personal appreciation is expressed to Professor and Mrs. Weeks who have been generous, kind, and especially patient during the years the writer was engaged in research. Since almost all citations to Devereux manuscript materials will be those in the Devereux Family Papers, all references cited will be as Devereux Papers unless otherwise specifically noted.

[2] John William Devereux, writing at Valverdi, Macon County, Alabama, May 20, 1840, in Record of the Devereux Family and Memoirs of John William Devereux. This magnificent piece of primary manuscript source material, owned by Colonel Homer Garrison, Jr., of Austin, is one of the few items dealing with Devereux family history that is not in the Weeks' collection of Devereux Family Papers. Colonel Garrison rendered many courtesies to the writer so that the contents of the diary could be used in this study.

figures as David Crockett, defender of the Alamo; Mirabeau B. Lamar, second president of the Republic of Texas; John C. Duval, first Texas man of letters; Pleasant W. Kittrell, educator and champion for The University of Texas; and the father and son team of John William and Julien Sidney Devereux.[3]

The background of the Texas branch of the Devereux family has been rather well recorded. John William Devereux wrote at least two brief accounts of the early family in France. One short history is found on the fly leaves of volume one of Louis Pierre Anquetil's (translator), *A Summary of Universal History*, and a second version appears in the manuscript history of the Record of the Devereux Family and Memoirs of John William Devereux. Concerning the family name, Devereux recorded:

> When the Salic Burgundians and Franks broke in upon Gaul they allotted to their conquering generals and most warlike men certain lands or feuds which they held under their kings or conquerers [sic] under tenures to render for them military services, etc. This was the origin of the feudal system afterwards continued under various modifications in France, Spain, Italy, and England. The head of the family from which I decended [sic] was a Feudal Lord (or Baron) and the residence was a Castle and fortified town call'd Evereux and now known by that name. it is situated 25 miles from Rouen & 55 northwest of Paris. . . . The heir was designated and known by the name of the castle in addition to the family name and in process of time the whole family assigned the name of d'Evereux or Devereux which is of Evereux.[4]

No documentary proof has been uncovered to substantiate John

---

[3]The name Devereux has various spellings. In ancient European and early American records the name is found in the forms of D'Evreux, De-Vreux, D'Evereux, D'Evereaux, Devorix, Devorax, Deveroe, Deverox, Deveroys, Deverois, D'Evus, Deverix, Deverieux, Deverex, Deverieus, Devereaux, Devereux, and others. Spellings of the name for the first United States Census of 1790 may be found in **A Century of Population Growth from the First Census of the United States to the Twelfth, 1790-1900,** p. 237. In the Devereux Papers many spellings of the name appear. John William and Julien Sidney Devereux always signed their names Devereux, and that is the spelling of the name to be used here.

[4]This particular account of the family background appears in the Record of the Devereux Family and Memoirs of John William Devereux. The account recorded on the fly leaf of Anquetil (trans.), **A Summary of Universal History,** is almost identical.

William Devereux's statements concerning the place of his Huguenot ancestors in Evreux.[5]

John William Devereux in his writings gave additional information on Huguenot history and the traditions of his own family's flight from France.

> The family of Devereux was driven out of France by Louix XIV when he revoked the Edict of Nantes. The Edict of Nantes was passed by Henry IV in the year 1598 of the Christian Era which secured to the Protestants religious liberty, or a free exercise of their religion. When Louis XIV revoked that edict the Roman Catholics commenced a persecution which compelled thousands to fly to other countries for refuge, and our family went to Britain —that part of them from which I am descended from have been long established in North Wales in the county of Montgomeryshire and own a valuable free hold estate.[6]

The Edict of Nantes, described as the first document in the history of Christianity to extend religious toleration in a country, was issued by Henry IV on April 13, 1598, and granted a

---

[5]Ministre Plenipotentiaire Jean Delalande of the Ministry of Foreign Affairs of France spent considerable time searching out information for the writer on the background of the Devereux family. On November 19, 1958, Delalande wrote, "I assure you that Evreux has not been a center of French Protestantism." On November 12, 1958, Delalande wrote, "Evreux has conserved a number of ancient homes of the XV and XVI centuries." Among the famous landmarks of Evreux is the cathedral Notre Dame d'Evreux, and Mr. Delalande kindly supplied the following information on the cathedral:

> The Cathedral of Notre Dame d'Evreux was built from the XII century to the XVII century. The nave is of the 12th Century (with the Roman Arches) and of the beginning of the 13th; the choir, of the end of the 13th; the side chapels, of the 14th; and the main chapel and the transept of the 15th.

> The famous Cardinal La Balue had the main chapel rebuilt, and in 1467 he constructed the two-story octagonal bell tower topped by a spire of lead 81 meters high.

> All the north side of the edifice was renovated from 1511 to 1531. The north facade is of the richest flamboyant style, and is flanked by two wrought turrets.

> The west facade (1575-1591), that dates from the Renaissance, is framed by two towers that, like the spire of the bell tower, were destroyed in part in 1940; the one on the right, originally Romanesque, was renovated in the Renaissance style; the left one is in the style of Louis XIII.

> The cathedral has a precious collection of stained glass windows of the 13th, 14th, 15th, and 16th centuries.

> The total length of the edifice is 106 meters; the width at the transept is 31 meters; the ceilings are 21 meters high in the nave and 24 meters in the choir.

[6]John William Devereux's comments on the fly leaves of volume one of Anquetil's (trans.), **A Summary of Universal History.**

large measure of religious freedom to the Protestant Huguenots.[7] Public worship was permitted, and Huguenots were granted all civil rights which included the right to hold public office and admittance to the universities. A major concession, which later caused trouble, was a provision that the Huguenots were also to be allowed to maintain a large number of fortified places, including such strongholds as the strategic seaport of La Rochelle.

The Huguenots during the early seventeenth century probably numbered around a million persons. France at the time had a population of approximately fifteen million, so the Huguenots constituted somewhat over one-fifteenth and perhaps never more than one-tenth of the French population.[8] Although the Huguenots were never more than a small minority of the population of France, their strength was far greater than their numbers would indicate. Writers such as H. M. Baird, Lucian J. Fosdick, H. A. Du Pont, and C. W. Baird[9] point out that Huguenots were recruited chiefly from the energetic and influential classes and included the industrial and commercial townsmen, the gentry, and a few nobles. Generally the Huguenots were characterized by rather high morality and had reputations as respectable and formidable groups.

The benefits granted to the Huguenot population by the Edict of Nantes in 1598 were not to be enjoyed for long. The Roman Catholic clergy had never accepted the Edict of Nantes, and their efforts were directed to obtaining its revocation. In 1617 Louis XIII came to the French throne. He felt, along with his close advisor Cardinal Armand de Richelieu, that Protestant Huguenots as a religious-political organization in possession of a number of fortified towns constituted a threat to the royal authority. Cardinal Richelieu determined to exterminate the Huguenots not solely on a religious basis but on the theory that they were undermining the monarchy, being as they were sort of republic within the kingdom. The Edict of Nantes had given the Huguenots not only religious toleration but a privileged political position. With fortified cities, Richelieu felt the

[7]The provisions of the Edict of Nantes can be found in **The Cambridge Modern History**, Vol. III, **The Wars of Religion**, 675-676; Encyclopedia Americana (1957), XIV, 482.

[8]Henry M. Baird, **The Huguenots and the Revocation of the Edict of Nantes**, I, 370.

[9]See H. M. Baird, **History of the Rise of the Huguenots**, Lucian J. Fosdick, **The French Blood in America**, H. A. Du Pont, **The Story of the Huguenots**, C. W. Baird, **History of the Huguenot Emigration to America**.

Huguenots formed a state within the state. Rebellions, supported in part by England, began to break out as early as 1624, and in 1627 a major revolt took place around the seaport of La Rochelle with England's giving active support to the Huguenots. With the fall of La Rochelle to royal troops in 1628, Huguenot power was broken and the French crown began doing away with the privileges granted at Nantes. Louis XIV took away additional privileges until finally, on October 18, 1685, came the formal revocation of the Edict of Nantes, abrogating all the civil and religious rights of the Huguenots. Royal troops were sent into the southern provinces to compel the Huguenots to abjure their faith. Following the revocation there was a mass exodus of more than a hundred thousand,[10] and to England, Holland, Germany, Switzerland, and America fled many of France's ablest subjects. The result was that France suffered a serious economic blow, for Huguenot skills were especially outstanding in the fields of industry and commerce.[11] The Huguenots took with them the secrets and knowledge of French industry and built up commercial competition with France.

In the Huguenot flight John William Devereux recorded that "My grandfather who was a younger son went to Glamorganshire . . ." in Wales.[12] The feeling in England was so strong for the Huguenots that the British monarch, James II, who had been on the throne of England for a little over eight months when the revocation of Nantes was promulgated, "signed a brief on March 5, 1686, taking the refugees under his protection."[13]

[10]Samuel Smiles, **The Huguenots: Their Settlements, Churches, and Industries, in England and Ireland**, 261. More than 400,000 Huguenots left France according to the **Encyclopaedia Britannica** (1951), XI, 872.

[11]Fosdick, **French Blood in America**, 15, states that, "The Huguenots represented the most sober, industrious, and intelligent class of the French people." Louise Seymour Houghton, **Handbook of French and Belgian Protestantism**, 18n, observes that, "The Huguenots were men of integrity, energy, economy and benevolence. 'Honest as a Huguenot' was a common saying."

[12]Record of the Devereux Family.

[13]Baird, **Huguenots and the Revocation of the Edict of Nantes**, II, 94. A later British monarch, William III, enlisted support of Huguenots in Holland. R. A. Brock, **Documents, Chiefly Unpublished, Relating to the Huguenot Emigration to Virginia**, viii, writes: "Of the army of William of Orange, numbering eleven thousand which sailed from Holland, and by whose aid he obtained the Crown of England, three regiments, each containing seven hundred and fifty effective men, were Huguenots. To these were added a squadron of horses. There were also about seven hundred officers distributed among other battalions of the army. In gratitude of these zealous and effective supporters, and in symppathy with the great multitude of their suffering brethren driven violently from their homes and

Many thousands did find refuge in England and Charles W. Baird, a leading writer of Huguenot history, has commented that "England was foremost in its offers of hospitality."[14] The British Isles profited by the Huguenot influx which "contributed immensely to the constituent population and useful citizenry of England, Scotland, Ireland and Wales. . . ."[15]

The first name recorded in the Devereux genealogy is that of Morgan Devereux (grandfather of John William and great-grandfather of Julien S. Devereux) who "was a native of Montgomeryshire North Wales."[16] Morgan Devereux married Elizabeth Hughs whose brother Sir Edward Hughs was a noted admiral in the British Navy.[17] Morgan and Elizabeth Devereux were parents of a son, Charles Devereux, who was born in 1740 in Glamorganshire, Wales, and was named for the mother's brother who "was a considerable freeholder."[18] In 1763 this Charles Devereux, in his twenties, left Wales and came to the then British colony of Virginia, becoming the first recorded member of the family to arrive in the New World.

---

native country simply for their religion, the king invited them to make their home in his new dominons."

[14]Baird, **History of the Huguenot Emigration to America**, I, 254.
[15]Brock, **Documents, Chiefly Unpublished, Relating to the Huguenot Emigration to Virginia**, vii.
[16]"Family Record" in Record of the Devereux Family.
[17]For an account of Hughs' career see **Encyclopedia Britannica**, II, 866. A portrait of Hughs was done by the famous English portrait painter Sir Joshua Reynolds and is in the Painted Hall at Greenwich.
[18]"Family Record" in Record of the Devereux Family.

CHAPTER II
On the Frontier

*I John William Devereux was born among
romantic scenery in the wildest part of the state
of Virginia at Chiswells lead mines in the year
of the Christian era 1769. . . .*

*I had all the hardships and privations incident
to the soldiers life on a frontier to perform and
suffer at 17 years of age.*[1]

CHARLES Devereux, a smelter and mineralogist by trade, arrived in the British colony of Virginia in 1763 "with many others to erect and carry on a lead works in (now) Wythe County then Fincastle"[2] at Chiswell's Mines west of the Allegheny Mountains in southwestern Virginia. Some three years later on October 7, 1766, Devereux married Nancy Woods,[3] "a native of Virginia and decended [sic] from Irish parents who had settled in that then colony at an early period."[4] Eight children were born to Charles and Nancy Devereux, and these included Elizabeth, born on December 7, 1767; John William, born March 15, 1769; James born October 7, 1771; Samuel McDowell, born December 7, 1773; Archibald McLelland, born August 20, 1775; John Bowyer, born September 7, 1777; Nancy, born November 16, 1779; and Charles Hughs, born March 7, 1782.[5] John William

---

[1]Record of the Devereux Family and Memoirs of John William Devereux.

[2]Ibid. One source, a Bible in possession of Miss Willa Allene Robinson, Evergreen, Alabama, has the following information written by Julien Sidney Devereux: "Charles Devereux . . . was born in 1743. He arrived in North America in 1760. . . ." John William Devereux in his Record of the Devereux Family gave the dates as 1740 and 1763, respectively, making a difference of three years in each instance.

All parentheses ( ) in quoted materials are those made by Devereux; the brackets [ ]are those of the writer. The original spelling, punctuation, capitalization, and syntax have been generally used except in certain instances when meaning would not have been adequately conveyed in the original form.

[3]Homer E. Davis, Hill City, Georgia, to D. W., February 22, 1953. Davis, a Devereux descendent, has in his possession a Devereux Family Bible which contains information on early members of the family.

[4]Record of the Devereux Family.

[5]Record of births in Devereux Family Bible in possession of Homer E. Davis, Hill City, Georgia.

Devereux was the second child born, and seventy-one years later on May 20, 1840, at Valverdi, Macon County, Alabama, he recorded: "I John William Devereux was born among romantic scenery in the wildest part of the state of Virginia at Chiswell's lead mines in the year of the Christian era 1769. . . ."[6]

Charles Devereux rendered service to Virginia troops at Chiswell's Mines during the American Revolution,[7] and records in the Virginia State Library reveal that Devereux provided "lead to the army."[8] It would be interesting to know how important Devereux's participation was during the fighting at Chiswell's Mines, for there was major activity in the area in 1779 and 1780 when Loyalists in southwestern Virginia formed a plot to seize the mines. The undertaking failed, however, and the mines were in production throughout the Revolutionary War.[9]

Identified also with the vicinity of Chiswell's Mines were two of the most significant persons ever to appear on the Texas scene—Moses Austin and his son Stephen F. Austin. In 1791, some thirty years after John William Devereux's birth, Moses Austin and his wife, Maria, moved from Richmond, Virginia, to Chiswell's Mines, and at this locality on November 3, 1793, Stephen F. Austin was born.[10] At the time of Stephen F. Austin's birth the country was on the southwestern frontier of Virginia,[11] for as late as 1790 the frontier line had moved just west of the locality.[12]

Charles Devereux's family had been reared at Chiswell's Mines two decades before the Austins arrived, and in the 1760's

[6]Record of the Devereux Family. Living in Texas in 1845, John William Devereux wrote: "I was born in the mountains of Virginia on the Kinawa [Kanawha] river amid romantic scenery."
[7]Calendar of Virginia State Papers, VIII, 149, 156.
[8]Ibid., 149; "Virginia State Troops in the Revolution," Virginia Magazine of History and Geography, XXXI, 328.
[9]H. J. Eckenrode, Virginia in the Revolution, 238, credits the term "lynch law" to have been derived from the action taken against the plotters by Colonel Charles Lynch, superintendent of the lead mines. Virginia Magazine of History and Biography, VI, 344.
[10]Eugene C. Barker (ed.), The Austin Papers, I, 1; Barker, Life of Stephen F. Austin, 17, 18. Moses Austin and Company had acquired the Chiswell lead mines in southwestern Virginia by 1789. The Austins worked the mines with slave labor and cultivated adjacent farms to provide food for the slaves and animals. A second child, Emily, was born at the mines on June 22, 1795.
[11]Ibid., 5, 18.
[12]See maps facing page 16 and on page 18 of A Century of Population Growth From the First Census of the United States to the Twelfth, 1790-1900.

and 1770's all the dangers and tribulations faced by early settlers were present in this frontier region. The Devereux boys
have been described as being large in stature, and John William
gave the following statistics on himself and his brothers:

Sons of Charles D[evereux] weights of the 5 Devereux's & one died before fully grown

JWD	180	6 feet 2½ inches, high
John B	180	6 feet 2 Inches
Archd M	250	6 feet 4 Inches
Charles H	250	6 feet 6 Inches
Saml M	350	6 feet 4 Inches
	1210	
James	180	died in the 21st year of his age
		Just 6 feet high[13]
	1390	

The only additional information located concerning Charles Devereux in Virginia is that in 1782 he acquired some four hundred
acres of land in Montgomery County, which he disposed of in
1784.[14]

On January 1, 1785, with eight children and six slaves,
Charles and Nancy Devereux "imigrated [sic] to the state of
Georgia and arrived at a plantation he had purchased in a
Quaker settlement near Wrightsborough [sic] in Columbia
County."[15] Earlier, on April 3, 1784, Devereux had applied for
a thousand acres of land in Washington County.[16] Wrightsboro,
presently a Georgia ghost town, was an early Quaker settlement
first known as Brandon. In 1770 Quaker Joseph Mattock obtained from the royal governor, Sir James Wright, a grant of
40,000 acres to revive the old settlement, and Mattock called
the new establishment Wrightsboro.[17] At the Charles Devereux
plantation the eldest Devereux son, John William, was made
overseer. In his "Memoirs of my own self" Devereux recorded:

I had no experience in farming nor no turn for driving
slaves[.] My father was dissatisfied with me and attempted to use severity[.] I did not submit to it and left him in

[13]J. W. Devereux Notebook (1847).
[14]Homer L. Davis to D. W., February 22, 1953.
[15]Record of the Devereux Family.
[16]This original petition is presently in Department of Archives and History, Atlanta, Georgia.
[17]Lucian Lamar Knight, **Georgia's Landmarks, Memorials and Legends,**
I, 481, 763.

my sixteenth year and through my mother procur'd a birth as clerk or storeboy with Mr. Rhesa Howard at Wrightsboro where I remained and gave entire satisfaction for three years. . . .[18]

From the age of sixteen to nineteen (1785-1788) John William Devereux worked in Howard's store, and during this time, at the age of seventeen, he had his first military experience. On the Georgia frontier he served six months as a "volunteer private soldier" against Indians in the Oconee War. During this first tour of military duty, young Devereux participated in fighting the Creek Indians at Shoulder Bone Creek, in the western part of Hancock County. The locality was the scene of a treaty on November 3, 1786.[19]

> My first three months was in the foot service and I had hard times—we made frequent excursions out on scouts and twice to bury the dead (a boy had been killed by Indians on Pistol Creek [was] buried & 2 negroes at the Rocklanding kill'd by Indians belonging to Bartlet only their bones remain'd to be buried) and I had all the hardships and privations incident to the soldiers life on a frontier to perform and suffer at 17 years of age—Dick Bonner who had been a revolutionary soldier was my Captain was kind to me and would have left me at the Fort when scouts were made but I was not willing to be left . . . "I would be a soldier."[20]

Devereux was able to enjoy some "army breaks," however, for on one occasion his commanding officer was his father's neighbor. The officer took young Devereux "into his mess and I did very well and had no cooking to do and only to wash my cloaths and take care of my horse whilst in quarters—and perform the usual share of garrison duty as belong to the guard etc."[21]

At the end of three years in Howard's store, Devereux borrowed money from the owner to "establish" himself in the merchandise business. In Hancock County "at a Baptist meetinghouse" Devereux set himself up in 1788 and stayed there two years until 1789 or 1790 after which he moved to Greensborough "which was just laid out for a County town." Green County

---

[18]Record of the Devereux Family.
[19]Knight, **Georgia's Landmarks, Memorials and Legends**, II, 790.
[20]Record of the Devereux Family.
[21]**Ibid.**

had been created in 1786 and named for Nathanael Greene, the second in command to George Washington during a portion of the American Revolution.[22] During the first two years in Greensborough, from about 1789 to 1791, Devereux purchased a lot, built a house, and paid back the money borrowed from Howard. The following year there was considerable excitement at this frontier settlement when the Creek Indians repudiated the treaty made in 1786 at Shoulder Bone Creek. Devereux recorded that: "The Indians broke out and did much mischief and my store was within six miles of the Indian boundary line (the Oconee). I had attach'd myself to a troop of Horse raisd in the county and was out on scouts after Indians every month for I made it a rule to go with every scout."[23]

So serious was the Oconee War that in 1792 the United States Congress authorized money to raise "a troop of Horse for the protection of the frontier," for Green County at the time touched the "Indian lands."[24] Officers for the military company included Captain Jonas Fouche, First Lieutenant John William Devereux, Second Cornet Zachariah Lamar, uncle of Mirabeau B. Lamar,[25] and one hundred non-comissioned officers and privates. Devereux soldiered "in good earnest" during 1792, 1793, and 1794, and recorded:

> I believe I spent more than half my days and nights in the woods winter & summer—the detachment under my command was stationed at Fort Twiggs most of the time and we had to cover the frontier of Greene and Hancock which were the most populous counties and both on the Indian line. . . .
>
> During my service in Fouche's troop I was in several skirmishes with the indians—once I had the command of

[22]Knight, **Georgia's Landmarks, Memorials and Legends,** II, 772.

[23]Record of the Devereux Family.

[24]**A Century of Population Growth,** 69. F. W. Hodge (ed.), **Handbook of American Indians North of Mexico,** II, 105, describes the Oconee as a small tribe of the Creek Confederacy, probably of the Hitchiti division, formerly living on the Oconee River in Georgia. The Oconee formed one of the parties to the treaty between the United States and the Creeks at Colerain, Georgia, on June 29, 1796.

[25]Members of the Devereux and Lamar families had close associations in Georgia. When John Devereux's son-in-law, Henry B. Holcombe, wrote to Mirabeau B. Lamar at Houston, Texas, on October 22, 1838, Holcombe mentioned that he had named a son Lucius Lamar Holcombe in honor of Mirabeau B. Lamar's brother. In the letter also mention was made to John William Devereux "whom you [Lamar] doubtless will remember as one of the oldest citizens of Milledgeville." See Charles Adams Gulick, Jr., and others (eds.), **The Papers of Mirabeau Buonaparte Lamar,** II, 258.

a detachment when we followed six warriors that had been on the frontier and surrounded them at their camp—they laid down their rifles and we took them prisoners—our orders from the governor were to capture if we could that they might be exchanged for white prisoners then in the nation—another time I commanded 26 men and overtook the Indians on the West fork of the Ocmulgee—they fired upon us at the river—we chargd through (the river) and put them to flight but lost one man (Named Lester) killd & two horses—the man killd was next to me & foremost in the charge (the men wanted to kill them) another time I had the command of 15 men and was sent from Fort Mathews in pursuit of Indians that had taken several horses and plunderd houses and pack'd their horses—my orders were not to pass the boundary line in the pursuit which was then the Apatatche river [Appalatchee, also spelled Apalachee.] and only 15 miles from Fort Mathews—Major Roberts the Federal Officer in Command caution'd me against crossing the line for that I would be arrested and broke for disobedience of Orders—when we reachd the line I consulted the men and they all were desirous to pursue farther and promised upon their honours not to inform against me—we continued pursuit that day and the following night without stopping—the next morning we discovered the indians at a conserable distance in the open woods and they discovered us—we chargd at the top of the speed of our weary horses and the indians threw off their luggage & mounted their horses and scattered each his own way and about a quarter of a mile from the start they enter'd a canebreak—we gather'd the plunder and return'd[.] from the time we were absent and bringing back the plunder'd property the commanding officer believd we had passd the temporary boundary line and had defeated the indians—a Federal Lieut not very friendly to me tamper'd with the men to find out what had been done—but as our scout seem'd to have more audit than it was worth the men kept our secret.[26]

After three years of military duty John Devereux had reached the age of twenty-five, and on Appril 19, 1795, he married sixteen-year-old Elizabeth Few, daughter of Ignatius and Mary Few of Columbia County. The Few family was prominent in American, as well as Georgian, history. Ignatius Few had held the rank of captain in the Revolutionary Army, while

---

[26]Record of the Devereux Family. A copy of the "Georgia Military Record Book. 1779-1839," W. P. A. Project No. 5993 (1941) p. 28, shows that from November 1, 1794, to December 31, 1794, Lieutenant John William Devereux was paid an allowance of $30.50 "for use and risk of his horse at 50 cts per day."

a brother, William Few, was a member of the Continental Congress and a delegate from Georgia to the Constitutional Convention of 1787.[27]

On January 15, 1799, while John Devereux was on a trip to New York, Elizabeth Devereux, at the age of twenty, died while giving birth to a son. She was buried at Mount Carmel, her father's plantation. The funeral for Elizabeth Devereux was preached the following March 5th by Abram Marshall, and John Devereux recorded that: "The flower garden was beautifully ornamented with a variety of flowers that bloom at that season. . . . The day was fine and a very numerous audience was seated around the parson who stood under a large cedar tree on a pulpit provided for the purpose."[28] Devereux gave back to his father-in-law the wedding gift of a plantation and slaves, and the following June Devereux left on another business trip to New York.[29] While there during August he "got a tombstone for my Eliza's grave—Spent some melancholy hours deciding on the inscription."[30]

Devereux then returned to his former occupation of merchandising and settled in Sparta, Hancock County. In addition to running a store Devereux served as justice of the peace from April 12, 1799, to December 4, 1801. He also held positions in Hancock County of justice of the inferior court for five years (1801-1806); was made a commissioner of Hancock County Academy on December 4, 1801; and was certified as a notary public on December 8, 1800.[31] On January 15, 1801, he married Sally Grigg, daughter of Jesse Grigg. A son Albert was born on December 6. The family moved to Montpelier and a daughter Louisiana was born there on September 16, 1803, and at the same place on July 23, 1805, son Julien Sidney was born. Dev-

[27]Charles C. Jones, Jr., **Biographical Sketches of the Delegates from Georgia to the Continental Congress**, 35.

[28]J. W. Devereux Scrap Book.

[29]For a most interesting account of this trip (June 23-November 18, 1799), see O. Douglas Weeks (ed.), "My Journal of One of My Trips to New York, by John William Devereux of Milledgeville, Georgia," **Georgia Historical Quarterly**, XV, 46-80.

[30]**Ibid.**, 54. The inscription selected was: "Sacred to the memory of Mrs. Eliza Devereux and her infant son. She was the beloved consort of J. W. D. and the affectionate daughter of Ignatius and Mary Few to whom she endeared herself by uncommon tenderness. She possessed a feeling and benevolent heart and was endowed with superior acquirements. Her departure was on the 15th of January 1799, in the 20th year of her life."

[31]Photostat copies of Service Card File, supplied by Department of Archives and History, Atlanta, Georgia.

[13]

ereux then moved with his wife and three children to Milledge-ville, Baldwin County, where a second daughter Antoinette was born on November 7, 1808. Both daughter and mother suffered ill health; the following year on November 1, 1809, daughter Antoinette died and then the wife died the following January 28. John Devereux recorded that "both were buried together at the Methodist burying ground—a melancholy coincidence—my two wives both died in childbed and both buried with their infants in the same coffin."[32] A funeral service was preached on March 4 by Reverend Miles Green, who had married the Devereuxs nine years earlier.

Devereux was closely identified with the early history of Milledgeville, and he was described as "an honest and enterpris-ing citizen"[33] of Baldwin County and one of "the most prominent of the early settlers."[34] A brother, Archibald M. Devereux, had helped select the site for the capitol on December 12, 1804, and was appointed one of the first justices of the inferior court of the county. The next year John William was chosen a commis-sioner to sell lots in Milledgeville to raise $60,000 for the erection of a capitol.[35] Devereux served several terms as Baldwin County justice of the peace from 1807 to 1817, and in 1811 he was elected to represent the county one term in the Georgia House of Representatives.[36] Devereux held the trusted position to re-ceive "the money for the stock in the state bank at Milledge-ville;" for many years he was elected a member of the corpora-tion of Milledgeville; and he was appointed commissioner for superintending the building of the Georgia State Penitentiary.

During the War of 1812 Devereux was not subject to mili-tary duty because of his age, forty-three, and because of the heavy responsibility he faced to support three small children. He had been appointed postmaster at Milledgeville, probably the most lucrative postal position at the time in Georgia, which was his "principal dependence" for support of his family.[37] Devereux did render service against the British, however, when he was appointed by Governor Peter Early to furnish rations to a regi-

[32]Record of the Devereux Family.
[33]George White, Historical Recollections of Georgia, 267.
[34]Knight, Georgia's Landmarks, Memorials and Legends, I, 274.
[35]Anna Maria Green Cook, History of Baldwin County, Georgia, 18, 19, 181. Milledgeville was the capital of Georgia until 1868.
[36]Photostat copies of Service Card File, supplied by Department of Ar-chives and History, Atlanta, Georgia.
[37]Record of the Devereux Family.

ment of some eleven hundred riflemen commanded by Colonel Jett Thomas. This wartime duty Devereux felt was "performed satisfactorily and with clean hands which is more than I can say for any other I knew who had anything to do with the quarter masters department from that day to the Semanola epocha [Seminole War]."[38]

In 1817, at the then advanced age of forty-eight, John Devereux made arrangements to move westward. Leaving daughter Louisiana, aged fourteen, with her uncle Samuel,[39] John Devereux took sons sixteen-year-old Albert and twelve-year-old Julien Sidney and headed west for the Alabama Territory.

---

[38]**Ibid.**

[39]According to a letter from H. E. Davis, February 22, 1953, "The town of Devereux [Hancock County], Georgia, was named for Samuel M. Devereux who gave the right-of-way for the Railway." In Hancock County Samuel M. Devereux was justice of the peace for many years, represented the county in the Georgia house of representatives in 1828 and 1829, and was elected to serve in the senate in 1831. Samuel owned considerable land and many slaves. He was a huge person; records give his weight at 350 and 400 pounds.

Interesting, perhaps, is that the Devereux grape was named for vintager Samuel M. Devereux. According to James C. Bonner in "The Georgia Wine Industry on the Eve of the Civil War," **Georgia Historical Quarterly,** XLI, 22, Devereux "grew one of these thrifty vines in the yard of his stagehouse between Sparta and Milledgeville, from which travelers secured numerous cuttings. Its fame, together with the name of the tavern owner, was spread throughout neighboring states."

CHAPTER III

"Gone to Texas"

Built it [the cabin]
occupied it &
left it and
gone to Texas
fool move[1]

THE exact date in 1817 has not been established when John William Devereux, at the age of forty-eight, pulled up stakes in Georgia and with his two sons, sixteen-year-old Albert and twelve-year-old Julien, headed westward for the Alabama Territory. Records indicate that as late as February 22, 1817, John William Devereux was still postmaster at Milledgeville, Georgia.[2] The reasons are not entirely clear why the Devereuxs decided to move; perhaps it was a part of the "Alabama fever" which came about when the War of 1812 ended. There were several factors which invited settlers to the new lands. The Indians in Alabama had been quelled by General Andrew Jackson and his Tennesseeans at the battle of Horseshoe Bend on March 27, 1814.[3] With the Indian menace removed there was speculation with Alabama lands, and great efforts by promoters were made to get persons to settle in the new territory. And for the pioneer there was always the bright prospect of making a fortune out of cotton.

There were several roads from Tennessee and Georgia into

---

[1]J. W. Devereux's Memorandum and Common Place Book.

The expression "Gone to Texas" came into use in the early nineteenth century when Texas had the reputation for producing and harboring outlaws. In many Southern States the letters G. T. T. were placed on the doors of houses to indicate where the occupants had gone.

[2]Clarence Edwin Carter ('comp. and ed.), **The Territorial Papers of the United States: The Territory of Mississippi, 1809-1817**, VI, 767.

[3]John Spencer Bassett (ed.), **Correspondence of Andrew Jackson**, I, 489-492; Albert Burton Moore, **History of Alabama**, 27. Jackson went from there to greater achievements at Mobile and New Orleans.

Mississippi and Alabama and these roads encouraged immigration. The Federal Road, which had been authorized by Congress in 1806 to connect Athens, Georgia, with New Orleans, Louisiana, had a connecting road to Milledgeville. This is probably the road the Devereuxs took to Alabama when they settled in Conecuh County in south Alabama west of the Chattahoochee River.[4]

The territory of Alabama was created out of the old Mississippi Territory, of which it had been a part since 1798, in an act approved by Congress on March 3, 1817.[5] Rapid settlement continued and in less than three years on December 14, 1819, Congress approved a resolution for admission of Alabama as a state into the Union.[6]

In the early history of Alabama as a state, John William Devereux appears as a prominent figure. Evidently he had a good reputation, and he may have commanded considerable respect with his record as a Georgia statesman, for Alabama Governor William Wyatt Bibb appointed Devereux justice of the county court of Conecuh on December 18, 1820,[7] a position he held five years. The United States Census for 1820 revealed that the Devereux family consisted of John William, Albert, and Julien, and there were fourteen slaves.[8]

The manuscript records in the Devereux Papers do not give much about the lives of the Devereuxs during these early Alabama years. Father John William Devereux once wrote that "My two sons Albert and Julien were six feet (and upwards) high,"[9] indicating that the sons were of about the same stature as their father and uncles. John William Devereux described son Albert's constitution as "delicate" and stated that "his father designed him [Albert] for a profession as best calculated to compart with his Physical and intellectual capacity—that of medicine."[10] Albert, however, decided against medicine and instead took up the study of law. He read law under Arthur

---

[4]See the map in Thomas Perkins Abernethy, **The Formative Period in Alabama, 1815-1828,** p. 163.
[5]Clarence Edwin Carter (comp. and ed.), **The Territorial Papers of the United States. The Territory of Alabama, 1817-1819,** XVIII, 53-57.
[6]**Ibid.,** 753-755.
[7]"Register of Gubernatorial Appointments Civil and Military, Territory of Alabama, February 9, 1818 - November 14, 1819,—State of Alabama, December 14, 1819 - October 4, 1822," **Alabama Historical Quarterly,** VI, 125.
[8]"Alabama Census Returns, 1820," **ibid.,** 367.
[9]J. W. Devereux Notebook (1847).
[10]Record of the Devereux Family.

Pendleton Bagley, who had married a niece of John William Devereux, and later served as Governor of Alabama and United States Senator. What Julien Sidney Devereux was doing during the early years in Alabama is not clear. Part of the time he was in Pensacola, Florida, looking after family interests there, and most probably much of his time was spent supervising the family plantation—experience he would put to use in later years when he would operate one of the largest of the East Texas plantations.

John William Devereux served for eleven sessions (9 annual and 2 extra) as state senator in the Alabama Legislature. His first term to represent Conecuh County was from October 25, 1819, to December 17, 1819, at the first annual session of the first general assembly at Huntsville when John Herbert resigned.[11] For the called session at Cahawba[12] from June 4, 1821, until June 18, 1821,[13] and at the third annual session of the general assembly at Cahawba from November 5, 1821, to December 19, 1821, Devereux represented Conecuh County in the senate.[14]

On August 5, 1822, Devereux again was elected senator to represent the counties of Conecuh, Covington, Henry, and Dale,[15] but before the end of the month real tragedy struck in the Devereux home; Albert Devereux came down with the dreaded yellow fever. Albert had been in Pensacola on family business when, on August 26, he became ill. The twenty-year-old son lived ten days, dying at his father's house on September 6. John William Devereux never stopped grieving about the loss of his son. Throughout all his notebooks, scrapbooks, memoirs, letters, and in all written memoranda until his death in Texas in 1847, the father was still mourning the loss.

At the time of Albert's death only John William Devereux was present because "my good neighors were afraid to stay with me least they might catch the fever."[16] Albert Devereux

[11]W. Brewer, **Alabama: Her History, Resources, War Record, and Public Men from 1540 to 1872**, p. 197.

[12]Cahawba was the capital from 1820 to 1826.

[13]William H. Brantley, **Three Capitals: A Book About the First Three Capitals of Alabama**, St. Stephens, Huntsville, & Cahawba, 233; B. F. Riley, History of Conecuh County, Alabama, 102; W. Brewer, **Alabama: Her History, Resources, War Record, and Public Men**, 197.

[14]Brantley, **Three Capitals: A Book About the First Three Capitals of Alabama**, 235.

[15]Certificate of Election, signed by J. J. Pleasants, Secretary of State, November 18, 1822, in Alabama State Department of Archives and History, Montgomery.

[16]Record of the Devereux Family.

was buried at the family residence "on the bank of the Conecuh River . . . under a small stooping white oak tree in a little Plumb Orchard."[17] The following obituary was written "To My Albert" by the father:

Obituary

Died in Conecuh County on the 6th of Septem (1822) at the residence of his father of the yellow fever which he caught in Pensacola where he had been on business, Albert Devereux[.] In the death of this amiable young man society has sustained a loss and his agent parent and friends a bereavement for which tears are shed in vain— In his early years of boyhood he evinced proofs of possessing an intellect of a superior cost and which if properly cultivated promised at some time to lead him to eminence and distinction— Although his person was of good statue and proportion and his complection flored and healthful his constitution was delicate and his father designed him for a profession as best calculated to comport with his Physical and intellectual capacity—That of medecine and was first resolved on and he read elementary books and appeared to be delighted with medical science but discovered that his natural disposition would be adverse to practice and having began to survey the great field of human effort and having formed an opinion that the richest harvests and choicest flowers were gathered and plucked by those who drank deep from the fountains of Coke, Hale, and Mansfield and being allowed to become the comptroller of his own distany he resolved that the profession of law should constitute the arena of his effort—with celerity almost unequal he mastered the elements and first principles of his favorite pursuits—was prepared for admittance to the bar—his prospects were such as to justify the highest expectations of his friends when alas he was not permitted to ripen into manhood nor to make one step upon the great theatre of life ere the cold and relentless arm of death arrested him in his youthful career—when he had lost hopes of recovery he relaxed into a mild and tranquil calm and seemed to turn his thoughts within and to hold converse with himself and at times raised his hands as if in prayer to his God when his heart-breaking and agonized father leaned over his pillow as if eager to unloose the grasp of death he turned his dying eyes and beged him to retire—thus perished at the early age of twenty and ten months a youth of unblimished character—the delight of his only parent his brother and sister and associates—the

---

[17]J. W. Devereux Notebook (1847).

tears that were shed at his grave and for his loss are the best comments upon his worth & virtues.[18]

In 1823, following Albert's death, the Devereuxs moved to Montezuma in adjoining Covington County, and during the fourth (November 18, 1822 - January 1, 1823), fifth (November 17, 1823 - December 31, 1823), and sixth (November 15, 1824 - December 25, 1824) sessions of the legislature Senator John William Devereux represented the counties of Conecuh, Covington, Henry, and Pike.[19] Devereux also served for ten years as judge in the county court of Covington and as postmaster for a time in Montezuma.[20] Devereux stayed in Covington County until 1833 when he headed to northeast Alabama for Macon County, which had been organized on December 18, 1832.

Julien S. Devereux, meanwhile, had become well established during the years the family lived in Covington County. In 1826 after he had reached the age of twenty-one, he was appointed to fill a vacancy as clerk of the circuit court of Covington County.[21] Before the end of the year, on December 28, 1826, he married Adaline Rebeccah Bradley. A newspaper account of the wedding titled Devereux as "colonel" and referred to his bride as the "daughter of Samuel Bradley, deceased, late of South Carolina."[22] Adaline had been born on April 6, 1803, and was two years older than Julien. The marriage would end in a separation some fourteen years later and then in divorce after Julien Devereux came to Texas. One child, Mary Emily was born to the couple at the "Hermitage," Covington County,[23] on Decemer 16,

---

[18]Ibid.

[19]Brantley, **Three Capitals: A Book About the First Three Capitals of Alabama**, 237, 239, 241.

[20]Record of the Devereux Family.

[21]Statement of Reuben Safford, Judge of Circuit Court of Covington County, September 22, 1826, Devereux Papers.

[22]**Alabama** (Montgomery) **Journal**, January 12, 1827.

[23]According to Willa Allene Robinson in a letter to D. W. dated May 15, 1950, "The Devereux home was called The Hermitage, and was near the foot of a very long, steep hill which was called Devereux Hill. It is still known by that name, although most people call it Debro instead of Devereux."

Concerning Montezuma, Miss Robinson writes: "There is no sign of, nor name of Montezuma now, however. The settlement was quite near the banks of Conecuh river, near the present site of River Falls, Alabama, and only a few miles from the present site of Andalusia, the present county seat of Covington County. Montezuma was the former county seat and at one time was a very wealthy village, or town. It was practically destroyed by flood waters, and later completely destroyed by fires." Records destroyed in this and other county seats in Alabama have made it difficult to work with original source materials.

1830, but she died on January 28, 1831.

Julien Devereux must have been considered among the learned men in Alabama during the 1830's. He was elected to membership in the Philomathic Society of the University of Alabama on November 13, 1831, when Washington D. Miller, who came to Texas in 1837 and served for a time as private secretary to Sam Houston, sent the following note to Devereux:

> Julien S. Devereux, Esq
> Montezuma
> Covington County, Alabama
>
> > University of Alabama
> > November 13, 1831
>
> Dear Sir:
> The members of the Philomathic Society of the University of Alabama having associated themselves for the purpose of promoting, so far as may be in their power the cause of literature and virtue—and with a desire to obtain an extensive acquaintance with historical, scientific and literary subjects the discussion of which may be attended with results beneficial to the youthful mind . . . have instructed me to request of you the favour of permitting your name to be enrolled among the honorary members of said society.
> Unanimous wish
>
> > Washington D. Miller
> > Corresponding Sec'y.[24]

In 1832 Julien Devereux represented Conecuh County in the Alabama Legislature,[25] and from 1833 to 1836 because of his "friendly disposition and liberal views"[26] he served as a trustee of the University of Alabama.[27]

Most probably by 1833 John William and Julien Devereux were living together. In October of that year the father and son headed north to the county of Montgomery which at the time bordered on land held by the Creek Indians. John William Devereux has recorded the account of this move:

1833

Mem We started from home in Covington County on the

---

[24]Washington D. Miller to Julien S. Devereux, November 13, 1831, Devereux Papers.
[25]William Garrett, **Reminiscences of Public Men in Alabama**, 747; B. F. Riley, **History of Conecuh County, Alabama**, 102.
[26]A. Woods to Julien S. Devereux, December 21, 1833, Devereux Papers.
[27]Garrett, **Reminiscences of Public Men in Alabama**, 792.

18th October 1833 with Waggon & team. Mr. Bond the
Overseer Julien & myself and 6 negroe men to build at
(Hobsons Choice Valverdi) in Montgomery County preparatory for making a crop the ensuing year—went
to Henry Jordans   15 miles
the next day rain'y & cold went to the Stinking
branch below Gainers Store   16 miles
next day to Baptist Meeting house at Double [?]
branches (Cold & Windy)   20 miles
next day to Wynns 6 miles above Boyds and 3 miles
above Devils Backbone   22   do
next day to the head branch of Conecuh found the
road stopd by Indians (We opend it)
                                                         18   do
next day to (Hobsons Choice Valverdi) our place
                                                         11   do
                                                         ─────────
                                                      102 total[28]

When moving to a new area the first thing settlers usually
did was to build a cabin. Many of the new settlers "built their
cabins in clearings, within call of each other, on a commanding
river bluff or near some bold spring in the interior."[29] The
choice spots for settlements usually included a water supply, a
river or creek for navigation, and soil suitable for crops.

Historians of Alabama and other localities have written at
some length about the log cabin and the role it has played in
the frontier way of life. Writers point out that once the pioneer
had selected the site for his new home he was faced with the
problem of providing shelter for himself and his family. The
new and primitive life was typified by the type of dwelling erected. Building materials were secured from the forest and the
log cabin was the most common type of abode. The cabin usually consisted of one or two rooms, depending on the size of the
family. There was virtually no iron in these cabins and the
floors were of dirt or split logs, called puncheon. No nails were
used and weighted poles held on the roof, which was made of
brush or crude shingles.[30] As the family increased in size, a
buckskin curtain was often strung up to divide the cabin into
more rooms. The younger children usually slept on pallets on
the floor, while the older ones slept in the attic "in the barn

---

[28]J. W. Devereux's Memorandum and Common Place Book.
[29]Peter J. Hamilton, **Colonial Mobile; an Historical Study,** 462.
[30]Edward Chambers Bettes, **Early History of Huntsville, Alabama, 1804
to 1870,** pp. 7-8.

loft . . . and even under trees and most anywhere."[31]

The settler who built the double log cabin joined the rooms with a passageway. Chimneys were usually built of clay-daubed sticks or stones and the large open fireplace served for cooking, heating, and lighting. For extra space the pioneer often constructed a lean-to behind his cabin. The walls were of notched logs and "the doors and shutters were of crude boards, and the shingles were hand-split . . ."[32] The hardships and privations of this type of home did not deter the newcomer. The spirit of cooperation of the frontier eased the problem of construction because, with the help of neighbors, a cabin could occasionally be built in about one day.[33]

When John William Devereux made the move to Hobson's Choice in Montgomery County he built his cabin as the other settlers had done. Although writers have had much to say about "cabin culture" on the frontier, it is rare to find information where a pioneer cabin builder wrote any instructions giving specific details on just how a log cabin was to be built.[34] John William Devereux did record the details of construction of his Alabama cabin and because this is a significant historical document his writings are quoted in full.

> *Mem* for my house at Hobsons Choice
> side logs 21 feet Long Hew'd after raisd
> end logs 17 feet long   do
> eaves 7 feet over wall Westside eave beams
> 24 feet long 3 of these and one pair more
> above 23 feet long eve 3 on each side to support the Roof
> foundation firstly on sills 23 feet long
> 7 to project at Westside for Piazza
> 2 other sills cross them 28 feet long
> 7 for End Piazza on North end
> Chimney south and to be 5 feet wide
> in front and 3 back & 3 deep &
> 4 (or 3½ feet high) door gap 3 feet
> 3 Inches Wide & 6 feet 7 inches high the cheeks 3 Inches thick
> shutter 2 feet 9 Inches wide—Window
> 3 feet Wide gap & 3 Inch Cheeks & 4½ feet high
> the side door to be on the West side &

[31]**Ibid.**, 8.
[32]Abernethy, **The Formative Period in Alabama**, 26.
[33]Moore, **History of Alabama**, 183.
[34]At least four authorities on log cabins have substantiated this statement: Roger N. Conger, Fred Cotten, Robert E. Davis, and Paul Ragsdale.

the window opposite East and
both this door and window *exactly*
8 feet clear from the North end
pitch about 10 feet from the floor
to Joists—or higher to suit eves—cover 4 feet Cypress
boards put on shingle fashion
either on Ribs lin'd and hew'd
or Rafters   *Mem* I think ribs with
rafters pin'd on them may be
best as planks for gables can't be
had—conveniently one End door
same size of side one to be in the
north end—Chimney stick & clay
good sized funnel and some feet
above ridge of roof cop'd to prevent
washing—the expos'd part to be of
Cypress   *Mem* one Joist to be exactly 8 feet from
North end for partition
Mem   first 3 places 7 feet from floor 23 feet
long to give 6 feet projection for side Piazza
& the Middle one to be exactly eight feet clear
from N end for partition—then 3 other plates
23 feet long to go over the others and to
project 3 feet each side to support the roof
then Ribs 24 feet long to give 4 to cover
the Chimney

Recapitulation

side logs 21 feet long
end   do   17   do long
2 sills 23 feet long bottom sills
2   do   28   do crossing the others
3 plates 24 do 7 feet projecting W. side
3   do   23 do over the others 3 feet projecting each side
Rafters 24 feet long to cover chimney
Roof plates
Mem   I conclude to alter the length of my first sills
to 22 feet to give five feet for piazza and
my plate from 24 to 23 feet to give
the projection 6 feet in place of 7
Mem   I think I will have two windows on
the East side—then the bedroom will have
a window East and door north in the end
and the other room door on West side Window
on East & chimney on the south—
Chimney outside back 5½ wide & 3½ feet
deep and inside front 5 feet wide 3 feet
deep back & 3 feet wide at back
    (take Julien's Chimney for pattern)
Mem   Measur'd ground in little field near

spring for my residence 105 yards wide
(1½ acre) and 150 yards long or 315 feet wide
& 450 feet long—trees to be planted 15 feet
apart E & W and 20 N & S—about 300 will
fill the space but room to be left for a small
flower Garden and for house & yard—30
pannels of fence on E. side bring 30 plumb trees
assorted to plant at corners of fence[35]

Macon County, organized and carved out of the region
ceded by the Muscogee Indians in 1832,[36] was the next place of
residence of the Devereuxs, and in 1835 Julien S. Devereux was
issued a commission in the county as justice of the peace.[37]
During 1835 and 1836 John William Devereux represented the
county in the senate.[38] In 1836 Julien S. Devereux had some
federal military service when he enrolled "6 June 1836 at Lime
Creek, Alabama, to serve for the period of 90 days, and was
honorable discharged 3 September 1836 at Montgomery, Alabama, a private of Sample's Company, Alabama Militia (Creek
War.)"[39]

The Devereux Papers preserved during the "Alabama years
(1817-1841)" are not nearly so extensive as those pertaining to
the family in Texas, but the available documents do reveal a
few facts about the professional and financial aspects of the
Devereuxs. Both Julien Sidney and John William Devereux had
rather large holdings in land and slaves. Julien may have acquired some additional wealth in his marriage to Adaline R.
Bradley, as members of the Bradley family later charged, for
the family was one of considerable means.

In the Devereux Papers there is frequent mention of plantation operations, but a complete picture of just what these Devereux plantations in Conecuh, Covington, Montgomery, and
Macon counties were like cannot be reconstructed. The operations of the plantations must have been of major proportions on

---

[35]J. W. Devereux's Memorandum and Common Place Book.
[36]Brewer, **Alabama: Her History, Resources, War Record, and Public
Men,** 336.
[37]Certificate dated April 28, 1835, signed by E. A. Webster, Secretary of
State, Devereux Papers.
[38]Brewer, **Alabama: Her History, Resources, War Record, and Public
Men,** 345.
[39]Department of the Army, to D. W., March 22, 1950. Nothing has been
found of record to show that this organization had any combat service, and
the Alabama Department of Archives and History cannot supply additional
information.

the Alabama scene in the 1820's and 1830's, for one document preserved, an agreement between Julien S. Devereux and his overseer Johnson Malone, December 28, 1839, would indicate that Julien S. Devereux was experienced in plantation operations.

Agreement between Julien S. Devereux & Johnson Malone This agreement entered into and signed between and by Julien S. Devereux and Johnson Malone both of the county of Macon and State of Alabama. Witnesseth. That the said Devereux has agreed to employ said Malone for the term of Twelve months to commence on the first day of January next (1840). The said Malone undertakes and engages to manage said Devereux farming business, and such other business, as said Devereux may require, such as taking care of stock, superintending and assisting in carrying on buildings, clearing land, or other improvements, giving and packing cotton, and all other services and duties, that are necessary to be performed by a successful sober and prudent overseer, his entire attention and services to be devoted to the interest of said Devereux as well on Sundays as any other days, he is to give his attention to the stock, Corn etc that is kept at the residence of said Devereux, and endeavor to prevent it from being destroyed and wasted as well as the stock, corn etc. that is kept for the use of the plantation, he is to use his best exertions to prevent the slaves of said Devereux from going about through the country of nights and Sundays, without the permission of said Devereux, and to prevent the slaves of other persons from coming on the plantation or at the residence of said Devereux, without written permits from their owners or employers. The said Malone is not to permit the negroes and work animals put under his charge to be employed in his own service or in the service of any other person without the permission of said Devereux. The said Devereux is to have the controul commonly exercised by employers, in having business carried on. Any time task by said Malone, other than working on roads, serving on Juries, attending elections and militia musters, is to be deducted from his wages and at the expiration of the said twelve months and upon the faithful performance of said engagements by the said Malone, the said Devereux is hereby bound to pay him the sum of Four Hundred and Twenty five Dollars, in money, or to be paid in Gin Cotton at Twelve and a half cents per pound, delivered at the Gin House of said Devereux, the amount aforesaid to be paid in cash or cotton at said price at the option or discretion of the said Devereux, provided however that this said Malone shall have the privilege at the end of said Twelve months of taking three Hundred and

fifty Dollars in full consideration of his years wages, in the place of the four Hundred and twenty five dollars in cotton at Twelve and a half cents per pound; and the said Devereux further agrees to furnish the said Malone, with a comfortable cabin to live in near the plantation and to furnish the said Malone with forty bushels of corn, to be measured and put in a house to itself for his use during the said Twelve months and the said Devereux does not agree to furnish the said Malone with corn for any other purposes whatsoever, the said Malone is to keep the cribs of said Devereux securely locked and attend to the feeding of the mules and horses at the plantation in person, and if the said Malone should keep a horse or mare of his own, the said Devereux agrees to have it fed the same as other work animals, provided that the said horse or mare, shall be used in the service of the said Devereux and to plough whenever the said Devereux may require it, and if the said Malone concludes not to keep a horse or mare of his own, then the said Devereux agrees that the said Malone may use a horse, or mule to ride to attend to the business of said Devereux, Each one of the parties to this agreement reserves to himself the right and priviledge to quit or seperate whenever he may become dissatisfied or, whenever he may think proper to do so. And if the separation is caused by the said Devereux, the wages of the said Malone up to the time that a seperation may take place, is to be considered due, in proportion to the time he may have remained in the employment of the said Devereux, and if the said Malone, quits of his own accord, he is to wait for whatever wages may be due him, until the expiration of the said Twelve months. The parties to this agreement, having signed two agreements of the same Tenor and date—this 28th day of December 1839
Witness

W. R. Wheelis
A. M. Devereux Julien S. Devereux
his
Johnson x Malone[40]
mark

While living in Macon County, which bordered on the Creek Indian Country, Julien S. Devereux did considerable speculating with Indian lands. A method used by white settlers to acquire choice Indian lands was to assist in the administration of a dead Indian's estate. Upon the death of the Indian, legal proceedings administered by a court or appropriate representative of the

[40]Agreement between Julien S. Devereux and Johnson Malone, December 28, 1839, Devereux Papers.

Office of Indian Affairs, would be held in order to determine the debts the deceased owed and to allow creditors to assert legitimate claims against the estate. In many instances land owned by the deceased would be sold, and the proceeds from the sale would be applied against those outstanding debts. A white settler would be appointed administrator of the estate, and at the foreclosure proceedings he would recognize the lowest bid of an associate. As a result the land could be acquired below its reasonable market value.[41]

Associated with Devereux in many land speculation deals was his partner Wildridge C. Thompson. On one occasion Devereux was charged with paying $1,000 to the heirs of a dead Indian for a valuable piece of land and later selling it for $10,705. When an investigation was held, however, Devereux was cleared of any misconduct and his operations in the land deal were described as "perfectly fair and honorable."[42]

This particular case, known as the Pen hadjo Case, was in the courts for four or five years, and although Devereux was cleared of any wrongdoing in the matter there came up the question of legal title and other persons became involved. Devereux and Thompson had a lawyer, Thomas Abbott of Washington, D. C., working on the case which went to the Office of Indian Affairs of the War Department. Secretary of War Joel R. Poinsett was advised in April, 1840, that the case had been considered by the Creek Commissioners and that, "They recommend the confirmation of the Administration sale, on the special condition that Julien S. Devereux & Wildridge C. Thompson pay the sum of $5,000 in such a manner as the President may direct for the use and benefit of the heirs & legal representatives of Pen hadjo deceased."[43] A second party in the case, G. D. Shortridge, appealed the ruling, however, and the outcome is not known for Julien Devereux left the next year for Texas.

Most probably there were losses in the land speculating business and perhaps also in the operation of his plantation, for Julien S. Devereux was faced with heavy financial obligations in the late 1830's and early 1840's. For a time he was associated in business matters with his cousin, Alfred M. Devereux, and his sister's husband, Henry B. Holcombe, who had business

---

[41]John B. Hogan to Julien S. Devereux, August 16, 1836, **ibid.**
[42]**Ibid.**
[43]J. H. Crawford to J. R. Poinsett, April 1, 1840, **ibid.**

interests of major importance in Mobile. These relatives suffered losses in many business ventures with Julien Devereux.

Between 1838 and 1841 Julien Devereux experienced considrable difficulty with creditors. During that period his debts piled up, totaling several thousand dollars, and he was threatened with court action on several personal notes and bills of exchange.[44] These transactions had an adverse affect on credit ratings and were always looked upon with dread.[45] Devereux's financial worries were typical of those faced by individuals during the general Panic of 1837, which was most severely felt in the West and South and lasted until 1843. Two main causes of the panic—expansion of credit and land speculation—were in large measure responsible for Devereux's precarious financial condition.

As early as April 5, 1838, when he was thirty-two years old, Julien S. Devereux had decided to move to the Republic of Texas, when he signed at Houston his intention to become a citizen.[46] During the summer of 1840 he was trying to sell his home and land in Alabama, and on July 25 Robert Dougherty agreed to buy. Dougherty wrote to an associate, Whiting Oliver:

> Upon consulting with my wife I found her willing to move to Macon. You may therefore see Col Devereux & say to him we will take his land & two thousand bushels of corn for twenty one thousand five hundred dollars. Thirteen thousand five hundred Dolls down. When we get possession & the ballance twelve months therafter [sic]. . . . Say to old Mr. Devereux that he may keep possession of *his house* & *his flowers* & *his fruits* (provided we trade) as long as he pleases.[47]

John William Devereux was seventy-one years old at the time and wanted to continue to reside in his Valverdi cabin.

On December 17, 1840, Julien Sidney and Adaline Rebeccah Devereux were separated. According to the "Articles of Agree-

[44]Citation to Sheriff, County Court of Macon County, April 30, 1838; Instrument of Protest, Tuskegee, Montgomery, Alabama, February 13, 1837; Citation, Montgomery County, Alabama, October 8, 1839; Citations, Montgomery County, Alabama, October 1, 1840; Citation, Macon County, Alabama, March 25, 1841, **ibid.**

[45]H. B. Holcombe to Julien S. Devereux, March 2, 1839, **ibid.**

[46]Undated affidavit, Montgomery County, Republic of Texas, **ibid.**

[47]Robert Dougherty to Whiting Oliver, July 25, 1840, **ibid.** Dougherty planned to move to Devereux's place by December 25.

ment"[48] it was "the pleasure, intention, and anxious desire of the said Adaline R. to leave the bed & board of her said Husband." In the settlement of property Adaline was to receive twenty-three slaves and "all the firnature [sic] of said Julien S. lately packed up with a view of being carried to Pensacola in Florida."[49] Julien was to pay a thousand dollars to Adaline for the "use and hire" of certain slaves during 1841 and the slaves were to be returned to Adaline on January 1, 1842. Descendants of the Bradley family have charged that during 1841 Julien Devereux "deserted his wife, took much of her money, many of her slaves and . . . [went] to Texas without ever having made contact with his wife or home and friends."[50]

Perhaps the separation from his wife along with heavy debts caused Julien S. Devereux to look westward, and in October of 1841 he headed for "Jasper County in Texas."[51] His reasons for leaving home and moving to Texas to get a new start in life were similar to situations faced by men like Sam Houston, Anson Jones, Mirabeau B. Lamar and others who had also experienced marital problems and political and financial reverses. Devereux

---

[48]Articles of Agreement, December 17, 1840, Macon County, State of Alabama, **ibid.**

[49]Ibid.

[50]Willa Allene Robinson to D. W., May 15, 1950. Miss Robinson writes that "Adaline Rebeccah Bradley and her sister, Margaret Matilda Bradley—who married her cousin James H. Bradley the year preceding the marriage of Julien & Adaline were the sole heirs to a great estate or plantation and many negroes, near Montezuma [Covington County]. At the death of Margaret Matilda Bradley—sister of Adaline Devereux—Adaline took Margaret's 3 week old infant daughter, "Margaret Matilda Bradley 2nd," and reared her to young womanhood, later moving to Brooklyn, Alabama, Conecuh County, where my grandfather—Julius Gurdon Robinson 'Sr., met and married Margaret Matilda Bradley 2nd. After their marriage—and at the death of Adaline Devereux, my grandmother (the niece of Adaline Devereux) became sole heir to the vast Bradley estate, a part of which Devereux had misused. My grandfather filed suits in court in an attempt to recover the property from Col. Devereux, but without success. It was never definitely known [in Alabama] what became of Devereux, as he could never be contacted by lawyers in the property cases. Therefore the property was lost by my grandmother." Mention should be made, perhaps, that on October 26, 1830, Julien S. Devereux was made administrator of the estate of his mother-in-law, and with John William Devereux presiding at the Covington County Orphan Court at Chamber on December 1, 1831, the "court order'd that said administrator [Julien S. Devereux] be authorized to sell the slaves belonging to the Estate of said Mary Bradley deceased." As early as January 18, 1831, Julien Devereux began to dispose of the Bradley estate and in February, 1832, he sold several slaves in the amount of $5312.25, and on November 2, 1832, Devereux had collected $1065.92 and had turned the amount over to "the clerk's office." Again on November 2, 1833, Devereux turned over to "the clerk's office" money collected from the sale of slaves and income from rent on the Bradley plantation.

[51]J. W. Devereux's Memorandum and Common Place Book.

was "well known in Alabama" in the early 1840's, and an acquaintance once stated that "a more honorable man than he while here could not have been found."[52] Devereux may have debated at some length about staying in Alabama for he wrote: "Reconsidered the matter [of removal] declined making a crawfish of myself and finally came to Texas."[53] Father John William Devereux was not far behind; he left "Valverdi Macon County Alabama on the 26th of April 1842 for the single Star Republic of Texas,"[54] and across the detailed description of his log cabin on the pages of his "Memorandum and Common Place Book" he wrote in huge letters what so many pioneers would say with "G.T.T." on the door of a cabin:

> Built it
> occupied it &
> left it and
> gone to Texas
> fool move[55]

---

[52]Nat Cook to Gustave Cook, March 16, 1852, Devereux Papers.
[53]Julien S. Devereux's Monte Verdi Plantation Account Book for 1849-1854.
[54]Record of the Devereux Family.
[55]J. W. Devereux's Memorandum and Common Place Book.

CHAPTER IV

Terrebonne Plantation

Bon Terre toute
Terre bon toute
or Terrebon do for
name of a farm
Terrebonne that's it[1]
O! Texas
You vex us
& perplex us
          how it rains
          how it rains[2]

JULIEN S. Devereux came to the Republic of Texas for the first time on April 5, 1838, almost two years after independence had been won at San Jacinto, and at Houston he filed a declaration of intention to become a citizen with E. H. Winfield, acting clerk of the District Court of Harrisburg County.[3] Julien Devereux's cousin, Alfred M. Devereux, who also came to settle in Texas in 1841, may have been influenced to come to the new Republic by some of the letters written by Alabama settlers newly arrived in Texas. One such letter was written by James R. Hines from Independence, Washington County, to Alfred M. Devereux on April 4, 1840, and gave a glowing picture of Texas:

> . . . Texas Alfred is undoubtedly the garden spot of the world. . . . I am going to examine Montgomery Cty in a short time and will then report to you [.] it Lies on the Sanja Sinto [San Jacinto] all so Liberty and Jasper Ctys and i think i shall Locate in one or the other [.] I have been offered Land on the Sanja Sinto at one Dollar pr acre

[1]J. W. Devereux Notebook ('1847).
[2]Record of the Devereux Family.
[3]Undated affidavit, County of Montgomery, Republic of Texas, Devereux Papers.

i will examine it and wright to you how i like [.] we have had a considerable difficulty with the Cumany [Comanche] Indians—their was a Treaty agreed upon the time and place the Parleys met⁴ the Indians Brought in a Miss Lockhart a prisoner and the whites told them that they might consider themselves all prisoners if they did not give up all the prisoners they had [.] at this demand they all being in the Council House one of the Chiefs struck at and killed one of the guard at the door with a knife [.] the fight terminated with a loss on the part of the indians 35 killed and 13 of them chiefs [.] this took place at St. Antonio [.] they are convalesant [.] it is reported Generally believed that Mexico has acknowledge the independence of Texas [.] it has given a great rise to business.

if you have any notion of this country do not think about money to by corne and meate for I shal [have] plenty for us both and you no you can have as Long as i have one *yeare* [ear] i have a fine stock of hogs and 3 cows and calves you shall sheare with me in all I have do not think of hard times [.] This is the easiest country to live in i ever saw [.]⁵

Such a letter as this did offer hope for a solution to the financial woes of Alfred M. and Julien S. Devereux. In the United States the effects of the Panic of 1837 were being felt while the Republic of Texas with its liberal land policy appeared as a "land of promise."

By June of 1841 Julien S. Devereux had sent to Texas an advance party with some of his slaves and personal possessions under the supervision of Andrew G. Scott. On June 22, 1841, Scott was within eight miles of the Mississippi border, and he wrote the following to Julien Devereux:

. . . Deer sir I will inform you that we are geting along but vary hilly and our load is so heavy for it is up one hill and down another all day till it is a nuff to kill the mules and horse and as for Rody⁶ it is impossable to do any thing with her for she will sleap inspite of everything that we can do for whiping will do her no good [.] she has come vary neer leting Antoynette⁷ fall out of the wagon several

---

⁴This is a reference to the Council House Fight episode in San Antonio on March 19, 1840, when representatives of the Texas government and leaders of the Comanche Indians met.
⁵James R. Hines to A. M. Devereux, April 4, 1840, Devereux Papers.
⁶Rody was a slave.
⁷This was most probably Antoinette Scott, an illegitimate daughter of Julien S. Devereux, born on May 1, 1840, in Macon County, Alabama. The mother of Antoinette was a sister of Andrew G. Scott.

times [.] now I will tell you that forage is vary scarse [.]
We has to pay from seventy five cents to a dollar and fifty
cents a Bushel for cor[n] in Alabamma and we heard that
in mississippi it is worse. . . . we hear that the roads is as
Bad on a head as any we have trveled [travelled]. we have
distributed all of our load that we can spair and it is all
that we can do to get along now. . . .[8]

The trip to Texas continued to be a trying one for Scott
and the party. The "bolster on the Big waggon broke" on June
23 and the same day there was a "vary Bad storm in the pine
woods."[9] The group faced a crisis at the Mississippi River for
"there the river had caved and taken in the road and we had to
cut a road about a quarter of a mile through the swamp."[10] On
July 8 the party arrived in Louisiana.

With additional possessions belonging to Julien Devereux,
Alfred Devereux left Macon County, Alabama, for Jasper County, Texas, on September 30, 1841. He took thirty-five slaves;
four of his own, twenty belonging to John W. Devereux, and
eleven owned by Julien Devereux. Alfred Devereux, according
to John William Devereux's account, left Alabama for Texas in
"a waggon drawn by 6 fine Mules to carry forage & provisions—
our light Waggon with two Mules (belonging to Alfred) and our
one horse Jersey drawn by our horse & he [Alfred] rode a fine
sorrel mare belonging to Julien. . . ."[11]

On October 8 Julien Devereux followed with "a Waggon & 6
mules with 19 negroes . . . and at the same time a Waggon with
2 pairs of Oxen & 14 negroes. There will make 23 for his wife's
share of the spoils."[12] Devereux's brother-in-law and business
associate, Henry B. Holcombe, was in the vicinity of Macon
County when the move to Texas was getting underway. John
W. Devereux had a dislike for his son-in-law and recorded at the
time that Holcombe "had gone to Montgomery probably to
spread the emigrating news and to offer his services as a *debtor-
catcher* to the Bank."[13]

No available records show just what debts Julien Devereux

[8]Andrew G. Scott to Julien S. Devereux, June 22, 1841, Devereux Papers.
[9]Andrew G. Scott to Julien S. Devereux, July 10, 1841, ibid.
[10]Ibid.
[11]J. W. Devereux's Memorandum and Common Place Book.
[12]Ibid. William B. Bond signed a receipt at Conecuh County, Alabama,
on October 22, 1841, to deliver to Julien S. Devereux at the "Court House
of Jasper County in the Republic of Texas" nineteen negro slaves and "Also
one six horse Road waggon, and eight mules and one gray horse."
[13]Ibid.

left behind in Alabama. Jointly Julien and Alfred Devereux had title to 2400 acres of land in Alabama[14] and this was sold in January of 1841 to William and Robert Dougherty for "20,500 or at the sales of $8.54 per acre $12,500 paid down and $8,000 in 12 months."[15] How far Julien Devereux's share of the land sale was used to clear up his own debts cannot be determined.

Thirty-six year old Julien Devereux was in Jasper County, Texas, in November of 1841, where at the time, he took an oath of allegiance to the Republic of Texas.[16] The next month he moved west some 125 miles to establish a home in Montgomery County, situated in the flat prairie and rolling wooded plains of Southeast Texas. For the next four and a half years Devereux would attempt to operate a plantation in this area.

Montgomery County, organized in 1837, comprised all of Washington County east of the Brazos River and extended to the Trinity, including all or parts of present Grimes, Walker, San Jacinto, Madison, and Waller counties. The county was named for General Richard Montgomery of American Revolutionary fame, as was the county seat, which was also created in 1837.[17] Located relatively near the coast, not too distant from the port of Galveston and the town of Houston, the county was ideally situated for commercial and agricultural purposes and experienced a steady growth in population. The first settlers who came developed their land by first clearing away the forests and then putting fields into the cultivation of corn and cotton. Many of the settlers, like the Devereuxs, were well-to-do planters possessing slaves. The first courthouse, a two-room structure, was erected at Montgomery in 1842, and by 1845 a newspaper, the Montgomery *Patriot*, was being published.[18] Montgomery was the only town in the county during the early years, and it rapidly developed into one of the important trading centers. Cotton and other products were taken to Houston, the nearest market, some sixty miles distant.

[14]Julien owned 1718 acres and Alfred owned 682 acres.
[15]Julien S. Devereux's Monte Verdi Plantation Account Book for 1849-1854.
[16]Undated affidavit, County of Montgomery, Republic of Texas, Devereux Papers.
[17]Some persons maintain that the town of Montgomery was named for the family name of Margaret Montgomery. W. N. Martin, A History of Montgomery, M.A. Thesis, Sam Houston State Teachers College, Huntsville, Texas, 1.
[18]The Choir Invisible: An Early History of Montgomery, unpaged.

Shortly after Julien and Alfred Devereux arrived in Texas they had some misunderstanding concerning the financial arrangements of expenditures for the move. Julien made a charge that Alfred owed him $500 while Alfred maintained that he spent $1014 of his own money to bring Julien's slaves and possessions to Texas and that Julien still owed him $514.[19] The case was in the courts for several years and evidence of the outcome is not available in the Devereux Papers.

After getting settled in Montgomery County, Julien Devereux sent word to his father who had remained in Valverdi, Macon County, Alabama, to join him in Texas. The aged father was anxious to join his only son and recorded: "I left my cottage at Valverdi Macon County Alabama on the 26th of April 1842 for the single Star Republic of Texas in the 74th year of my age and arriv'd at Terrebonne my sons plantation in Middle Texas on the 26th of May."[20] John Devereux kept a careful record of his expenses to Texas and these totaled $548.65. Devereux went to Mobile and then to New Orleans where he took a steamer for Galveston.

Julien Devereux received a letter from his sister Louisiana Holcombe written on May 4, 1842, in which she expressed surprise that her brother had left "for Texas so soon." She discussed his debts and observed that she "regretted exceedingly" that Devereux "had not been more scrutinizing into the matter before you adopted the alternative you did—your sacrifices have of course been much over any amount you could have lost by

---

[19]"Julien S. Devereux vs. Alfred M. Devereux," undated item, Devereux Papers. Alfred Devereux noted that on October 30th he "crossed the Sabine $1.00" and the next day "feriage at the Sabine . . . $8.75."

[20]J. W. Devereux's Memorandum and Common Place Book. The elderly father dreamed of building a cabin in Texas and wrote the following just before starting on his journey to Texas:

 Mem If I shall live to build a house in Texas I think the best dimensions for my cottage will be one about 20 feet long in the clear or (22) logs long and 16 Clear wide or logs 18 long—the three Cross or ends to project about 6 feet one at each end & one in the middle—window and door next the fire place near the partition projecting log door south & window opposite the other end door in the middle of end & window south about 10 feet 8½ do between floor & joists—fire place 5 feet wide & 3½ high 3½ deep sills framed together & end from the chimney projecting for Piazza 6 feet on blocks 18 Inches—door to be cut 3 feet 4 Inches wide to allow cheeks 2 Inches & leave 3 feet door shutters—Windows 4 feet high & 3 feet wide allowing for 2 Inch cheeks which will take sash for 12 lights of glass 8 by 10—plates long enough to cover chimney.

remaining."[21] Bad times still prevailed in Alabama, however, and Louisiana described her own family financial affairs as being "just about in as bad a condition as they can be."[22]

Devereux's land in Montgomery County, consisting of 495 acres in the William M. Rankin league situated a few miles west and southwest of the town of Montgomery, was purchased on December 3, 1841, from Cyrus Dikeman.[23] Lake Creek, which rises in Grimes County and flows southeast for thirty miles into the West Fork of San Jacinto River in south central Montgomery County, ran through the Rankin league. Important also to the Devereuxs and other early settlers in the area were such waterways as the San Jacinto River, which traverses Montgomery County, and Spring Creek, which forms the boundary line between Montgomery and Harris counties.

Julien S. Devereux's plantation was called "Terrebonne," a French word meaning good land. The use of the name was decided upon when several versions and combinations of the French words for good land were considered:

> Bon Terre toute
> Terre bon toute
> or Terrebon do for
> name of a farm
> *Terrebonne that's it*[24]

The land of Montgomery County was highly productive and the Devereuxs had great hopes of success during the first years in Texas. An early general description of the new Texas country by John William Devereux was:

> Texas is in general a Prairie Country[.] near the sea coast particularly there are plenty of Timbered land in Eastern Texas and East of the Trinity—There are Timbered lands in Eastern Texas that have not much under growth and the range is fine for all kinds of live stock—there they have good water—it may be called the Paridice of Inferior animals but only "the land of promise" to man[.][25]

---

[21]Louisiana Holcombe to Julien S. Devereux, May 4, 1842, Devereux Papers.
[22]**Ibid.**
[23]County Clerk, Montgomery County, Texas, to D. W., April 18, 1961; May 6, 1961.
[24]J. W. Devereux Notebook (1847).
[25]Record of the Devereux Family.

A newspaper clipping pasted in J. W. Devereux's Memorandum and Common Place Book gave the following description of the Texas Republic:

> There are but few belts of alluvial bottoms, and according to the information of every traveller, they are all either sold or mortgaged. Only the most miserable, most barren, or the most swampy lands are remaining, and are as yet not in the hands of the speculators. In summer the rivers dry up in the sand, and in winter they swell into lakes. The yellow fever and all billious diseases reign there, and along the whole extent of the coast of the Gulf of Mexico. He who settles in the dry and high country, lives, and wars with the Commanches, and is hardly better off. There are some very small strips in the interior more densely peopled: the whole mass of the country is a wilderness.

For this description Devereux wrote "Smack" and commented that the "discription of Texas exagerated but too much truth in the statement as relates to Middle and Western Texas."[26]

Julien Devereux filed a divorce petition on February 10, 1843, against his wife, Adaline Rebeccah, from whom he had separated in December, 1840, and who had remained in Alabama. In the petition Devereux charged that Adaline possessed "such unmeasured and uncontrolled excesses of passion & ill temper and such outrageous conduct . . . to render the life of your petitioner one of Extreme Misery."[27] Patrick C. Jack, member of Stephen F. Austin's second colony and an important figure in the period of colonization and the Republic, presided as judge of the Sixth Judicial District and heard the divorce case at the spring term of 1843. John William Devereux gave the following deposition concerning Adaline's conduct:

> She was of the most violant and passionate temper. the bursts of passion to which the defendant was subject brought on frequent hemhorrege which eventually disqualified her entirely from the duties of a wife[.] her conduct as a mother was so inconsiderate and neglectful that the only child of the parties to the suite died for want of attention and proper maternal treatment. She the defendant would neither suckle the infant herself nor suffer a wet nurse to do it and the child for want of suitable nurishment

---

[26]J. W. Devereux's Memorandum and Common Place Book.
[27]Divorce Petition, County of Montgomery, Republic of Texas, February 10, 1843, Devereux Papers.

died. She was so extravagant and wasteful that it was with difficulty that her husbands whole income could meet and supply her unreasonable and exorbetant demands. In spite of all her husbands remonstrances she would upon the slightest grounds and generally without any cause beat and abuse the servants of the plaintiff in the most unmerciful and unwarrantable manner. at the slightest check given any of these outrages she would throw herself on the ground and give vent to her passions by the most violent cries and exclamations inconsistent with the proper delicasy of a female. . . . She became addicted to habits of intemperance and when in that situation would lie cursing and swearing in the most vulgar and unfeminine manner. . . .[28]

The jury on March 29, 1843, ruled for the plaintiff and granted the divorce.

Three months later on June 27, Julien Devereux was married to Sarah Ann Landrum in a ceremony performed on Lake Creek by Samuel D. Hay.[29] The bride, who described her husband at the time as "a man of wealth and high standing," was sixteen years old and twenty years younger than Julien. She had been born on May 1, 1827, in Marengo County, Alabama, and was the daughter of John and Mary Wells Landrum, who had arrived in Texas on December 31, 1829.[30] John Landrum

---

[28]**Ibid.** The United States Census for 1850 reported Adeline R. Devereaux [sic] resided in Conecuh County, Alabama.

[29]Family Record, Devereux Papers.

[30]E. L. Blair, **Early History of Grimes County,** 125. After Sarah Devereux had reached an advanced age she wrote the following notes concerning her family background: "My father came to Texas in the winter of 1829 or 30 from Maringo [Marengo] County, Alabama. Came overland to Natches Miss. Took Boat and came up Red River to Alexandria [Louisiana]. I have heard my Mother often relate a little incident that occurred there. I was not quite three years old. She had some purchases to make preparatory to starting on the road for Texas. While she was busy with her shoping a woman came in and seeme[d] very much attracted & amused with my childish prattle. I became quite friendly with her[.] She then asked mother to let her take me to her house only a little way. She would bring me back in a little while. After the woman had been gone with me some time, Mother had gotten through attending to her perchas [purchases], I had not returned. She began to feel that she was very thoughtless and imprudent in permitting me to go with a stranger. Still waiting the more she thought about it the more anxious and frightened she became. After she could wait no longer she went out on the street. Rushing up one street & down another. Knocking at one residence after another and not finding me she was becoming thoroughly alarmed. She came to a house and knocked. No answer. She opened the door and went in. After passing through a room or two, she heard voices and recognising her little ones prattle she rushed in without ceremony and caught me up and out again without apoligy, always believing the intention was to kidnap.

The company then left Alexandria on their way into Texas, after a

had served in the Texas Army during the Revolution from March 12 to April 17, 1836.[31]

Julien and Sarah must have been permanently established within six months after their marriage for when William Bollaert, the British writer and ethnologist, was travelling through Montgomery County in November of 1843, he made mention of passing Julien Devereux's plantation. Bollaert recorded in his diary that on: "Saturday, November 11th, 1843: . . . Two miles brought us to the bridge over Lake Creek and 6 miles more to Montgomery—full of farms and plantations and some comfort. Before we arrived at Lake Creek, passed a large plantation belonging to Colonel Julian [sic] Devereux. He has all his slaves together forming a 'Nigger Village' . . . ."[32] Bollaert made drawings of many scenes he viewed in Texas and thirty-eight of his sketches and 1,274 pages of manuscript Texana are now on deposit in the Ayer Collection of the Newberry Library, Chicago. One sketch done of a "Texan Farm in Montgomery County" of "Mr. Lewis' Plantation n[ea]r Montgomery" was most probably situated near Devereux's plantation and is reproduced in this book to give an idea of the farm buildings and topographical surroundings at the time Devereux lived in the area.

On December 30, 1843, John William Devereux drew up his will, and the contents provide some additional information on the Devereux family. John William owned twenty-two slaves at the time and stated that eleven slaves were to "decend to the legitimate child or children of my son Julien S. Devereux

---

weary journey of weeks. The company consisting of my grandfather Landrum two sons & families and a son in law settled in Austins Colony. My maternal grandfather (Martin Wells) was one of the early settlers of Bastrop."

[31]Landrum's military record is somewhat confusing. A photostat copy of Muster Rolls of the Veterans of Military Engagements Fought Before and During the Texas Revolution and During the Period of the Republic, Archives Division, Texas State Library, shows in Part I, 44, that Landrum enlisted on March 18, 1836, in "Capt Wares Co. San Jacinto Volunteers" and "deserted." On page 54 Landrum is listed as a member of "Capt Thomas Robbins Co. Cavalry, formerly Wm. H. Smith and subsequently John Dyers Company in the Campaign of 1836." Most probably John Landrum was no deserter for in the Audited Military Claims, Republic of Texas, Archives Division, Texas State Library, there is a statement signed by Captain William Ware, March 23, 1836, granting John Landrum twenty days leave of absence "to confound rumors among his friends." From May 29, 1836, Landrum again served as a volunteer in the Texas Army until he was discharged with "an affection of the breast" on July 7, 1836.

[32]W. Eugene Hollon and Ruth Lapham Butler (eds.), **William Bollaert's Texas**, 266.

but not to includ any that may be borne by Barbara Way[33] or any sister of Andrew Gilbert Scott even if it or they should be legitimatized by law or otherwise. . . ."[34] The remaining eleven slaves were to go to the four youngest children of daughter Louisiana A. Holcombe. Henry B. Holcombe, husband of Louisiana, was not to be appointed guardian because "he has no feeling or regard for the comfort or the morals of slaves but would take them to Houston or Galveston and let them to the highest bidder."[35] If Julien had no legitimate children, after his death the slaves were to go to his sister's children. While Julien lived, however, the twenty-two slaves were to remain in his possession. Louisiana was excluded from a direct inheritance, and she would later contest the will.

During these first years in Texas Julien Devereux must have been kept busy operating his Terrebonne Plantation. Unfortunately, the records for this plantation are not extant and almost no generalizations can be made concerning the actual operations at Terrebonne itself. Almost all purchases for the Terrebonne Plantation were made in Houston and during 1841 and 1842 Devereux did a considerable trade with the firm of F. Gassiot. Devereux wrote to Gassiot on January 5, 1842, to "Permit me once more to assure you of my intention to deliver you cotton in payment of what I owe you as early as I can get it Gin'd and the roads will allow it to be hauled."[36] On March 3, 1842, when Devereux had sent for $30.76 worth of supplies and had them charged, Gassiot reminded his customer that:

> You will remember that we Texians have no credit in the States to purchase our goods & that we have to pay the cash for them— You will therefore oblige me to put me in funds as immediately as possible as at this

---

[33]Julien Devereux had an illegitimate son, Julien Sidney, by Barbara Scott Way. The United States Census for 1850 recorded the boy as being eight years old and having been born in Texas. Seventh United States Census (1850), Population Schedule, Microfilm, University of Texas Library, Austin. In another will filed in Rusk County, Texas, on September 4, 1845, John Devereux stated: "I add with some reluctance and hope I may not hurt feelings, that I am not willing that any child or children of the sisters of Gilbert Scott particularly of Barbara Way formerly Barbara Scott shall inherit any property I may leave for my son whether legitimatized or not as I have good reasons to believe that children bourne by that woman will not likely be natural children of my son." Copy of will of John W. Devereux, September 4, 1845, Devereux Papers.

[34]Will of John W. Devereux, December 30, 1843, **ibid.**

[35]**Ibid.**

[36]Julien S. Devereux to F. Gassiot, January 5, 1842, **ibid.**

present time I want money in a very uncommon urgency to be able to meet my engagements abroad—I depend upon your punctuality in doing this as soon as possible.[37]

By November 15, 1842, Gassiot was pressing Devereux to pay and wrote that, "I shall be happy to receive some cotton from you soon as convenient. Cotton is losy and the times are hard here. . . ."[38]

In 1843 during a trip to Houston, Julien Devereux purchased among other things for his plantation, "1 Barrel of sugar, 1 Barrel of flour, 100 lbs coffee, ½ doz. weeding hoes, 7 axes, some good spirits of wine, quinine, castile soap, candle moulds, looking glass, fine comb, and Black ink."[39] A typical transaction made was on July 6, 1844, when Devereux purchased items from J. Shackelford, Jr., at Houston, and made payment with four bales of cotton:

Mr. J. S. Devereux
Bot of J. Shackelford Jr

4 Sacks Salt 3/275 1/300		11.25
100 lb Bro. Sugar	10c	10.00
2 pt. Ky. Bagging 90 90 180c	20	36.00
1 Coils Rope 146 128 274	10	27.40
1 Blanket		2.50
2 Axes	2.25	4.50
1 Barl. Irish potatoes		3.50
1 Set Cups & Saucers		.75
1 " Knives & forks		1.50
1 " Dining plates		1.00
½ Bus. Onions		2.00
2 lb Pepper	25	.50
4 Papers Garden Seeds	12½	.50
2 lb Rifle Powder	57	1.25
11 Yds. Calico	37½	4.13
1 Pr. Morocco Shoes		2.00
1 lb Ginger		.25
1 lb Salt Petre		.25
1 lb Roll Sulphur		.25
12 lb Blester Steel	20	2.40
7 ½ lb tobacco	6½	4.69
3 Gals. Vinegar	50	1.50
2 " Whisky	.75	1.50

[37] F. Gassiot to J. S. Devereux, March 3, 1842, **ibid.**
[38] F. Gassiot to J. S. Devereux, November 15, 1842, **ibid.**
[39] "Mem of Articles to be purchased in Houston [1843]," **ibid.**

2 lb Bailing Wire	50	1.00
Amt. paid Howell & Vanalstyne		10.25
1 Barl. Apples		5.00

	$135.87
To Cash & Bal:	38.05

By 4 Bales Cotton 2319 lbs 7 ½c

173.92	$173.92

E&OE
Houston July 6th 1844   J Shackelford Jr[40]

Among the Houston establishments with which Devereux did business was the firm of Rice and Nichols, owned by William M. Rice, who later endowed the William Marsh Rice Institute, and Ebenezar B. Nichols, noted Houston and Galveston business executive who later served as a member of the Secession Convention. On November 8, 1844, when Devereux ordered a hundred pounds of coffee from Rice & Nichols, the merchants informed Devereux that, "Coffee is very scarce with us—in consequence of which we send on half of the quantity you ordered. We expect a supply of coffee in a few days when we will forward balance of your order."[41]

Paul Bremond, for whom the town of Bremond in Robertson County was named, was another Houston merchant who sold to Devereux. On May 22, 1845, Devereux purchased such things as "1 Tweed coat $6.00, 1 Silk Handk $1.00, 1 cloth frock coat & vest $30.00, 1 pr. calf boots $5.00, and 6 violin strings $.75." The total bill for purchases came to $474.73 and payment was made with eighteen bales of cotton at "9263 lbs @ 5 ⅛¢ a pound.[42]

During 1843 Devereux paid $23.03 in "Republic & county taxes," while in 1844 the payment was $27.33.[43] Devereux appointed Maxwell W. Field to be plantation overseer on January 1, 1844, at a yearly salary of $250.00, and on January 1, 1845, the agreement was renewed for a year at $225.00.[44] Devereux was to board Field and have his washing done.

[40]J. S. Devereux Bill, July 6, 1844, **ibid.**
[41]Rice & Nichols Bill, November 8, 1844, **ibid.**
[42]Paul Bremond's Account, May 22, 1845, **ibid.**
[43]Bills and Receipts, April 9, 1845; March 2, 1847, **ibid.**
[44]Agreements Between Julien S. Devereux and Maxwell W. Field, 1844, 1845, **ibid.**

An important anticipated event in the Devereux home, which ended in sadness, occurred when Julien and Sarah's first child, a daughter, "was still born on the 8th January A. D. 1845."[45] On May 5 of the same year the board of land commissioners of Montgomery County approved a request Devereux had filed on May 6, 1844 for 640 acres of land.[46] The land was located in what later became Wise County.

Julien S. Devereux had little leisure time in Montgomery County to record the details of either his work or business, or his general observations. Conditions of the times, and especially those in Terrebonne and Montgomery County, have been recorded at some length by the aged father who was then in his seventies. John W. Devereux recorded what many Texans felt during the period of the Republic when he wrote, "Our Continent can boast of having the largest Rivers—the largest Lakes—the largest Cateracs & the highest mountains in the world (and their men particularly in Texas can *whip their weight in wildcats*)."[47]

The environments of Montgomery County produced a special breed of Texans and there was a

> *Toast to suit Lake Creek & San Jacinto*
> Citizens of Montgomery County — they have
> hearts for their friends as warm as the
> sun in their clime and hands for their foes
> as deadly as their night dews and morning fogs.[48]

Attitudes of the Devereuxs toward this "land of promise" began to change. The rains, northers, mosquitos, malaria, and other hardships recalled fond memories of the earlier home in Alabama. Scorpions were a constant problem and persons were advised to "come to Texas to see real scorpions plenty."[49]

The climate of Montgomery County was hard on both humans and animals. John Devereux wrote of its general effect:

> I consider this part of Texas unhealthy and the Climate very unsuitable for old persons on account of the humidity of the atmosphere and the extremes of heat and cold—my friends told me I wou'd do very wrong to go into a land of

[45]Family Record, **ibid.**
[46]"File 1865, Fannin 3rd Class, Cond'l Cert. 640 acres, Julien S. Devereux, Filed March 5/55," General Land Office, Austin, Texas.
[47]J. W. Devereux's Memorandum and Common Place Book.
[48]Record of the Devereux Family.
[49]**Ibid.**

strangers at my time of life and to a Country at war etc but certain considerations influencd me connected with my son's affairs and I also suppos'd I wou'd be in a more temperate climate than Alabama in this I am *egregeously* deceiv'd—our land is as rich as we cou'd desire it to be and produces abundantly—our residence is in the fork of the San Jacinto and Lake Creek both of which streams have very many Lakes on them which fill in the winter and evaporate during the hot months (May and June) when we generally have a drought—during the dry weather we never see the sun in the mornings until about 9 & 10 OClock being abscur'd by fogs—the slaves are shelter'd from the heat of the sun during the continuance of the fogs but they get wet to their necks with the heavy dews & when the sun comes out it is like "fire itself"—white people cannot work out in this part of Texas—our slaves have not work'd half as much as they did in the states—we are oblig'd to indulge them and have considerable sickness at that but none died yet and half a dozen more born & doing well—I have seen warmer and Colder weather here than I ever saw before—we frequently have what is call'd *northers* which when accompanied with rains produce the heaviest kinds of sleets and perhaps in 48 hours it is as warm as in summer.[50]

The Texas climate seemed to affect the birds' singing for Devereux recalled that back in Alabama:

How I have lov'd to climb the Hill
Where sings at eve the Whippoorwill
Also in leafy foliage he'd
sings loud the little Katydid
But now they sing no more for me
the Climate stops their minstiley.

John Devereux also observed that, "The whippoorwill is sometimes seen here but don't locate—the Katy did that is green in the U. S. is a pale red sickly colour and makes a different noise— a more harsh Ghastly rasping cry."[51] There were no "singing birds" at Terrebonne Plantation—only crows and woodpeckers —although "We have plenty of old field Larks that pull up our Corn but sing not—no don't sing here."[52]

Heat stroke was frequent in the area and care had to be exercised in working the slaves. On one occasion "an unfor-

[50]Ibid.
[51]Ibid.
[52]Ibid.

tunate adventurer" named Sacket, who had been to San Antonio, came through Terrebonne in the heat of the summer, "receiv'd a stroke of the sun *coup de sol Eil*," and died there among strangers. John Devereux "sat many hours beside poor Sackets grave" where "his wife who resides in some of the northern States caus'd a coarse paling to be put around his grave."[53] Devereux wrote the following lines in memory of the man:

THE PRAIRIE GRAVE

The one that sleeps in this lowly spot
Left love and fondness behind him
And there are them who have not forgot
and hope in heaven to find him

the lonely mound in the Prarie wild
comes oft to a mothers musing
when she bows & prays for her long lost child
who she sorrows for ever since losing

no words were read—over his head
no sculptur'd praise to save
the fame of the pilgrim pale and dead
in his lonely Prairie Grave

The whispering breeze that wanders here
and clear blue sky above him
and the twinkling stars that look down so bright
Are like spirits that watch and love him

and the breezes that blows near his repose
and the Prairie's rich grasses wave
seems to sigh as they hurry by
The lonely—the Prairie Grave

O. the silence then of the broad broad sky
and the wide spread green below
seem to hush the fierce winds rolling by
into strange and solemn woe

a coarse little paling only—is there
enclosing the lonely mound
the grass it is green & the flowers are fair
that are growing there around

no words to be read are over his head
nor no sculptur'd praises to save
the fame of the pilgrim—pale and dead
in his lonely Prairie Grave[54]

[53]Record of the Devereux Family.
[54]Ibid.

Malaria was a frequent threat to the settlers. During one particular epidemic in 1844, John Devereux planned to spend the "sickly season" in Galveston and started for the port on June 14. Upon arriving in Houston he was informed that "yellow fever prevailed to an alarming extent at Galveston" so he returned home to characterize his newly adopted country in these words: "O! Texas—Texas—not only *the home* but the grave of the brave,"[55] and wondered, "How many valuable lives have ended in 'this war and Pestilence' land Texas."[56]

The Terrebonne area was one where: "Here Natures stinking fogs we have to share, As they scatter stench upon the poison'd air,"[57] and also:

> Here youl always find an ague
> & venemous reptiles & insects to plague ye
> Rattlesnakes, constrictures & copperheads
> Tarantulas, scorpions and centepedes
>
> From ponds comes Fogs fill'd with Miasmata
> which in clouds comes pouring at ye
> Causing fevers, nervous and billious
> Also conjestive (most sure to kill us)
>
> Surviving this a cronic stops ye
> first enlarged spleen then die with dropsy
> you risque more each year than going into
> The famous battle of Jacinto[58]

The country offered little hope for survival and Devereux cautioned: "Fly from extremes of wet & dry, or stay & live until you die," because "you will not live out half your days."[59] The situation became more and more unbearable:

> O! Texas
> You vex us
> & perplex us
> how it rains
> how it rains[60]

Devereux had been disillusioned and came to feel:

[55]Ibid.
[56]Ibid.
[57]Ibid.
[58]Ibid.
[59]Ibid.
[60]Ibid.

Texas is an empty show
for man's delusion (Illusion) given
where we are taught to feel & know
it is far from being Heaven (more Hell than Heaven)

where damps and Cold Rocks blood & bone
when freed from burning heat
and when our toils and labours done
to make our Crops compleat

cold rains come down and drive us out
from saving what is made
our hands are sick both young & stout
and languish in the shade

our roads are stop'd—our market roads
and our market has yellow fever
we cannot send a single load
If we did so endeavour

no Baggins nor no rope can get
to put up what we geather
we are stop'd by mud high creeks & wet
by lasting rainy weather

Our Doctor bills we have to pay
from the little we may save
and think ourselves well off to say
we remain out of the grave

We are threaten'd with invasion too
and may be call'd to fight
to us such prospects are not new
what ever is—is right[61]

By the spring of 1845 John William Devereux had experienced enough of "Middle Texas" and wrote:

Deo Volente I will take myself away from middle Texas (in all) June next—I'll be seen no more between San Jacinto and Lake Creek—I have been three years in this poison'd atmosphere—drank bad water and breath'd foul air—have borne northers and scorchers—inundations drouths—pestilence endemic and epidemic—chilld with cold & moisture and again panting and exhausted with hot sirocco air surcharged with malaria from stagnant lakes—the sun is obscur'd every morning until nine oclock and constant rains from October until June and drouth from June until October —we frequently experience a feverish heat like a day in

[61]Ibid.

July and the next hour a norther as cold as we might expect in January—however a man may distrust his own judgement in other matters he can at least guard against the tyranny of climate and not do violence to his common sense by continuing (if there) in the most variable of all variations the weather in Middle Texas

J.W.D. 1845 April[62]

The question of annexation was of much interest to Texans in late 1844 and early 1845. In the presidential election of 1844, James K. Polk, who favored annexation, was elected, and John Tyler, the presidential incumbent, urged annexation by a joint resolution which was adopted on February 28, 1845. John William Devereux favored annexation, stating:

Give us annexation (as offer'd) let no one say no
Let the star spangled banner borne Westward ho![63]

Julien S. Devereux was an active supporter for annexation in Montgomery County,[64] and John Devereux, with the experience he had had in the legislative bodies of Georgia and Alabama, was urged by his friends to become a candidate for the convention to meet on July 4, 1845, to draw up a state constitution for Texas. Devereux was seventy-seven years old at the time and considered himself "consequently unfit for such employment."[65] He issued the following statement:

NOTICE

The Undersigned would respectfully make known to his fellow citizens of Montgomery County that he declines being a candidate for a seat in the convention to be elected to form a constitution for the state of Texas
May 24th 1845   J. W. Devereux

By early 1845 Julien S. Devereux must have made up his mind to move his family from Montgomery County and to look elsewhere for a homestead. On February 1, he hired Henry Goffe for three months "to go in company with, and take charge of a certain number of slaves, a waggon and mules which the said Devereux is about to take up into the county of Rusk or

[62]Ibid.
[63]Record of the Devereux Family.
[64]Houston **Telegraph and Texas Register,** May 21, 1845.
[65]Record of the Devereux Family.

Nacogdoches for the purpose of making a crop on the plantation recently occupied by Col Robert Smith, or such other plantation as said Devereux may conclude to occupy the present year."[66]

Julien, Sarah, and John William Devereux left Terrebonne Plantation on June 13, 1845, for southwestern Rusk County to occupy a place rented from Colonel Robert W. Smith, participant in the battle of San Jacinto and first sheriff of Rusk County. The Devereux party arrived at the Smith place on June 27, after fifteen days of travel.[67] In addition to the Devereuxs, there were ten slaves and "forty-head of cattle (cows and calves) . . . and a waggon heavily loded with Bacon etc drawn by 4 pair of oxen. . . ."[68] While Julien Devereux was in Rusk County making the necessary arrangements to establish himself, the Terrebonne Plantation was left in charge of the overseer, Maxwell W. Field. During the summer months Field kept his superior informed and wrote to Devereux on July 30 and presented a bright picture of the condition of the cotton and corn crops. Field wanted his employer to know that "Your Doctors bills is not 1 cent for neither of them has given a doce of medicine here since you left and god grant that it may remain so."[69]

On August 15 Field wrote another letter to Devereux and reported the condition of the slaves as "remarkable healthy." Field then engaged in some tall Texas talk:

> Tomorrow i have set a part to make an attack on the cuccleburs growing around the fence corners and in the lane but a hell of a job it is[.]   for mere curiosity this morning i measured an averaged size one and it measureed 13 inches in diameter[.] it takes many severe blows with a grubin hoe to get them up in many places[.] where the tops of them fall on the fence break the rayls and rock the fence considerable but i have the bodey of them cut off ten feet long so that they will answer in place of the broken rayls when they get season[.] the land in Rusk County cannot produce such coccleburs as them.[70]

Field felt the outlook for the cotton crop was good at Terrebonne and engaging in another little Texas brag he wrote:

[66]Agreement Between Julien S. Devereux and Henry Goffe, February 17, 1845, Devereux Papers.
[67]Record of the Devereux Family.
[68]**Ibid.**
[69]Maxwell W. Field to Julien S. Devereux July 30, 1845, Devereux Papers.
[70]Maxwell W. Field to Julien S. Devereux, August 15, 1845, **ibid.**

As you know i am a tolerable good rough hand to brag[.] i will not say much about the cotton just merely mention that you never had anything growing on your plantation that you could call cotten before.[71]

Devereux was assured that "youre business has not nor shall not be neglected in your absence."[72]

Julien and Sarah Devereux returned to Terrebonne at the end of summer to gather the crops and sell the plantation. Devereux felt Field had somewhat overrated things because not as much cotton had been picked by October 22 as Devereux had expected. He felt that the cotton crop would total between sixty-five and seventy-five bales and that "If cotton continues at the present price I think the crop will be ample to meet all my present engagements, but nothing to *brag on.*"[73] Devereux told his father he would return to Rusk County in December and make arrangements to build a home, for he had no intention of staying in Montgomery County.

I find the same old cloudy mornings and cold damp air that we always have here. My spleen has not hurt me much since I commenced travelling, but my appetite is not very good owing I believe partly to my having been so accustomed to Tabby's kind of cookery and I have not had a *drink* of water since I returned to the county, the difference in the water alone would be a sufficient reason for me to move[.] Sarah complains all the time of the water here and is very unreserved and determined in her preference for Rusk County.[74]

Julien's health must have improved in the Rusk County climate for he remarked to his father: "Every person I meet here congratulates me on my appearance and improvement in health so I am induced to believe my stay in Rusk has been of some service."[75] Julien Devereux spent Christmas of 1845 at Terrebonne and returned to Rusk County on January 8, 1846. He could not bring Sarah this trip as she was expecting a child. After taking care of a few essential matters, such as engaging

---

[71]**Ibid.**
[72]**Ibid.**
[73]Julien Sidney Devereux to John William Devereux, October 22, 1845; October 30, 1845, **ibid.**
[74]Julien S. Devereux to John William Devereux, October 22, 1845, **ibid.**
[75]Julien S. Devereux to John William Devereux, October 30, 1845, **ibid.**

overseer A. C. Heard, Devereux left again on January 17 for Terrebonne.[76]

A change in overseers took place at Terrebonne early in 1846 when Devereux replaced Maxwell W. Field with William Howerton. Devereux was happy with the change and observed that:

> Howerton is getting on very well. there is altogether a difference movement in everything about the plantation since he got underway. the negroes like him very well and appear much more cheerful and lively than they did under Fields administration. he has done more work himself in one month such as repairing the waggons etc. than Fields did the whole year. his ploughs and gearing are kept in the neatest order—and he is always in a good humour, but exacts strict obedience from the negroes and thus far they render it cheerfully even Anderson appears to be entirely changed he is punctual at his work and quite lively, and told Howerton that although he would rather not go up to Rusk but that he thought more of his master than his wife and was ready to go whenever ever [sic] the rest was carried etc. and I have no fears of being troubled with any of them when I move, which I shall certainly do whenever a sale of the place can be effected even after the crop is planted.[77]

The time was getting close for Sarah to have her baby and with the loss at birth of the first child in January of 1845, the approaching event was looked forward to "with interest and anxiety." John William Devereux was told that, "Sarah promises herself a great deal of pleasure in presenting our *little boy* to you this Spring."[78] The baby arrived before spring, however, and in his last letter from Terrebonne on March 7, 1846, Julien Devereux wrote to his father:

> Dear Papa
>   I have more that I wish to say and feel less qualified to express it than on any occasion I have ever written to you—on Tuesday the 24th of February about 9 Oclock at night our little boy was born, and you can imagine our delight and happiness than I can possibly express it. we have however suffered a good deal of uneasiness and anxiety for several days past as he has been quite sick with some thing

---

[76]J. W. Devereux's Memorandum and Common Place Book.
[77]Julien S. Devereux to John William Devereux, February 4, 1846, **ibid.**
[78]**Ibid.**

like the croup but he is considered out of danger at this time. he is in truth a stout promising boy. and is by common consent named John William Devereux Junr he is already known as little 'Billy' the negroes can inform you all the little particulars—Mr. Howerton and his cavilcade of corn grinders will start in the morning and their appearance at the Hutton place will be sufficient evidence that I have sold out here. the trade is by no means as good a one as I made with *Old precisely* last December, but it was the best I could do. and I was fully determined not to refuse an offer. that would half way do. and if corn can be had to keep us from starving I know that I shall be satisfied with the arrangement for I have been in dread all the time at the idea of another sickly season on Lake Creek. the trade is 900 dollars cash $1,000, next January and $600 the January thereafter. Bond given for titles. my note given him for 600 taken up with corn at 50 c per bushel. the $900 is all I have to go on at present as I have not made sale of the cotton. If you can engage corn to be paid when I get there, it will be well to do so, if not i expect I can buy enough when I go up even if we have to haul it a long ways. I wish Mr Howerton to return as soon as the animals are rested a little, with 10 mules one mule waggon and the ox waggon, to move the balance of us and drive the cattle. . . . I have no regular plan of operations. only *to get away from here with all hands, stocks & as soon as possible,* as to how we will make out when we get there I leave that for future reflection—Mr Howerton will continue in my employ as the overseer and in fact I dont know how I could get away from here without his services. Mr Heard I presume will continue at the $15 per month as long as we may need him which will in all probability will be 6 months. or we may conclude to carry on two farms and continue them both in business if they wish it—I want you to advise and consult with Howerton as to what hands to send back to drive cattle and help us move[.] there will have to be one in the place of Jess who will be needed to drive the carriage or if Scott could be spared to drive the carriage and continue Jess with the wagon. any way however that will get us away from here as soon as possible—

9th march last night Stoneum arrived with all hands to take possession and this morning we are all in a bustle and confusion trying to make a start. perhaps it will be best for 3 waggons to come back as Mr Howertons family will go up with us and I can work oxen in the blue waggon. Dock remains here for the present and is very much averse to going at all write me what is the best you will take for him if it becomes absolutely necessary to sell him—Mr

[53]

Howerton can explain all our difficulties with the negroes
I have sold my cotton to Mr Willis and will weigh [?] it tomorrow $900—is to be paid and the balance he is to assume
my debts here, the balance about 7 or $800 — I have many
things I ought to write about but cant not compose myself
sufficiently to do so—I hope that with your advise, Howerton will get things started up there and return as soon as
possible as we are all more than anxious to get away from
here==when Wells returns he will leave no person there
but Henry and Allen and I want you give them some assistance in there crop so as not to let it suffer. I will be
under some obligations to Mr Landrum in assisting me to
move, and I would regret very much that his crop at the
Smith place should be injured for want of attention, when
all hands get there perhaps you may be able to spare some
help a day or two occasionally I shall feel considerable
anxiety to hear how Howerton and all under his charge gets
on and I would have been very glad to have went up with
him. but it is out of the question for me to leave home at
this time. if there should be any clearing commenced befor
I get there let them commence near the Vaughn place after
clearing up what woods inside of the fence.

Yours in haste
J. S. Devereux

P. S. Sarah and our little boy are well at this time[79]

Julien and Sarah Devereux arrived in Rusk County to reside
permanently on May 12, 1846, and John William Devereux made
the following notation in one of his diaries:

Tuesday 12th clear day—Julien & wife arrivd at one
oclock—left rest over the Trinity waiting for the water to
fall—all well—brought a fine child with them (Johnny
Billy) born since I parted with them[.][80]

---

[79]Julien S. Devereux to John William Devereux, March 7, 1846, **ibid.**

[80]J. W. Devereux's Memorandum and Common Place Book. In the Record
of the Devereux Family the route from Montgomery to Rusk County was
recorded as follows:

Distance to Terrebonne Lake Creek	
from Huttons to Douglass—	18 miles
there to Angelina River—	3 ¼
there to Neches River—	14 ½
to McLeans 6 ¼ to Martns 10 ½	16 ¾
to Crocket—	9 ½
to Parkers 12 Spring lake 6.	18
to Trinity River—	5
to Mitchells 6 ½ Lake 1 ½	8
to Rivers 13 Pine spring 13 ½	27
to Roans 6.—	8
to Lake Creek plantation	18
	144 Miles

Julien Devereux had settled for good in Rusk County, and here he would live for the next ten years and operate his Monte Verdi Plantation.

CHAPTER V

Early Years in Rusk County

If you are Rich come here and purchase cheap land—If poor come here to get a home where you can have health and be able to labour for the support of your family and increase your property. . . . If you have committed crimes and have a bad character go else where[.] Rusk County will not do for you.[1]

RUSK County, located in the northeastern part of Texas, is situated in the "Red Lands" section of East Texas, on the divide between the Sabine River on the east and the Angelina River on the west. The physical setting of Rusk County must have been inviting to the Devereuxs who were totally dissatisfied with Montgomery County. The new locality had gently sloping hills, narrow valleys, and dales, and the 750-foot altitude in the southwestern part, where the Devereuxs settled in 1845, was considerably higher than was Terrebonne in Montgomery County. The new area had good drainage, rich soils, adequate rainfall, an abundance of mineral and forest resources, and excellent game range—all factors which were considered by early settlers.

The southwestern section of Rusk County had been crossed by at least three early Spanish expeditions: Domingo Terán de los Rios in 1691, José Domingo Ramón in 1716, and Joseph Francisco Calahorra y Saenz sometime in September of 1760. Several early grants, in what became Rusk County, were issued by the Mexican government for titles to land located on the "waters of the Angelina," and with Texas independence, after the battle of San Jacinto in 1836, settlement began to increase. Not until the Cherokee Indians were defeated in 1839 in the battle of the Neches, however, was there a great increase in population. Within three years there was sufficient population for a separate county, which was created on January 16, 1843,

[1]Record of the Devereux Family.

[56]

and named for General Thomas J. Rusk, Secretary of War under Sam Houston and later United States Senator. The county seat of Henderson, laid out in 1843 in the center of the county, was named for James Pinckney Henderson, who was attorney general, secretary of state, minister to England and France during the Republic and later elected first governor of the state of Texas. Early settlements in the county included Mount Enterprise, located in the southern part of the county and settled in 1832; Camden, settled in the early 1830's, located on a bluff on the south bank of the Sabine River in the northeast corner of the county; and Millville, nine miles northeast of Henderson and known as Liberty Hill during the 1840's. Other early settlements were Harmony Hill, located about fifteen miles northeast of Henderson; New Salem, in southwestern Rusk County not far from the Devereux residence; and Pinehill in extreme eastern Rusk County.

Population figures for the early years after the creation of Rusk County are not available, but the increase must have been rapid because when the first United States Census for Rusk County was taken in 1850, the population was 8,148, surpassed only in the state by adjoining Harrison County with a population of 11,822.[2] The county attracted a number of early planters like Albert Tatum, John Graham, James Smith, Richard B. Tutt, Milton M. Boggess, William Wright Morris, and Julien S. Devereux.

The Devereuxs were favorably impressed with Rusk County from the time of their arrival on June 27, 1845, for less than three weeks later, on July 15, John William Devereux gave this description of the new surroundings:

> I am in Eastern Texas Rusk County breathing pure air and drinking pure water—If you are Rich come here and purchase cheap land—If poor come here to get a home where you can have health and be able to labour for the support of your family and increase your property—If you have been unfortunate and met with reverses in your pecuniary affairs come to Texas (Eastern Texas) and avoid the affected pity and sincere contempt of quondam friends consequent attendants on misfortunes—here you will find many who will exchange sympathies with you and unite in fellow feelings having had similar difficulties to encounter—If you

[2]Seventh Census of the United States: 1850, p. 504.

have committed crimes and have a bad character go elsewhere Rusk County will not do for you—no such will meet
with encouragement here.[3]

The Devereuxs rented a temporary home, situated near the village of Gourdneck, from Robert W. Smith.

In Montgomery County the residents wanted the Devereuxs
to return and on July 17, 1845, one neighbor, William Fowler,
wrote Julien Devereux a favorable account of conditions there.

I am told no country ever presents more promising prospects—the seasons have been regular—corn well matured.
. . . In short portions of Montgomery are not surpassed by
Mississippi cotton—If you could now see your plantation
all health—*goardneck* would continue *goardneck*—The negroes are well—the country generally healthy however the
MDs ride about & prescribe.[4]

John William Devereux remained in Rusk County on the
rented Smith land after Julien and Sarah returned in late summer, 1845, to Montgomery County where they stayed until the
following May.

On September 11, 1845, Julien Devereux made one of his
first purchases of land in Rusk County, which would later total
more than ten thousand acres, when he bought for $500 the
land called the Hutton Place from Winchester Doyel and James
Hutton.[5] Father John William had only praise for the new purchase and commenting on the new situation in Rusk County
he wrote:

I admit our Meats are nice and sweet
And our Milk and Butter hard to beat.

-       -   -

Here undisturb'd you traverse O'er the fields
Share the rich pastime which the country yields.[6]

Julien Devereux, while closing out his operations at Terrebonne, wrote his father that Sarah's parents, John and Mary
Landrum, would move to Rusk County shortly. Julien also
mentioned to his father what William Beck Ochiltree, a significant lawyer during the Republic who later had a Texas county

[3]Record of the Devereux Family.
[4]William Fowler to Julien S. Devereux, July 17, 1845, Devereux Papers.
[5]Bills and Receipts, May 26, 1846, **ibid.**
[6]Record of the Devereux Family.

named in his honor, had to say about the Devereux land purchase in Rusk County:

> Judge Ochiltree attended the late district court here and gave them all such a high colorued description and character of the Hutton place that we are really envied by a good many—the Judge told them that it was the best place in all respects of any other place between the Sabine and Brazos Rivers.[7]

Most of the actual supervision of the work at the Hutton Place was in the hands of the father while Julien was in Montgomery County. John William Devereux kept a diary for the year of 1846, and some excerpts from this source provide an interesting picture of early life on an East Texas farm. On the first day of January, Devereux wrote:

> Thursday first day of January year of the Christian era 1846 and of the Higerra or flight of Mahomet 1259 at Hutton in Rusk County Texas I commence my diary for the present year.—this Morning showery and windy—hands commenced grubbing—expected Julien before this time but have not heard from him for two ½ Months—Negroes under Management of negro Scot no overseer young Reed's time out—all on foot and well except poor Henry and I don't expect he will ever see another *well day*—clear'd away and wind from north—sun set beautifully[7a]

On January 15, 1846, Julien Devereux hired A. C. Heard to "oversee & work 6 months for 80 dollars or for a shorter time at 15 a month."[8] Devereux "had formed a very favorable opinion of Mr. Heard as an industrious prudent young man. . . ."[9] The new overseer accomplished much and on January 26, John Devereux recorded that "all hands busy and Heard continues to rush a head with their work & all cheerful."[10] Considerable time was devoted to clearing new land, planting crops, and erecting buildings, and on March 26 an entry in Devereux's writings read: "Men building cabbins and women grubbing and burning

[7]Julien Devereux to John W. Devereux, October 30, 1845, Devereux Papers.
[7a]J. W. Devereux's Memorandum and Common Place Book.
[8]Ibid.
[9]Julien S. Devereux to John William Devereux, February 4, 1846, Devereux Papers.
[10]J. W. Devereux's Memorandum and Common Place Book.

brush."[11]   John Devereux supervised the buildings constructed on the Devereux land, and on January 25 he recorded that the hands had "finished smoakhouse last night—3 days from the stump."[12]

The Mexican War broke out in April of 1846 and on May 24, twelve days after Julien and Sarah Devereux had returned to Rusk County, overseer "Heard started on Kitty the Mule on the expedition in the Rusk Company of Mounted Volunteer Rifle men for the Rio Grande to fight the Mexicans."[13]   The company was raised by Captain John McClarty, a Henderson merchant, and the following account has been given:

> The company performed a march of over two hundred miles, the distance from Henderson to Lynchburg, without tents or camp conveniences of any kind, under the direction of an officer who had started upon the campaign without one dollar in cash to defray expenses; but by energy and appeals to the liberality of the citizens residing upon the line of march, succeeded in reaching the point of rendevous, Galveston, and afterward the headquarters of the army of occupation in Mexico.[14]

A former Devereux overseer, James B. Reed, had also entered the service against the Mexicans, and he wrote some rather interesting letters to Devereux.   On August 21, 1846, from "Republic of Mexico Near Camargo," Reed wrote:

> We were nearly seven days marching from Matamoras to this place.   Our trip was one of hardship and dangers, on account of our exposure to the rays of the sun, that poured down on us as hot as ever mortal man felt them. The trees were so small and low, that it was almost impossible to get a shade in the heat of the day, for man or beast. And the water was distressingly scarce, and very bad, being such as we could get out of the ponds along the road.[15]

Since many men in Rusk County were fighting in the Mexican War, news from the scene of battle was of great interest. One veteran, "Old Bailey," returned home and on November 6,

---

[11]Ibid.
[12]Ibid.
[13]Ibid.
[14]Wm. DeRyee and R. E. Moore, **The Texas Album, of the Eighth Legislature, 1860,** p. 119.
[15]James B. Reed to Julien S. Devereux, August 21, 1846, Devereux Papers.

"Lully and Julien went to Baileys yesterday to hear particulars of the Monteray [sic] battle—Bailey sent me about fifty segars taken at the capture of Monteray. I have smoak'd real Mexican *booty.*"[16]

In the Devereux Papers is a copy of an undated letter written by Julien S. Devereux to a party outside of Texas with his comments on the Mexican War:

> You perhaps expect me to say some thing on the subject of the war with Mexico or it would appear to you reasonable that I should give you some information on the subject from the fact of my living in Texas—but I assure you that the people of Eastern Texas are among the last in the United States to receive news from the seat of War—We have overland communication with the Rio Grand and our news is recd through the New O. paper by the way of Red River —a great many of our *boys* are there but as they are *in during the war* we seldom ever see or hear from any of them— as to my politics I will only say that I am a *Texan* in the full sense of the term, and the friends of Texas are my friends=the United States are fighting our quarrel and in our cause and Henry Clay and all others out of Texas that were opposed to annexation and all others *in and out* of Texas opposed to the War I look upon as enimies to Texas and consequently enimies of mine at least politicaly so— therefore you may set me down as a Democrat.[17]

There was much sickness during the summer and fall of 1846. Dr. William H. Beers spent much time at the Devereux home looking after the young son, John William Devereux, Jr., and there were numerous cases of the fever among the Negroes. Overseer William Howerton, who had moved to Rusk County when the last of Devereux's possessions were brought from Montgomery County, was also ill as was his son. On August 17 the weather was described as sultry and damp with the sun "out blazing at times."[18] Sickness continued and when the young Devereux child almost died, a second physician, Dr. Allen, was called.

During the first week in September Julien Devereux came down with the fever, and on September 8 John William Devereux wrote that, "One day the persons who came to see us was of the

---

[16]J. W. Devereux's Memorandum and Common Place Book.
[17]Portion of letter, date and address not given, Devereux Papers.
[18]J. W. Devereux's Memorandum and Common Place Book.

opinion that Julien and his child & myself would all die. . . .
Doctor Allen makes this his head quarters and is sent for several times every day."[19] There was considerable sickness in the
neighborhood and persons called frequently at the Devereux
home for "medicine and spirits etc. etc." The Devereuxs' supply
was running low and on September 18 some ten cases of fever
existed "and as many more unable to go about or do anything."[20]
Neighbors "call as if we kept an apothecarys shop to get medicine and we yet continue to be able to supply them—Julien had
in enough a supply when at Shreeveport [sic] to supply our own
people for some years."[21] During the height of the sickness,
which lasted until late October, "hardly ever less than three and
often six applications for medicine" were made at the Devereux
home. Other items were secured from the Devereuxs and on
October 27, John William Devereux noted that "Three days ago
Vaughn came to get Shrouding to bury Corderay's child—got 5
yards of fine cotton cloth . . . they got the last of a whole piece
given away for shrouding."[22] The first Devereux home had
been "too near the Angelina River," and three days before
Christmas, 1846, Julien Devereux occupied a new house he had
built. John William Devereux had Christmas dinner with his
son, daughter-in-law, and grandson.

During the first year in Rusk County Julien Devereux con-
tinued to acquire land. On June 20, 1846, he bought from W. D.
Henry and Levice Henry their "square section of Land in the
South West corner of William F. Allison head right League."[23]

Devereux purchased his provisions from Charles Vinzent at
Mount Enterprise, from Sam McClarty in Henderson, and at
times some of his supplies, such as the gin bought on December
15, 1846, came from Shreveport, Louisiana, some 91 miles and
five days' travel from Devereux's place. Taxes on Devereux
property for 1846 totaled $18.35.

On March 15, 1847, John William Devereux celebrated his
seventy-eighth birthday. This was an advanced age at the time
and the old man was in poor health. He knew his life was near-
ing its end and on May 3 he noted he had "no appetite and
weaker every day "travelling" "travelling" travelling as the

[19]Ibid.
[20]Ibid.
[21]Ibid.
[22]Ibid.
[23]Julien S. Devereux, Bills and Receipts, June 20, 1846; Devereux Papers.

Methodists song says to lay my body down."[24] Just before his death John William Devereux wrote:

> To Julien S. Devereux . . . I hope you will keep my memoirs sacred during your life as they have been made with a hope and expectation that you will not allow them to be made *spinning* paper as my fathers papers were. . . . You will recollect that your father spent many hours in collecting for his scrap book such pieces as he had written on the blank leaves of his book etc. to be examined by you when he is no more.[25]

On June 22, 1847, with "cronic dysentary and dropsy" John William Devereux died. His religious faith had been that of a "Unitarian Quaker," and he had probably acquired this as a young boy when his father had moved the family from Virginia to a Quaker settlement in Columbia County, Georgia. Devereux had once recorded that, "I differ only with the Quaker in his non resistence principle—I cant agree to allow any man to smite me & not return the complement nor allow my country to be invaded without giving my physical assistance to defend it."[26] In the Record of the Devereux Family and Memoirs of John William Devereux, son Julien made this entry some years later:

> Monte Verdi Rusk County. Texas 31st December A D 1851 I now proceed to comply with the request of my dearly beloved and worthy Father by stating that his health continued to decline although his mind continued clear and vigorous. he kept a daily Journal of his health and condition and passing events in a small mem Book up to the 10th June 1847. On the 15th of June my sister Mrs Louisiana A. Holcombe arrived at our residence and remained until my Father died which was on the 22d day of June A D 1847. he departed this life on that day at the going down of the sun surrounded by the family and his friends and neighbours at peace with his creator and all the world. his remains now lie about 300 yards from our dwelling on an eminence Southwest from our house where also is buried our beloved little son who bore the name of his Grand Father and who died on 25th September 1848=
> Our present intention is to have them both removed to the

---

[24]Diary Kept by John William Devereux for Year 1847.
[25]Record of the Devereux Family. Fortunately for Texas history, Julien S. Devereux and his descendants have preserved the writings.
[26]**Ibid.**

burying ground at the Baptist meeting house[27]

The will John William Devereux drew up in Rusk County on September 4, 1845, was executed, and its contents caused a misunderstanding between son Julien and daughter Louisiana A. Holcombe. John Devereux had willed his twenty-four slaves to Julien for his use and benefit during his life. On Julien's death twelve slaves, including the oldest slaves Scott and Tabby, would go to Julien's legitimate children, and the other twelve slaves would go to Louisiana's sons Julien and Lucius Holcombe, provided they would change their names to Devereux.

Louisiana felt that her father's "mind was not right when he made the will."[28] She urged her brother to give her half the slaves she felt entitled to, because Julien was "rich as the world would call it" while she was "very poor as regards property."[29] Louisiana had found out about the will shortly before her father died, and she wrote Julien that if he had informed her earlier of the contents she could have reasoned with her father.

For more than a year no satisfactory solution was worked out concerning the will. Louisiana's son-in-law in Marshall, Dr. W. S. Taylor, decided to take the case to court and declare the will null and void on the grounds that John William Devereux was not of sound mind at the time he made the will and also because he was under the "control" of Julien Devereux when the will was made. The case went to the District Court of Rusk County in November, 1848, and in the agreement reached Louisiana was to receive her portion of the slaves at Julien's residence on February 1, 1849.[30] In the settlement of the father's slaves, valued at $8,450, Julien received eighteen, including several of the old slaves, while Louisiana received eleven. According to the apppraisement the average price of the slaves was $291.37; the average price of those selected by Julien was $275 while those going to Louisiana were valued at $318.[31]

Julien and Sarah Devereux lost their only son, John William

---

[27]**Ibid.** The remains of John William, Julien, and some other members of the family are interred in the family burial plot about a mile due east of what became in the late 1850's the last home of the Devereux family.

[28]Louisiana A. Holcombe to Julien S. Devereux, August 10, 1847, Devereux Papers.

[29]**Ibid.**

[30]Articles of Agreement between J. S. Devereux and Holcombe [1848], **ibid.**

[31]Julien S. Devereux's Monte Verdi Plantation Account Book for 1849-1854.

Devereux Junior, on September 25, 1848. The child, two and a half years old, had been in poor health much of his life. Another son, Albert, named for Julien's deceased brother buried in Alabama, was born on December 15. Julien's daughter Antoinette always resided in the Devereux home and Julien's son Sidney, by Barbara Way, was with the Devereuxs much of the time. Julien Devereux, at the age of forty-three, was assuming a responsible place in his community and the county, for on August 7, 1848, he was elected justice of the peace in Beat Number 3,[32] a position he held through 1851.

As a cotton planter Devereux did amazingly well during his first years in Rusk County. His cotton crop for 1847 was recorded as 104 bales and Devereux noted that, "I have made more cotton and corn this year than I did the year before I left Lake Creek (which was considered a very good crop)."[33] By 1849 he ranked high among the successful planters in Rusk County. During that year, according to his own figures, he paid taxes on the following property:

Taxable property for 1849.
62 slaves valued at 300 each total $18,600
Land 2040 acres head right of Wm F Allison
   467   head right of Romana Gonzales
   320   Isaiah Call
   200   Wm M Kettell

3027	Valued at one dollar per acre	3,027
150 head of cattle valued at $4 per head—		600
400	hogs	400
20 horses & mules—		1,200
3 waggons valued at		300

         $24,127[34]

Julien Devereux had ample reason to feel good about things as the decade of the 1840's came to a close. He may have expressed his feelings at the time in a "Texas Toast" he composed which read:

---

[32]Certificate of the Election of Julien S. Devereux as Justice of the Peace in Beat No. 3, August 14, 1848, Devereux Papers.

[33]Copy of letter, Julien S. Devereux to "Willis," October 5, 1847, *ibid.*

[34]Julien S. Devereux's Monte Verdi Plantation Account Book for 1849-1854.

Wealth by our Labor
Independence by our Sword
Honey in the Bee Gum
& Sugar in the Gourd[35]

During the 1850's, when Texas experienced rapid growth, Devereux, with his operations at his Monte Verdi Plantation, would assume a position as a major cotton planter in Texas.

[35]Ibid.

CHAPTER VI

Monte Verdi Plantation

"Monte-Verdi"
Is the name I have concluded
to give to my place of Residence
in Rusk County Texas=
Julien S. Devereux[1]

THE earliest date found with Monte Verdi designated as the name for Julien Devereux's plantation has been on March 7, 1849, when Devereux purchased an account book from a Henderson merchant, Major Sam McClarty, and wrote the following on the front side of the book:

"Monte Verdi"
Terre Le Oriente
Julien Sidney Devereux
Gourd Neck Rusk Co. Texas
7 March 1849

One cannot be certain whether Julien Devereux had the French or Spanish language in mind when he named his plantation, for the word *verdi*, meaning green, becomes *verte* in French and *verde* in Spanish. A literal French translation would mean green elevation, while a recent Spanish dictionary defined *monte* as "a high natural elevation of land; virgin land covered with trees and underbrush."[2] Probably Devereux intended to use French spelling because his subtitle to Monte Verdi of *Terre Le Oriente* is French for "Land of the East." "Green wooded area," a most appropriate and descriptive translation, has been

---

[1]Julien S. Devereux's Monte Verdi Plantation Account Book for 1849-1854.

[2]**Diccionario de la Lengua Espanola**, 893.

[67]

selected by one person[3] to describe the area where Julien Devereux lived in 1849 when he determined that:

"Monte-Verdi"
Is the name I have concluded
to give my place of Residence
in Rusk County Texas=[4]

Julien Devereux's Monte Verdi Plantation, situated in Rusk County in the so-called "Red Lands" section of East Texas, was finally settled upon for a number of reasons. The owner was influenced by the richness and fertility of the soil which would grow crops like cotton, corn, and vegetables; the facilities for marketing with Shreveport, Louisiana, on Red River, a distance of around ninety miles; and the environment of Rusk County which suited Devereux for raising a family. Julien Devereux, like most of the plantation owners of Texas during the 1840's and 1850's, had previous planting experience for he had operated an Alabama plantation with his father before arriving in Texas.

Plantations which were established in Texas and the Old South before the Civil War, were organized to facilitate large scale production and the accumulation of wealth. No doubt, Devereux had these two purposes in mind when he undertook the establishment of Monte Verdi. In the successful operation of the plantation there were three human factors: the master, the overseer, and the slaves. The plantation owner was the master, and full responsibility for success or failure depended on his decisions. He was responsible for the care of his slaves; he had to go in debt to make the crop for the ensuing year; and he always was concerned about too much rain or a lengthy drought. With good management and reasonably favorable weather, a plantation like Monte Verdi had many compensations for its owner.

A main factor in the success or failure of a plantation was the overseer, and Devereux was fortunate much of the time in his choices to fill this most important position. The ideal qualifications for an overseer were honesty, industriousness, and to know farming and be able to handle Negroes. Most overseers

---

[3]D. O. Blaisdell, Bastrop, Texas, Spanish teacher, suggested "green wooded area" to the writer.
[4]Julien S. Devereux's Monte Verdi Plantation Account Book for 1849-1854.

were young men and their activities were supervised by the planter when he was in residence. Devereux did not keep the Terrebonne overseer, Maxwell W. Field, but secured the services of William Howerton, an able man who stayed with Devereux for a number of years. When the planter hired his overseer, the two signed a contract setting forth the terms of the overseer's employment. The following "Agreement" was signed between Devereux and Howerton for 1846, while Devereux was still in Montgomery County:

This Agreement entered into and signed between Julien S. Devereux and William Howerton both of the County of Montgomery and Republic (or State) of Texas. Witness that the said Devereux has agreed to employ said Howerton for the term of twelve months, commencing on the first day of January 1846. the said Howerton undertakes and engages to manage said Devereux's farming business and such other business as said Devereux may require such as taking care of stock superintending and assisting in carrying on buildings, or other improvements, Giving and picking cotton and all other services and duties, that are necessary to be performed by a successful and prudent overseer, his entire attention and services to be devoted to the interest of said Devereux. the said Devereux is to have and retain the control commonly exercised by employers in having business carried on. any time lost by said Howerton except that of working on roads serving on Juries and attending Elections is to be deducted from his wages. and at the expiration of the said twelve months and upon the performance of said engagements by said Howerton the said Devereux is hereby bound to pay him the sum of Two Hundred and fifty Dollars. the said Devereux further agrees to furnish said Howerton with Twenty bushels of corn to be delivered at the Commencement of the time or as soon as the same can be measured and received conveniently, the said Howerton to find himself and family in all other respects with the exception of the said Twenty bushels of corn. Each one of the parties to this agreement reserves to himself the right to quit or seperate whenever he may become dissatisfied or whenever he may think proper to do so, and if the seperation is caused by the said Devereux, the wages of the said Howerton up to the time that a seperation may take place is to be considered due in proportion to the time he may have remained in the employment of said Devereux and to bear interest until paid, and if the said Howerton quits of his own accord whatever wages he may have earned is not to be considered due until the expiration of the said

twelve months. The parties to this agreement having signed two agreements of the same tenor and date this day of 1846
Witness[5]

From 1847 through 1849, Howerton's salary was $300 a year;[6] in 1851 the salary was increased to $325 and in 1852 to $350.[7] Howerton, like many industrious overseers, was able to establish himself in the neighborhood and gave up his job at Monte Verdi. Relations between Howerton and Devereux remained close, and in 1855 Devereux took Howerton on one of his tours.

The overseer was an interloper between the master and slaves, and at times he faced many problems. The overseer had long hours; he was the first to get up and was late to bed. The overseer did hard work and was exposed to sun and rain as the following accounts concerning overseer Ansel Heard reveal:

> February 18, 1846 — Raind gently all night and now *misting* and cold— Heard out ploughing with his hunting shirt wet with the hands ploughing in a cut of the dryest land—weather too bad to be out but I dont control him in pushing ahead as he wants to plant next week—they finished the cut at dark—heavy rain.
>
> - - -
>
> March 6, 1846—This morning raining—hands continued planting through the day in drizzles of rain—light rains dont drive Heard out.[8]

On occasions, when a planter could not secure the services of an overseer, an able Negro slave would be placed in charge. At Monte Verdi the position was usually filled by the devoted slave, Scott.

In 1850 Devereux was searching for an overseer and wrote to Mark Stroud in Henderson that he "would like to employ a man with a small family (or at least not a large family), who will undertake to manage my plantation affairs and attend to taking care of the stock &c I have about 25 good hands all family negroes, and easily governed I am contented with having moderate work done & I would not have a severe or cruel overseer

[5]Agreement between Julien S. Devereux and William Howerton for 1846, Devereux Papers.
[6]Monte Verdi, Texas, Plantation Book.
[7]Julien S. Devereux's Memorandum and Record Book, 1840-1856.
[8]J. W. Devereux's Memorandum and Common Place Book.

on any terms."[9] Devereux was willing to pay three hundred dollars in cash for an overseer and furnish "his bread corn for the year."

Devereux was not always fortunate in securing the services of an able overseer, as was the experience with one [John W.?] McKnight. Things at Monte Verdi became so unsatisfactory about the time Devereux took his seat in the Texas Legislature, in November of 1855, that he was forced to make a change. The plantation under McKnight's management had gotten into a "shackling condition" and Devereux hoped things would improve with the new overseer Ramsey's direction.[10] Writing from Austin about the situation Devereux said:

> Since I have been here and have had time to reflect on the subject it is a matter of wonder with me that we have got through as well as we have in the management of our affairs and more especially as relates to the plantation, when I reflect that my plantation and hands has been under the control of such a worthless, drunken, stubborn ill natured fellow as McKnight, I wonder things are no worse (it is true however that we have made scarcely any cotton crops for the last two or three years) and if McKnight had continued a year or two longer my plantation would have been broken up & we should have been compelled to sell our home or some of the negroes. I am now surprised at myself for having such a fellow about me at all, and under that we have escaped so well. I very much hope that our affairs at the plantation will be better conducted for the future. If it had not been for the sale of the Dodson place & the Doctor Jourdan land I dont now see how I could have held up—[11]

Perhaps the experience with McKnight led Devereux to write home that, "Since I left home I have seen and conversed with a great number of planters and I find none of them spoil their overseers as I do."[12]

The third human element in the operation of a plantation was that of the slaves, and the Negroes at Monte Verdi accounted for a huge investment. On August 3, 1850, Devereux listed seventy-four slaves, forty males and thirty-four females.[13] In 1853 the total number of slaves had increased to 84. Total num-

[9]Copy of letter, Julien S. Devereux to Mark Stroud, November 4, 1850, Devereux Papers.
[10]Julien Devereux to Sarah Devereux, November 13, 1855, **ibid.**
[11]Julien Devereux to Sarah Devereux, December 10, 1855, **ibid.**
[12]Julien Devereux to Sarah Devereux, November 5, 1855, **ibid.**
[13]Julien S. Devereux's Monte Verdi Plantation Account Book for 1849-1854.

bers do not indicate a working force, however, because there were children and many old slaves who could not do manual labor. The Devereux family frequently mentioned that their slaves were "family Negroes" and took pride that their Negroes were well treated. Julien's sister, Mrs. Louisiana Holcombe, once wrote to her brother that "you know well that any slaves we have ever had in possession are well treated and only a reasonable service required of them."[14] The Devereuxs had a strong attachment to their slaves and in Alabama, when Louisiana was considering a move to Texas, she wrote Julien that she had no intention of parting with her slaves while she lived and added that, "The children all love Jincey and call her Granny and she takes care of them and loves them."[15] Louisiana also remarked that, "Family negroes are the most unenviable property that we can own, as we cannot bear to separate them and . . . we do not like to hire them out for fear of not being treated well."[16]

At Monte Verdi the slaves were treated with kindness. Two of the oldest slaves, Scott and Tabby, are mentioned often in the Devereux Papers with much affection. In most letters written between members of the Devereux family there can be found messages to slaves, as for example on January 25, 1849, in a letter from Dr. William S. Taylor, son-in-law of Louisiana A. Holcombe, written to Julien Devereux:

> I was sorry to hear that the negro woman Polly was dead. I will see that her children are well taken care of[.] I will be obliged to you if you will get Mr. Howerton to go a part of the way with the negroes[.] he knows the roads well & will *understand best how to get* them across the bad creeks between your house & Henderson.[17]

Negro morale probably was high most of the time at Monte Verdi Plantation. Julien Devereux would not compel his Negroes to work when sick or in bad weather, and the house servants, when ill, were not to do washing and milking. John William Devereux wrote on January 2, 1846, that "all [slaves] in good spirits & happy singing and carroling at their work,"[18] and on

---

[14]Louisiana A. Holcombe to Julien S. Devereux, December 6, 1848, Devereux Papers.
[15]Louisiana Holcombe to Julien S. Devereux, September 12, 1852, **ibid.**
[16]Louisiana Holcombe to Julien S. Devereux, February 7, 1854, **ibid.**
[17]William S. Taylor to Julien S. Devereux, January 25, 1849, **ibid.**
[18]J. W. Devereux's Memorandum and Common Place Book.

May 30, 1847, that he "heard the hands carrolling their melodies and at 12 heard their large horn call them off and on to their labours."[19]

Two or three episodes involving discipline of Negroes are mentioned in the Devereux Papers. On May 19, 1846, there was a *"Fracas* with Negroes and Heard—he gave July and Flora and Seven a good thrashing which they well deserved for impudence."[20] July must have been a problem for on January 5, 1852, Julien Devereux recorded that he had paid to a Mr. Birdwell a ten dollar gold piece "for bringing negro man July home when Runaway (the first occurrence of the kind ever happened with me)."[21] One other entry Devereux made, payment of $3.75 to William Reagan in March of 1850 for "clog made to put on negro man Ben the iron weighing 15 lbs at 25c pr. lb,"[22] may indicate that Ben was being punished for some reason.

Marriages were arranged by the plantation owners, and when a marriage between slaves on different plantations took place the children belonged to the mother's master. Planter B. V. Loftus sent the following note to Julien Devereux to promote a slave marriage:

> January 24th 1846 Mr. Devereux the Boy-Sam wants to have one of your negro girls for A Wife[.] the Boy is onnest I think for I have raised hime he is under a good carracter as Enny Negro
>
> Yours with Respect
B V Loftus[23]

The next day there was "a marriage between Sam Loftus and Eliza Henry Maria by consent of all parties—Sam brought a consent & a good recommendation from his master."[24] Devereux was interested in the spiritual attention of his slaves and on September 26, 1850, he wrote the Reverend J. B. Renfro the following:

---

[19]Diary kept by John William Devereux for Year 1847.
[20]J. W. Devereux's Memorandum and Common Place Book.
[21]Julien S. Devereux's Monte Verdi Plantation Account Book for 1849-1854.
[22]Julien S. Devereux's Memorandum and Record Book, 1840-1856.
[23]B. V. Loftus to J. S. Devereux, January 24, 1846, Record of the Devereux Family.
[24]J. W. Devereux's Memorandum and Common Place Book.

Dear Sir
     I write you a few lines at the request of my man Jack. who believes that he has some religious impressions and is very desirous to make his feelings known to you and thinks that he can be relieved and comforted by a conference with you—I have no slave who needs or who has needed a change or reformation more than Jack, and I would be well pleased if he shall become reformed—

truly yours &c
Julien S. Devereux[25]

Slave holders in East Texas were concerned for a number of years with the work done by the abolitionists, the extreme section of the antislavery party in the United States which advocated by means of the press, lectures, and petitions to Congress the immediate abolition of Negro slavery. The abolitionists were opposed to the annexation of Texas as a slave state in 1845, and by 1852, with the publication of Harriet Beecher Stowe's *Uncle Tom's Cabin,* the abolitionists were looked upon with hatred and fear throughout the South.

With selected biblical scriptures many southern planters justified a system of slavery, and the Devereuxs recorded the following sources:

Exodus 21. 2d V. he that stealeth a man &c our law the same
Deutronomy. 21. 2 Hebrew men servants free after 7 years
     now women &c children
Exodus 21. 3. 4. women not free nor children
Deutronomy 15. 12 v female Hebrew women slaves were
     free after 6 years servitude. Exodus 21.20.21 slaves
     considered (money) or property) Leviticus 25-46.v
     slaves were inherited & may be beat until they die
     and slaves forever
New Testament Titus 2.9v & 10 Peter 2-18v 20 I Timothy
     6.12v [1-2] & 3. 4 .5 —(see Leviticus Chap 25 where slaves
     are inherited from father to son) Chapter 25th Leviticus
     Mem it will be seen by reference to the foregoing and examining the parts of the Old & new testament that slavery has been tolerated among the Jews and persons represented as *God's people* —how do the Fanatics urge that slavery is forbidden by the scriptures—I am more oppos'd to slavery than Moses for he tolerated or sanctioned slave killing by their masters   JWD

---

[25]Julien S. Devereux to J. B. Renfro, September 26, 1850, Devereux Papers.

58th chap Isaiah text for Abolitionists[26]

At least twelve of the slaves on the Monte Verdi Plantation were permitted to cultivate cotton, corn, and vegetables, and when these products were sold the slaves received the money. For the year 1850 the total value of the Negro crop was $737.05, and in 1853 merchant Charles Vinzent at Mount Enterprise sent three hundred dollars to Devereux to be distributed to the slaves whose cotton crop Vinzent had bought.[27] Vinzent also wrote Devereux, "I should be glad to have a chance to sell them anything they want of such things as we keep for sale. I would sell goods to them *really very low*[.]"[28] Devereux permitted his Negroes to handle money, and when slaves made trips to Shreveport for supplies they frequently had from eight to twelve dollars in their pockets.

Julien Devereux was interested in the well-being of his slaves, and at times his doctor bills ran high for medical services rendered to the blacks. No doubt much time was lost by Negroes during sickness, as on August 13, 1846, when "Negroes half of them sick and convalescent—the rest nursing the sick."[29] In the case of a Negro birth, a midwife in the neighborhood was called in, as on April 25, 1846, when "Henry Maria was delivered of a child last night—the child was safely forth coming by our own folks but we had to send for Mrs. Wornell to do some winding up business."[30]

No record exists that Devereux ever hired out his slaves. Once he did permit a slave to do washing for a neighbor whose wife was ill, and when Dr. P. T. Richardson needed help for his "gin raising" Devereux permitted five of his slaves to assist with instructions to "caution them about getting killed or crippled."[31]

---

[26]Record of the Devereux Family. The **Weekly Delta** (New Orleans), June 2, 1860, reported the following abolition activity in Rusk County: "**Abolition Bibles**—Quite an excitement prevailed lately at Henderson, owing to the sale there by a book agent, of several copies of the Cottage Bible. This edition of the Bible was prepared for the press by an Abolitionist. It has copious notes whenever these notes can be made to bear on the slavery question, and they evidently are not fitted for the South. The agent was required to take back all the copies he had sold, and leave for the North at once."

[27]Charles Vinzent to Julien S. Devereux, April 21, 1853, Devereux Papers.
[28]**Ibid.**
[29]J. W. Devereux's Memorandum and Common Place Book.
[30]**Ibid.**
[31]Note from Julien S. Devereux to Mr. Few, September 4, 1853, Devereux Papers.

Proper management of a slave force the size existing at Monte Verdi was no small problem for Devereux or his overseer. The Negroes had to be fed, clothed, and housed during the years of lean crops as well as in seasons of abundance, and care was necessary for those slaves too young or too old to work. With a large labor force it was essential to have proper division of work laid out at all times. Most of the time was spent in the fields, but when there was no field work to be done and in bad weather, slaves had to be kept busy splitting rails, killing hogs, shelling and grinding corn, building fences, or burning brush.

Probably most of the Monte Verdi slaves were devoted to their master. When a drunk resident, Andrew Jourdan, Sr., met one of Devereux's Negro slaves on the road and "without any provocation or justification did cruelly, unreasonably treat and abuse said negro man" Devereux wrote to D. W. Field, district attorney in Rusk County, with a request that an indictment be issued against Jourdan.[32] The Devereux slaves probably gave faithful service as is indicated in 1855 while Julien Devereux was in the legislature when his wife wrote, "Martin says they are trying to do their best."[33] In a later letter she wrote that, "Jim tell[s] me to say to Jesse[34] that they are all well and heap of work ahead of them but think they are get[t]ing on finely and in a fair way to get through with it in good time."[35] Devereux must have felt pleased when Sarah wrote him that the slaves, as well as his family, were anxious to see him and that, "There never was a set of people that want to see any body as we all want [to] see you and Jesse."[36]

Cotton was the most important crop grown on the Monte Verdi Plantation, and Devereux followed the plan of most planters to break the land in December or January so that the earth could mellow and permit early planting. Devereux frequently planted some fields early and some late so that if there should be a frost not all the crop would be lost. Abigail Curlee in her dissertation on A Study of Texas Slave Plantations, 1822 to 1865, has given an excellent summary of what steps went into planting cotton:

[32]Julien S. Devereux to D. W. Field, May 13, 1850, **ibid.**
[33]Sarah Devereux to Julien S. Devereux, November 20, 1855, **ibid.**
[34]Jesse, a slave, was with Devereux in Austin at the time.
[35]Sarah Devereux to Julien S. Devereux, January 1, 1856, **ibid.**
[36]Sarah Devereux to Julien S. Devereux, December 27, 1855, **ibid.**

Planting usually started with the ploughs opening a shallow furrow on top of the ridges which were from four to eight feet apart, depending upon the fertility of the soil. The thickly planted seed were covered over with a harrow, or a plough, or a board attached to the heel of a plough. Many rolled the beds to settle the dirt about the seed and to facilitate capillary action. According to the season, cotton reached a stand in two or three weeks, when the hoe hands scraped down the sides of the bed to break the crust and remove all grass and weeds. Sometimes rain prevented the scraping until the weeds had so choked the cotton that the planter was forced to plow it up and replant. The ploughs followed the hoes and threw the dirt from the tender plant, only to throw it back again in another two weeks. About the third week in March, when the cotton had three to six leaves the hoe gangs chopped it to a double stand, leaving two or three stalks in a place for protection against cold, cut-worms, or rain. In another two weeks, if frosts or rain had not intervened, the "choppers" went over the cotton again, leaving a stalk every two or three feet. If other work was not pressing, the planter had the Negroes go over his cotton every two or three weeks until the bolls began to form or the plant shaded the ground. Early cotton put on forms the first of May, bloomed in two or three weeks, and the blossoms gave place to boll in June. Bad weather upset this schedule; however, a late season did not necessarily mean a failure. The year 1850 turned out to be an average one although in May the crop was no further advanced than usual in March. Boasting that it was not necessary to cultivate cotton as often in Texas as in other states, many planters contented themselves with three or four cultivations, but most of them found that loose topsoil paid.[37]

Since the year of 1850 has been considered an average one for cotton production in Texas, Devereux's operations in this year may be examined to see what he produced and where he ranked as a planter on the Texas scene. Devereux mentioned that he started picking cotton on September 2, 1850, and recorded these additional statistics:

First frost to kill vegetation was the 26th Oct 1850
First ice was on the morning of the 17th Nov.   "
Finished picking out our cotton on the 12th Dec 1850
Finished Gining Cotton on the 16th Dec 1850

[37]Abigail Curlee, A Study of Texas Slave Plantations, 1822 to 1865, Ph.d. Dissertation, The University of Texas, Austin, Texas, 157-159.

Finished packing cotton on the 21st Dec. 1850[38]

Abigail Curlee utilized the United States Census of 1850 for her study of Texas slave plantations and drew the conclusion that, "If forty 400 pound bales of cotton or forty hogsheads of sugar[39] be taken as the basic production of a planter, the Census of 1850 reveals that there were 375 planters in Texas; only ninety-one of whom produced one hundred or more bales of cotton or hogsheads of sugar."[40] Devereux ranked with the top ninety-one planters in Texas for during that year he produced one hundred and twenty 400 pound bales of cotton.[41] Only one other Rusk County planter, B. F. Thompson, with one hundred and twenty-five 400 pound bales of cotton, ranked with the top ninety-one planters in Texas. The largest plantations in 1850 were in the area of Brazoria, Austin, Matagorda, and Wharton counties, and on the basis of planters in the hundred unit class, only three East Texas counties had planters listed; Devereux and Thompson in Rusk County and one planter was listed in the counties of Cass and Harrison.

Devereux's rank among slave holders in Texas is also interesting. With seventy-five slaves in 1850 Devereux was among the ninety-two slave holders in Texas who owned fifty or more slaves.[42] The complete inventory Devereux made to census taker Thomas M. Likens on November 24, 1850, was as follows and covered the period for the year ending June 1, 1850:

Acres of Land—Improved 420
Acres of land—Unimproved 3892
Cash Value of farm $16,000
Value of Farming Implements

[38]Julien S. Devereux's Monte Verdi Plantation Account Book for 1849-1854.
[39]"One hogshead of sugar may be roughly considered the equivalent of a bale of cotton, therefore the unit of measurement is derived in both cases," according to Abigail Curlee, A Study of Texas Slave Plantations, 1822 to 1865, p. 218.
[40]**Ibid.**, 219.
[41]"Schedule 4, Production of Agriculture in 1850, Census of the United States," M.S., Texas State Library, Austin, Texas.
[42]Curlee, A Study of Texas Slave Plantations, 1822 to 1865, p. 27. The breakdown for slave holders in Texas in 1850 was as follows:

1 slave	1,935	20 and under 50	374
2 and under 5	2,640	50 and under 100	82
5 and under 10	1,585	100 and under 200	9
10 and under 20	1,121	200 and under 300	1
		Total	7,747

Devereux Family Papers

Record of Devereux Family

Typical Pages in Record of Devereux Family

Devereux Cathedral

Samuel M. Devereux   Julien S. Devereux

John William Devereux's Cabin

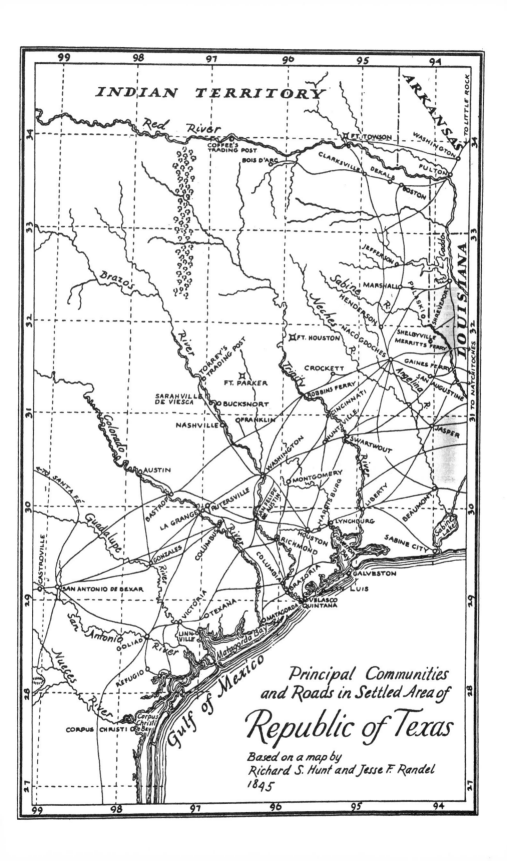

INDIAN TERRITORY

ARKANSAS

Red River

TO LITTLE ROCK

FT. TOWSON
WASHINGTON
TO LITTLE ROCK

COFFEE'S
TRADING POST
BOIS D'ARC
CLARKSVILLE
DEKALB
PULTON
BOSTON

Brazos

JEFFERSON
MARSHALL
TISKIO
SHREVEPORT

LOUISIANA

Sabine R.
HENDERSON

River

TORREY'S
TRADING POST
FT. HOUSTON
NACOGDOCHES
SHELBYVILLE
MERRITTS FERRY

TO NATCHITOCHES

FT. PARKER
CROCKETT
GAINES FERRY

Trinity
Angelina R.
SAN
AUGUSTINE

SARAHVILLE
DE VIESCA
BUCKSNORT
ROBBINS FERRY
CINCINNATI

NASHVILLE
FRANKLIN
HUNTSVILLE
JASPER

Colorado
AUSTIN
WASHINGTON
SWARTWOUT

TO SANTA FE
MONTGOMERY
River

Guadalupe
BASTROP
RUTERSVILLE
SAN FELIPE
DE AUSTIN
HARRSBURG
LIBERTY
BEAUMONT

LA GRANGE
COLUMBUS River
LYNCHBURG
Sabine Lake

CASTROVILLE
GONZALES
RICHMOND
HOUSTON
SABINE CITY

San
River
COLUMBIA
BRAZORIA
GALVESTON

SAN ANTONIO DE BEXAR
VICTORIA
SAN LUIS

San Antonio River
TEXANA
VELASCO
QUINTANA

Nueces
GOLIAD
LINN
VILLE
MATAGORDA

REFUGIO
Matagorda Bay

River
Corpus
Christi
Bay

CORPUS CHRISTI
Gulf of Mexico

Principal Communities
and Roads in Settled Area of

Republic of Texas

Based on a map by
Richard S. Hunt and Jesse F. Randel
1845

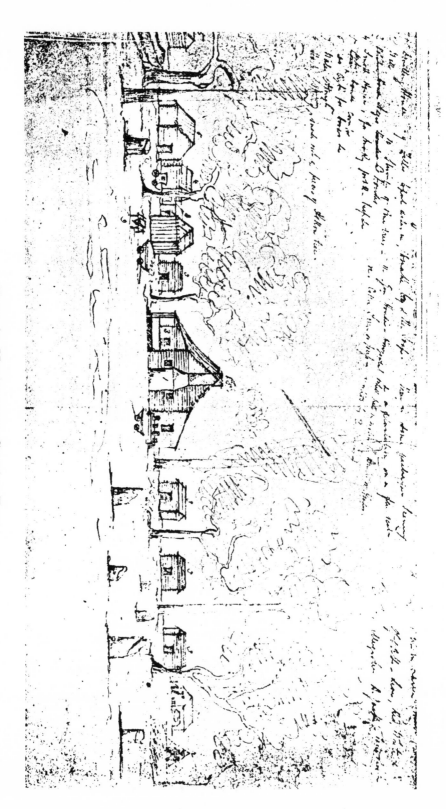

Farm in Montgomery County, Texas

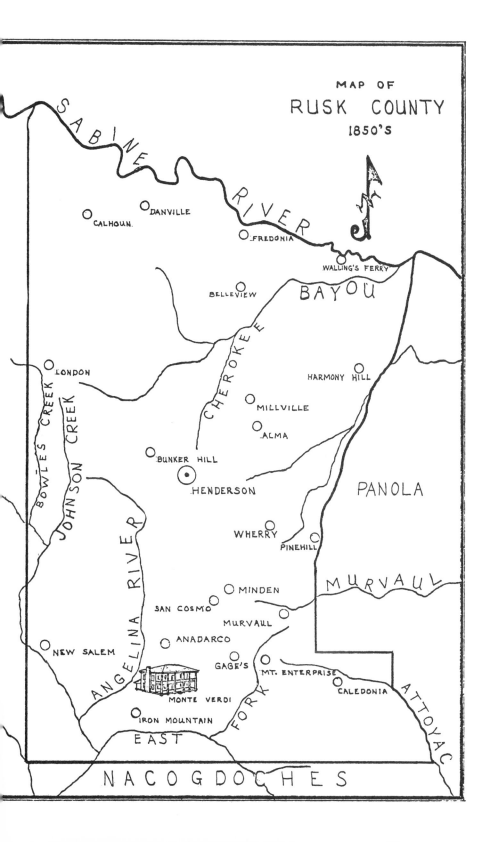

MAP OF
RUSK COUNTY
1850'S

Julien S. Devereux's Monte Verdi Plantation
Account Book for 1849-1854

Julien Sidney Devereux   Sarah Ann Devereux

Albert and Julien Devereux

TO THE VOTERS OF RUSK COUNTY.

The Democratic Convention which recently assembled at Henderson, nominated me a candidate to represent Rusk county in the lower branch of the next Legislature. Within the last few days, I have concluded to accept the nomination, which I should have done with more alacrity, but for the condition of my health which at one time rendered it doubtful whether I could stand the fatigues of the canvass. I am now, however, a candidate before you, and a such acknowledge your right, before giving me your support, to require an expression of my views in reference to State and national policy; and as I am not in the habit of public speaking, I have adopted this mode of giving you my opinions.

The question of as much, or perhaps the most importance of any that will come before the next Legislature for its action, is the acceptance or rejection of the so called Texas Creditors Bill, as passed by the late Congress of the United States. The Legislature of the State of Texas some years ago, established the terms on which she was willing to pay her public debt, and in the bill alluded to, Congress has impliedly said that these terms are inequitable and unjust, and thus reflecting to some extent upon the justice and good intentions of our State Legislature. For this reason, I think the bill objectionable. But as the bill probably contains the most favorable terms that Congress will concede to us, I am willing to accept it as a final settlement of the whole matter, and thus put to rest a fruitful source of expense and legislation. But I must have unqualified assurances that it will be a final adjustment of the vexed question, otherwise it cannot receive my sanction.

The question which next claims my attention, is State aid to projects of internal improvement. No one can appreciate the advantages of Railroads more highly, or feels the want of them more sensibly, than I do; and yet, I should be unwilling to see the State engage in a general system of building Railroads, for which she would be under the necessity of imposing taxes upon the people, which might prove onerous and burthensome, especially when we can have no assurance that our immediate section would be benefited by such works. It has been ascertained, however, by calculation, that if the Texas Creditors Bill is accepted by the Legislature, (and of which there can be but little doubt,) there will be in the Treasury of the State, unappropriated, about four millions of dollars. This money can be of no benefit to the people, so long as it remains in the vaults of the Treasury; but, on the contrary, will be a bone of unceasing strife and contention in the Legislature. I am, therefore, willing that this money shall be loaned in equal proportions to two or three, or even four, Railroads, the terminus and course of which shall be designated, and to run through the most populous sections of the State, and connecting the interior and other portions of the State with the Gulf, in such a manner as to be of the greatest benefit to the greatest number. I propose then to secure the repayment of the money, by having it applied exclusively to the purchase of iron, and by taking a mortgage upon the road, or undoubted personal security. By this policy, the State will not be involved a cent—the people will be subjected to no additional taxation, while the construction of Railroads will be greatly facilitated. I am, moreover, in favor of the repeal of the Pacific Railroad charter, or at least such a modification of its

provisions as will release any particular lands now held in reserve for that road, as I think the present reservations will retard, if not prevent for years to come, the settlement of one of the best portions of our State—the consideration of our State Constitution. I am not at all clear that it is necessary to alter any portion of the Constitution; but if it should be ascertained that any of its parts conflict with legislation necessary to the interests of the people, I am willing that it should be amended in the manner pointed out by the Constitution itself,—in other words, that the amendments thought to be necessary may be submitted by the Legislature to the people for their action.

I am opposed to a call of a convention for such a purpose, because I believe the Legislature has no constitutional right to call such a convention; but if it had the right, I should oppose its exercise, because it would subject the State to vast expense, when the same ends might be accomplished without one cent of expense, in the legitimate manner pointed out by the constitution.

I will next proceed to give you my views on Federal or National Policy. As I am the nominee of a Democratic Convention, it may be needless to say that I am a Democrat of the Jeffersonian school. Through all the vicissitudes of that party, I have given it my firm adhesion, and humble support. I have been with it in six troubles, and never deserted in the seventh. The principles adopted and affirmed time and again by the Democratic Baltimore Convention, have ever met my unqualified approval. My opinions in respect to those principles have undergone no change, and my firm convictions are that the safety and perpetuity of the Union depends in a great measure upon keeping up the organization of that party. No national party can occupy the Democratic Baltimore platform and be radically unsound upon the constitutional rights of the South. So long, then, as our party organization is kept up on such a basis, it will constitute one of the strongest, if not the very strongest, ligaments that binds together the two sections of the Union. Entertaining such views, it may be needless to add that I shall oppose, in my humble way, all parties, whether whig or know nothing, which may conflict with the democratic party, or which seeks to subvert or overthrow it. I have many objections to the party recently sprung into existence, under the name of the know nothing or American party; but if I had no other than those which I have already enumerated, I should feel constrained to oppose it.

I have now, fellow-citizens, given you a synopsis of my views upon State and national policy. My reasons for these views are not given as fully as I could desire, but they are at least as full as would be consistent with convenience in an address like this. It is my purpose, however, to canvass the county, and as I have no concealments and nothing to disguise, it will always be my pleasure, as it is my duty, to give my views to any and all who may feel an interest in knowing them, upon all topics of public interest.

It is hardly necessary to add, that I should be pleased and duly grateful to receive your suffrages.

I am, respectfully,
Your obedient servant,
JULIAN S. DEVEREUX.

Political Broadside Issued by Julien S. Devereux

RAILROAD Independent Freemen's TICKET

For Governor.
D. C. DICKSON.

For Lieutenant Governor,
W. G. W. JOWERS.

Commissioner of the Gen'l Land Office,
STEPHEN CROSBY.

For Congress,
L. D. EVANS.

For the Legislature,
S P Hollingsworth
William Stedman
Allen Birdwell
Mark Stroud
J C Spinks

For County Commissioner,
P R Lilly
Henry Berry

DEMOCRATIC ANTI-KNOW NOTHING TICKET.

For Congress.
MAT. WARD.

For Governor.

E. M. PEASE.

For Lieut. Governor.
H. R. RUNNELS,

For commissioner of Gen'l Land Office..
WILLIAM FIELDS.

FOR REPRESENTATIVES,

J. S. DEVEREUX,
J. HARVY PARSONS,
M. D. ECTOR,
W. B. HOLLOWAY.

For county Commissioner,

HENRY BERRY.
JAMES BAGLEY.

For the Texas Debt Act.

Rusk County Ballots, 1855

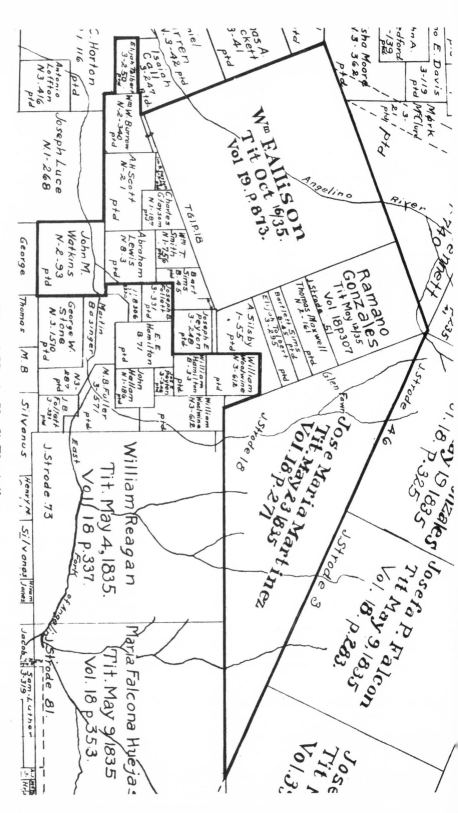

Map of Monte Verdi Plantation

No: _45_ Depot No. 1.

No. _174_ **Confederate Tax Receipt.** $ _____

Received of _Sarah Beaver own_

the sum of _Three hundred Four 80/100_

Dollars, in Confederate Treasury Notes, being the full amount of Confederate Tax due by him for the year 186_7_

Dated _20th May 1864_ _F. S. Young_

Collector District No. _14_

Rush County. _Aprile_ 1864

Received of _Mrs S Beaver_ of

Rush County. _eighth hundred_

and fifty six lbs of _bacon_ on

account of _C. S. Tax in Kind._ _N. G. Bagley_

QUALITY: _good_

Agent, Depot No. 1, Rush County.

No | ESTIMATE OF GRAIN, FORAGE, POTATO AND WOOL TITHES, DUE BY _Mrs S A Beaver_ FOR 186_

POTATOES		CORN.		WHEAT.		OATS.		RYE. BUCK-WHEAT. PEAS		HAY.		FODDER.		PEAS & BEANS.		WOOL.		TOTAL VALUES.
Bush.	Val. $	Bush.	Val. $	Bush.	Val. $	Bush.	Val. $	Bush.	Val. $	Lbs.	Val. $	Lbs.	Value $	Bush.	Val. $	Lbs.	Val. $	Dollars.
2½	2 00	533	2.50	7½	5.00	17	2.00					2433	2 00			3	2 00	1463 50

Names of Appraisers or Assessor. _S Lawler_

Dated _____ 186___

Mrs S A Beaver
Tax Payer.

NOTE.—If not delivered within 60 days from date hereof, the producer will be liable to 50 per cent. ADDITIONAL, and in ALL CASES when not paid IN KIND, the transportation is to be ADDED to the tax at the rate of 20 cents per 100 lbs.

No. _362_ Estimate of Cotton, Sugar, Molasses, Tobacco and Bacon Tithes, due by _Mrs S A Beaver_ for 186_

COTTON.		SUGAR.		MOLASSES.		TOBACCO.		BACON.		TOTAL VALUES.
Pounds.	Value. $	Pounds.	Value. $	Gallons.	Value. $	Pounds.	Value. $	Pounds.	Value. $	Dollars.
750	20							856	80	834.80

Names of Appraisers or Assessor. _S Lawler_

Dated _July 22d_ 186_4_

Mrs S A Beaver
Tax Payer.

NOTE.—If not delivered within sixty days from date hereof, the producer will be liable to 50 per cent. ADDITIONAL, and in ALL CASES, when not paid in KIND the transportation is to be added to the tax at the rate of 20 cents per 100 lbs.

Confederate Tax Receipts

The Texas Capitol, 1853-1881

Monte Verdi, 1920

Monte Verdi, 1950

Artist's Drawing of Abandoned Monte Verdi

Monte Verdi Before Restoration

Monte Verdi Before Restoration

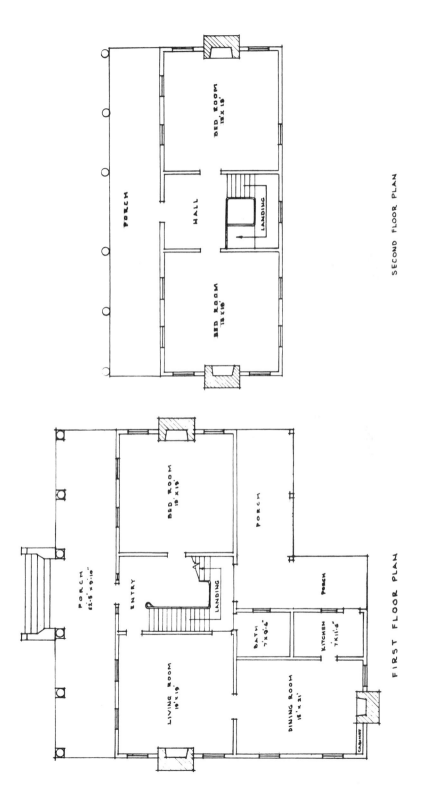

BED ROOM
18 X 18'

PORCH

HALL

LANDING

BED ROOM
18 X 18'

SECOND FLOOR PLAN

BED ROOM
18 X 18'

PORCH
21'-5" X 9'-10"

ENTRY

LANDING

PORCH

LIVING ROOM
18 X 18'

BATH
7 X 9'-6"

KITCHEN
7 X 11'-6"

PORCH

DINING ROOM
18' X 21'

CABINET

FIRST FLOOR PLAN

Monte Verdi Restoration Plans

Monte Verdi Restored, 1961

Monte Verdi Restored, 1961

DEVEREUX FAMILY

MORGAN DEVEREUX = ELIZABETH HUGHS

CHARLES DEVEREUX (b.1740-d.1805) = NANCY WOODS (m.OCT.7,1766-d.1793)

Children of Charles Devereux and Nancy Woods:

- ELIZABETH (b.DEC.7,1767-d.1821?)
- JOHN WILLIAM DEVEREUX (b.MARCH 15,1769-d.JUNE 22,1847) = (1) ELIZABETH FEW (m.APR.19,1795-d.JAN.15,1799) (2) SALLEY GRIGG (m.JAN.15,1801-d.JAN.22,1810)
- JAMES (b.OCT.7,1771-d.OCT.20,1780)
- SAMUEL M. (b.DEC.7,1773-d.?)
- ARCHIBALD M. (b.AUG.20,1775-d.1809)
- JOHN B. (b.SEPT.7,1777-d.1800)
- NANCY (b.NOV.16,1779-d.OCT.24,1779?)
- CHARLES H. (b.MAR.7,1782-d.?)

Children of John William Devereux:

- ALBERT (b.DEC.6,1801-d.SEPT.5,1822)
- LOUISIANA (b.SEPT.16,1803-d.?)
- JULIEN SIDNEY DEVEREUX (b.JULY 25,1805-d.MAY 1,1856) = (1) ADALINE REBECCAH BRADLEY (b.APRIL 6,1809-m.DEC.28,1826) =(2) SARAH ANN LANDRUM (b.MAY,1827-m.JUNE 27,1843-d.APR.25,1900)
- ANTOINETTE (b.NOV.7,1808-d.NOV.1,1809)

Children of Julien Sidney Devereux and Adaline Rebeccah Bradley:

- MARY EMILY (b.DEC.16,1830-d.JAN.28,1851)
  - (x) BARBARA SCOTT WAY
    - SIDNEY WAY (b.JAN.,1845?-d.1890's.)
- CALEB JACKSON GARRISON = ANTOINETTE SCOTT (b.MAY1,1840-m.MAY 15,1856- d. AUG.25,1872)
  - JULIEN ABBIE HOMER ARTHUR
- JOHN WILLIAM (b.MARCH 7,1846-d.SEPT.25,1846)
- ALBERT (b.DEC.15,1846-d.MARCH 7,1910) = ELIZABETH A.STAMPS (m. FEB.11,1869)
  - JULIEN O'GILVIE WILLIAM EDWARD ALBERT HARPER SARAH ANTOINETTE FRANK LEE CHARLEY HOWARD LEILA BELLE ALBERT
- JULIEN SIDNEY (b.FEB.2,1851-d.JUNE 9,1896)

Children of Julien Sidney Devereux and Sarah Ann Landrum:

- WILLIAM PENN (b.APR.11,1850-d.DEC.6,1928) =(1) MARY DOLTON (2) JENNIE MILLER DOUGLAS (3) MARY PERKINS
  - JEWEL PEARL WILLIAM MILLER
  - WILLIAM PERKINS JULIEN = O. DOUGLAS WEEKS
    - SARAH JULIEN
- CHARLES (b.AUG.15,1855-d.SEPT.30,1884)

Devereux Family Genealogy Chart

and Machinery $2,000
Livestock:
    Horses 4
    Asses and Mules 21
    Milch Cows 40
    Working Oxen 16
    Other Cattle 100
    Sheep 25
    Swine 300
    Value of Livestock $2500
Produce during the year:
    Indian Corn, bushels of 3000
    Oats, bushels of 100
    Ginned Cotton, bales of 400 lbs each 120
    Wool, lbs. of 100
    Peas & Beans, bushels of 200
    Sweet Potatoes, bushels of 1000
    Butter, lbs. of 500
    Value of Animals slaughtered $360[43]

Devereux does not record how much money the crop for 1850 yielded, but the previous year he sold his cotton for "$53.62¢ per bale"[44] in Shreveport, Louisiana, and if this price can be taken as average the amount cotton brought Devereux in 1850 would be between $6500 and $7000. Some Devereux cotton in 1849 brought 9¢ a pound while some, sold in 1850, brought as high as 12¢ a pound.[45] Of the twelve bales Devereux packed on October 10, 1850, the average weight was 503½ pounds.

In 1851 Devereux reported that he had planted cotton on March 18, 21, and 26, and that on June 9 was the "first cotton blooms seen this year. One turned red suppose to have been in bloom a day or two."[46] The cotton crop for 1851 totaled 85 bales weighing 44,197 pounds.[47] Devereux sometimes sold his

---

[43]"Schedule 4, Produce of Agriculture in 1850, Census of the United States," M.S., Texas State Library, Austin, Texas.

[44]Julien Sidney Devereux's Memorandum and Record Book, 1840-1856.

[45]Ibid.

[46]Julien S. Devereux's Monte Verdi Plantation Account Book for 1849-1854.

[47]Julien S. Devereux's Memorandum and Record Book, 1840-1856. A first glance in comparison of 1851 cotton to that of 1850 would indicate a drop. Devereux's figures "for a year" are not based on the same period of time as are the figures of the United States Census. The Census figures were from May 31, 1849, to June 1, 1850, while Devereux figured from January 1 to December 31 for his calculations. Frequently cotton grown in the autumn of one year would not be picked, ginned, and marketed until the following year. Devereux's calculations of ninety-one bales of cotton for 1850, recorded in his Monte Verdi, Texas, Plantation Book, are understandably not for the same time period as the 120 bales accounted for by the census enumerator.

cotton to merchants in Mount Enterprise and Henderson and frequently he sent it to Shreveport, Louisiana.

Julien Devereux owned two gins, and he usually did the ginning for the smaller farmers in the neighborhood. In 1853 Devereux took out insurance at a cost of $75 on his two gin houses. One gin was described as a building "41 feet square containing a 50 saw improved Pratts Gin and Burrows improved patent corn mill with cast iron segments and running gear for Gin and mill complete valued at $1500," while the second gin house was "36 feet square containing Pratts 45 saw gin. Cast iron segments and running gear complete" was valued at $1000.[48] Most probably Devereux realized a healthy income from his gin operations, and in October of 1848 the following "Notice" was circulated among Rusk County residents:

NOTICE

All persons that haul cotton to the subscribers Gin are requested to bring bagging, rope and twine with the first load or it cannot be received, as there will not be room to store cotton only as it is ready to be ginned—all cotton will be considered delivered as soon as it is packed—The subscriber will not be liable for accidents either at the Gin or mill and will not be accountable for sacks or bags of corn or meal unless the sacks are plainly marked
this 26th October 1848

Julien S. Devereux

N. B. Corn, and Corn meal, for sale——[49]

The second most important crop grown at Monte Verdi was corn, the staple food of Texas as well as the South. Corn was eaten from the table as roasting ears, corn bread, grits, and hominy. During the early years at Monte Verdi corn was frequently hard to obtain and journeys of several days' time had to be made to secure the needed supply. The following procedure was used by Devereux to prepare his corn for planting:

Corn prepared for planting

Tar the Seed corn thus: Fill a barrel two thirds full of seed corn. add water enough to cover it ten inches deep; let it soak some twenty hours, pour off the water and replace it with that which has been made pretty hot (warm) and just

[48]Julien S. Devereux statement, April 3, 1853, Devereux Papers.
[49]"Notice," October 26, 1848, **ibid.**

enough to cover the corn; when the corn feels warm: add a gallon of hot water having a pint of (new) tar mixed with it; stir till every grain is varnished over with the tar. drain and roll in plaster and ashes or ashes only till dry enough to plant[.] neither birds squirrels or cut worms will injury corn thus prepared

The above is taken from Morris Shreveport Almanac for 1852 I have tried it and know that it [will] do—[50]

In 1848 Devereux planted corn on February 11 and 12, but there are notations of later planting on March 5 in the years 1850 and 1851. The next year, 1852, corn was planted on February 14. September was usually the month when "pulling" the corn began, and the following yield was recorded for Monte Verdi in 1850:

Mem of Corn made in 1850 Monte Verdi
Sept 16th 2 loads with large waggons—

" Estimated at 40 bushels pr load	80
Tuesday 17th 8 loads ditto	320
18th 4 loads with large waggons etc	160
3 loads with small waggon	80
19th 4 loads with large waggon etc	160
3 loads with small waggon	80
20th 8 loads with large waggon	320
21st 8 loads with large waggon	320
23d 6 loads " " "	240
24th 8 loads " " "	320
25th 10 loads " " "	400
26 9 loads " " "	360
	2840

72 large waggon
240 bushels or 6 loads of the above corn was cribed in the Gin lot to feed the mules in the Gining season and the balance of 2600 bushels was hauled and cribed in the mule lot near the Quarter[51]

The next year, 1851, Devereux recorded making 2450 bushels.[52]

Other crops in cultivation at Monte Verdi included sugar cane, planted on March 5, 1851, and on February 14, 1852; oats

[50]Monte Verdi, Texas, Plantation Book.
[51]Julien S. Devereux's Monte Verdi Plantation Account Book for 1849-1854.
[52]Ibid.

sowed on January 29, 1851;[53] and wheat sowed on October 27, 1848.[54] Turnips, rye, and potatoes were put out on February 8, 1851,[55] and on February 29, 1848, Devereux "planted the last irish potatoes, and some beans, squashes & cucumbers & okra."[56]

The success or failure of crops depended of course on favorable climate and Devereux in his writings gave much space to weather. An early comment was, "The great Frost was on the morning of the 16th April 1849. Corn-Cotton and all tender vegetation killed. Upwards of 100 acres of our corn & 60 acres of cotton appears to be entirely destroyed."[57] During 1850 Devereux's writings give a rather good picture of the hardship and ruin brought about by bad weather:

> Rainy Season commenced in Dec 1849. & rained all through the month of January and up to this time in February 1850 8th February 1850. the Angilina has been 2 feet higher in the month of January than was ever known by the *Oldest inhabitants*—great rain commenced on the night of the 11th February & rained 26 hours without abating which was followed by a Norther which produced the most intense cold weather we have had this winter[.] the Sun is now shining this 10 oclock the 14th and freezing=
>
> - - -
>
> Great Snow on the morning of the 27th March 1850 Leaves on the trees nearly full grown, half dozen different kinds of Roses and a great many other flowers in our garden in full bloom. Now 10 oclock in the morning all nature clothed in white and the snow falling rappedly cleared off in the evening. Large white frost on the morning Of the 28th March 1850= the Spring has continued so cold and wet that we have not been able to plant or do any thing in the farm in regular order & I have not attempted to keep a Memn of planting. On the 21 & 22d May we planted the cut of corn lying between the Weaver cut & the Mastadon it being the 3d time planted in corn this year. . . .
> The Great Cold Spell of weather was the first week in Dec 1850. began the 3d and continued until the 9th. The 6th 7th 8th the ground trees etc. all covered with sleet & snow. small streams frozen entirely over etc. etc.
>
> - - -

[53]Ibid.
[54]Monte Verdi, Texas, Plantation Book.
[55]Julien S. Devereux's Monte Verdi Plantation Account Book for 1849-1854.
[56]Monte Verdi, Texas, Plantation Book.
[57]Julien S. Devereux's Monte Verdi Plantation Account Book for 1849-1854.

the mornings of the 16th & 17th Feby [1851] the ground hard froze & thick ice.

- - -

the largest rain that has fallen thus far in the year was on the 19th Feby 1851. had to send to the Spring at the Quarter on the morning, of the 20th for water for house purposes.

- - -

On the night of the 26th Feby one of those kind of Rains that are always *unknown* to the Oldest inhabitants fell in perfect torrents, which together with the already high state of the water courses will most likely not cause them to fall *suddenly*

the 27th wind came from the north & during the night commenced snowing & freezing and on the morning of the 28th as cold as I ever have known it to be. Peach trees in full bloom. (mem. it appears there was only a portion of the trees in bloom which were killed)[58]

Before the end of 1851 Rusk County was having a severe drought, and Devereux noted on October 10 that Monte Verdi had the "first rain to wet the earth in about five months."

Julien Devereux took pride in his orchards, and peaches, plums, figs, and apples did well on the land at Monte Verdi. From Nacogdoches Adolphus Sterne sent cuttings to Devereux,[59] and James Harper Starr and Devereux exchanged fruit trees as well as "sprouts and cuttings of Altheas, Roses, or anything in that line."[60] From Augusta, Georgia, in 1855 came a request to Devereux for "rooted vines of his favorite variety of wild grapes, mustang grape, post oak grape, summer grape."[61]

Some figures on livestock at Monte Verdi are available. For the winter of 1848-1849 (December 8 and 22, 1848; January 10, 1849), sixty-one hogs were killed and 10,444 pounds of pork were put up. In 1850 pork totaled 12,059 pounds; in 1853 the figure was 13,695 pounds; and in 1854, between January 7 and January 12, there were 119 hogs killed totaling 14,793 pounds.[62] In 1855 Devereux sold the following cattle:

---

[58]Ibid.
[59]Adolphus Sterne to Julien S. Devereux, February 22, 1849, Devereux Papers.
[60]Julien Devereux to James Harper Starr, February 21, 1849, James H. Starr Papers, University of Texas.
[61]D. Redmond to Julien S. Devereux, January 2, 1855, Devereux Papers.
[62]Julien S. Devereux's Memorandum and Record Book, 1840-1856.

116 head of stock cattle sold Mr. Cason &
Son and delivered on the 18th October 1855
at $7.00 per head rec'd payment in Gold $812.00
7 Cows and calves sold to Doctor John A.
Jourdan 6 cows & calves at $10 & one at $15   75.00
one beef to Dr. Jourdan 582 lbs   16.00
one cow sold to David Basinger   10.00[63]

Devereux also had sheep, horses, and as many as twenty-three
mules on January 19, 1853.[64] Most stock thrived on the abundant vegetation at Monte Verdi.

It was no small job to supply the needs of a plantation the
size of Monte Verdi, and Julien Devereux had to purchase large
quantities of food, clothing, and articles such as rope, bagging,
and twine needed to carry on plantation operations. It was not
unusual for Devereux's accounts to run up to large amounts, as
was the bill for $3123.48 paid to McClarty & Son in Henderson
on June 30, 1852, and the one for $3552.34 paid to Charles Vin-
zent at Mount Enterprise on August 15, 1854.[65]

Typical items Devereux purchased when he made trips to
Henderson and Shreveport may be found listed on this "Memorandum" which he wrote out and carried with him:

small grind stone, candle sticks & snuffers, umbrella
set of caston,—flints & percussion caps. powder,
shot & lead—stretcher chains & log chains hoop iron.
Sheet iron for making bells—spade—shovel plough
moulds leather for bell collars & harness fish hooks
assorted fiddle strings—Saddle bags Side saddle—
Stirup irons—Tin buckets with strainers—2 pair
blankets—1 churn-milk pail—2 small waters-2 counter-
panes—1 set plates—1 set of knives & forks—1 small
frying pan—one set of cups & saucers—1 fine shawl—
8 yards of striped or ribbed muslin for a dress—
1 net cap with large border for winter—6½ yds white
bishop lawn for dress—nut megs & graters-sperm
candles. medecine of different kinds for family purposes—
nails—waffle irons—Sugar kettle at Shacklefords.
Lands Sassaparilla—1 barrel of flour—brandy & wine—
Molasses—Tea. (Tobacco cut). bagging rope & twine—
fire dogs. Moffatts pills & bitters Brandettes pills Mackel—
eye water & lip salve. Calomel Castoroil laudrum.
quinine. Morphine. Rhubarb, aloes. camphor. blister

---

[63]Monte Verdi, Texas, Plantation Book.
[64]Ibid.
[65]Bills and Receipts, June 30, 1852; August 15, 1854; Devereux Papers.

salve. Epecac—h peppermint. Specticles—water buckets
with brass hoops. fire dogs & Shovel & tongs—Starch
wafers   1   paregarec   Batemans drops
              Glister pipe
Inquire if Judge Norton wants to purchase Mr Landrums
place.—Inquire for a carriage or carriage repairing
one side of fine upper leather or one calf skin
some brand iron for Mr Landrum
2 or 3 pair of white Ladies stockings
2 pair shoes for Antoinette[66]

An idea of prices during the 1850's can be had by examin-
ing some of the purchases Devereux made.   In Shreveport on
October 17, 1850, Devereux bought "36 prs Rusetts shoes" at
$1.15 each; "6 pairs boys Rusetts shoes" at $1.00 each; 10
pounds of tobacco at 35 cents a pound; a barrel of flour for
$7.00; and 2 sacks of coffee weighing 328 pounds at 14¢ a
pound.[67]   In 1851 Devereux was paying 62¢ for a carriage whip,
$3.75 for a Panama hat, 20¢ for a doll for Antoinette, 40¢ for a
plug of tobacco, 25¢ for a bottle of Cologne, $5.00 for a satin
bonnet, and 50c for a hand saw.[68]   Huge quantities of clothing
and cloth were bought for distribution among the slaves, and
Devereux usually picked up something for members of his family like a silk dress or shawl for Sarah, song book for Antoinette,
and marbles and knives for the boys.

Devereux was once described by John McClarty in Henderson as a planter who "has always been our most prompt and
acceptable customer."[69]   Occasionally, however, Devereux would
be urged to pay a portion on his account, as in March, 1852,
when Dr. Elijah Dodson begged Devereux to pay his medical
bill saying, "I am trying to get money to send on to Philadelphia
to pay for the stock of medicine I purchased there last year.   Unless I pay for it I shall not be able to get another supply."[70]

In November, 1849, after marketing a portion of his cotton
crop, Devereux paid his account with Charles Vinzent and had
a balance of $203.07.[71]   Conditions locally such as drought, or
a war or panic on the national scene, could bring a shortage of

---

[66]Undated "Memorandum," **ibid.**
[67]G. M. Nichols to Julien S. Devereux, October 17, 1850, **ibid.**
[68]"J. S. Devereux's acct with T & W. T. Smith, 1851," **ibid.**
[69]John McClarty to Julien S. Devereux, January 19, 1855, **ibid.**
[70]Dr. Elijah Dodson to Julien S. Devereux, March, 1852, **ibid.**
[71]"Statement between Charles Vinzent and J. S. Devereux, 13 November
1849," **ibid.**

money in New Orleans, and this would be felt among Rusk County merchants. Under some conditions a merchant might have to call for assistance from planters.

Confidential   Mt Enterprise Tex
                                                  Febr 20 1854.
Col Devereux

D Sir

The object of my present is to ask a particular act of friendship of you.—Money matters are in at N Orleans worse than they have been for ten or fifteen years.—On next Sunday morning I start to N Orleans with the view of relieving to the best of my ability, the wants of some friends, who for ten years have stuck to me through thick and thin.—I wish to get one thousand dollars from you by Saturday evening next or more if it be possible.

It is a matter of necessity not on my own account, as on account of my friends.—The recent decline in cotton in N.O. = is solely caused by the tightness of the money market.

Yours very respectfully
Charles Vinzent

P.S.

I can replace the money in Two or three weeks. .—
Please dont look on this matter as a dun[72]

Once when Devereux ordered a "Bathing Tub" the merchant could not supply it but he wrote Devereux that, "I have ordered the Tub to be made."[73] The merchants made every effort to satisfy Devereux's specific needs, and one Shreveport merchant wrote, "The currant jelly was in small jars, so we purchased two of each glass & tin jars. The white wine we could not get by the gallon and we send you a case, which we think is a good article."[74]

Julien Devereux, like most Texas planters, was not a careful accountant, and no statistics are available in the Devereux Papers to show the profits or losses for a year's operation at Monte Verdi. Abigail Curlee has described the problem faced by writers who attempt to analyze plantation records:

The planter was not a scientific accountant. He did not reckon value upon the basis of cost and price. It is ex-

---

[72]Charles Vinzent to Julien S. Devereux, February 20, 1854, **ibid.**
[73]G. M. Nichols to Julien S. Devereux, May 28, 1849, **ibid.**
[74]J. N. Howell to Julien S. Devereux, April 24, 1856, **ibid.**

tremely doubtful whether the majority of the planters ever actually analyzed their economic situation and determined what per cent their investments were returning. Most of them are said to have contented themselves with the yearly statement of their accounts from their factors, and to have kept meager records, if any. A few kept diaries of daily happenings. Thus only once or twice a year must the planter have realized what his financial condition was— when his factor sent in his statement, or "dunned" him for cotton to balance accounts, or when taxes were due. The whole system was one to entangle in its meshes even a good business man, but especially a man unaccustomed to think in terms of money. The planter had to buy on credit for a large number of people over a long period of time. He was not required to make payment until his crop was harvested. He often overbought, if his prospects were favorable, only to have a month's drought bring partial or complete failure. If he and his slaves had lived easily and comfortably during the year and the annual settlement with his merchant in January found a substantial balance left after payment of accounts and the charges for marketing, he was content.[75]

Devereux's record of plantation management appear in a variety of books, diaries, and data books. It is frequently extremely difficult to determine the income and outgo of operations because complete records seldom were kept over a long period of time. Gaps exist over periods for so long as half a year, as in 1853, when Devereux left on June 2 on his "Southern trip" and did not keep a memorandum for the balance of the year.

The health of Monte Verdi Plantation was of major concern to Devereux, and the medical bills paid indicate that doctors W. W. Freeling, Elijah Dodson, A. P. Galloway, P. T. Richardson, and William H. Beers were on the premises quite often, caring for slaves and members of the Devereux family. During August, 1848, while Devereux's son was ill, Dr. Beers paid a visit and doctored the boy for five days and nights charging $100.[76] Dr. Dodson made some thirty visits during 1851. His charges on February 6 included $5.00 for "one visite and medicine in the night to Mary and Delivering her of child," and 50¢ the same day for "pulling a tooth for a negro."[77] On January 9,

[75]Abigail Curlee, A Study of Texas Slave Plantations, 1822 to 1865, p. 223.
[76]Dr. William H. Beers Medical Bill, 1848, Devereux Papers.
[77]Dr. Elijah Dodson to Julien Devereux, December 10, 1851, **ibid.**

1856, Devereux paid a medical bill of $121.95 which was in payment for calls to administer to slaves for such things as $1.50 for "salve & dressing Boys finger" and "visit with Shelton & setting arm & leg."[78]

The doctor was not always called in when sickness came about on the plantation, and remedies and cures for all sorts of ailments were jotted down in scrapbooks, diaries, and the like kept by the Devereuxs. Some remedies may have come down as "old wives tales" as indicated by the notation that on January 19, 1848, "Old Bailey and a cagen called—got my wildcat skin to cure his wife's breast—recommended by Doctor Rains as a Specific."[79] The "cure for Hydrophobia" recommended was:

Cure for Hydrophobia

soak a Rennet in a tumbler of water for a few minutes—add a pulverized savadilla as much as you can hold between your thumb and three fingers mix it thoroughly and give it to the patient (confine him and force him to swallow it if not willing) then place him in the sun or near a fire have him well warmed—if he is not tranquelized with one dose give a second and it will be certain to succeed.[80]

The cure for a sore leg was to "apply scrape turnips to the effected part until cured which will be completed in a short time," and a quick remedy for scalds and burns was to "Let clarified honey be applied in a linen rag and in a moment the pain will cease."[81] Cures were suggested for cancer, fevers, lock jaw, snake bite, coughs, and the like. For rattlesnake bite a victim was to take "the expressed Juice of the Cuchold Burr taken inwardly plentifully with sweet milk and some mashed bound to the wound." The simplest remedy recorded was for a nervous headache:

Many persons who are engag'd in sedentary occupations are afflicted with this kind of headache and the following is a simple remedy—Take a sponge and wash the body thoroughly with cold water after which wipe with a course Towel or Cloth so as to undergo a good scrubbing—besides

[78]W. W. Freeling to Julien S. Devereux, January 9, 1856, **ibid.**
[79]J. W. Devereux Memorandum and Common Place Book.
[80]Record of the Devereux Family.
[81]J. W. Devereux Scrapbook.

affecting this special good such a practice contributes in the highest degree to improve and invigorate the system.[82]

Monte Verdi Plantation was large and wealthy as evidenced by the listing of taxable property Devereux recorded during the 1850's. By 1852 Devereux valued his holdings at $47,824 broken down as follows:

seventy-one slaves valued at	$28,000
8424½ acres of land in Rusk County valued at $2.00 per acre	16,849
25 horses and mules valued at	1,500
150 head of neat cattle valued at	750
Stock of hogs & sheep valued at	400
One pleasure carriage	325
	$47,824[83]

Three years later in 1855, the year before Devereux's death, his taxable property was reported to be:

Seventy five slaves (75) valued at $30,000
3624 acres of Land on the Wm. F. Allison League
  347 acres on the Romana Gonzales ¼ League
  416   ”   ”   ”   Abram H Scott head right
  320   ”   ”   ”   Josiah Call   ”   ”
  320   ”   ”   ”   Elijah Talbot   ”   ”
  500   ” (in two surveys) on Thomas Maxwells head right
  320   ” (in two surveys) on Bartlett Simms head right
  259½ ” (in two surveys) on Joseph Peyton head right
  640   ” in the John M Watkins head right
  320   ” on the William Burrows   ”   ”
  320   ” on the Abram Lewis   ”   ”
  370   ” of the A Silsby head right
  497   ” of the grant of J M Martinez

8253½ Acres

            All the above described tracts of Land situated in Rusk County Texas and valued at $2.00 pr acre— $16,507
30 horses and mules valued at $18.00   1,800
300 head cattle valued at $15.00   1,500
    Miscellaneous   5.00   500

total amount of taxable property $50,307[84]

---

[82]Record of the Devereux Family.
[83]Monte Verdi, Texas, Plantation Book.
[84]"List of Taxable Property Given in by Julien S. Devereux, March, 1855," Devereux Papers.

These figures, as well as those from 1846 on, indicate that Devereux's outlook was one of optimism for generally he tended to farm more land and acquire more slaves each year. Management of Monte Verdi during the first few years occupied most of Devereux's time. He did like to fish and hunt, and there were wolves, bears, wildcats, turkeys, ducks, deer, and panthers in the nearby "Angelina bottoms." Devereux noted on January 30, 1852, that:

> Basinger, Howerton & myself went hunting in swamp. killed a Panther & Bear, both very large and fat. the bear much the fatest that we have known of any this season. the days hunt was a very exciting one and required great exertions to save the bear which was finally killed in the East Angelina River.[85]

Devereux could afford to travel and stay in fine hotels, but no where was he so happy and contented as in the serene and peaceful life at Monte Verdi. He loved the out of doors of his plantation and the kind of life it had to offer. Perhaps Devereux expressed his feelings best when, as a member of the Texas Legislature, he declared that, "I would greatly prefer to forego all the honor & glory and be places where I could step to back gallery of an log cabin and call out to Bill to feed them hounds & saddle old John for a hunt at the pine Island or the pine log crossing or any where on my own dominions."[86]

Devereux spent much time reading. He subscribed to newspapers outside of Texas, including several published in Alabama and in New Orleans. In Texas he took the Houston *Telegraph and Texas Register*, the *Texas State Gazette*, published in Austin, and the Marshall *Texas Republican*. Numerous agricultural magazines were received at Monte Verdi such as *De Bow's Review*, a New Orleans publication which presented factual information on Southern agriculture, transportation, and manufacturing. Devereux kept informed concerning significant books being published from time to time such as the Thomas Jefferson writings and the *Harper Family Library*. Devereux was notified

---

[85]Julien S. Devereux's Monte Verdi Plantation Account Book for 1849-1854.
[86]Julien S. Devereux to Sarah Devereux, December 11, 1855, Devereux Papers.

by one dealer that the *Writings of Benjamin Franklin* by Jared Sparks could be supplied to his residence "complete in ten (10) vol Octave . . . at $30.00 pr copy," which the dealer said was the price of the books in New York and Boston.[87] Typical books read by Devereux were Charles Lyell, *Principles of Geology*, Washington Irving, *Astoria*, George White, *Historical Collections of Georgia*, and George Combe, *Constitution of Man*.

As mistress of Monte Verdi Sarah Devereux had to supervise the care of her own household while frequently playing the role of mother and nurse in the care of slaves. Guests dropped in often at Monte Verdi and sometimes there was overnight company for weeks at a time. Monte Verdi gained a reputation as a place for friendly hospitality and good food, as exemplified in a friend's letter to Sarah:

> I am sorry that I am not with you to enjoy some of the green peas, but the tommatos [sic], and egg plant will still be plentiful. O how I wish I were with thee to get some nice clabber, and butter milk.[88]

Sarah Devereux enjoyed pleasures at Monte Verdi. She went to quiltings and sometimes Julien would share her company at a Baptist preaching. Occasionally the family could get together and hunt chinquipins. While her husband was in the legislature, Sarah wrote to him that, "Antoinette and Albert and I had gone to Salem today to attend a Masonic and Odd Fellows Procession and Installation of officers and a nice dinner prepared by Mrs. Nelson it was a very nice affair and plenty for everyone there and as many more."[89]

Devereux was happy with the calm and quiet life at Monte Verdi. As he became more successful as a planter, however, greater demands were made upon him by his associates. Monte Verdi offered much in "A Way of Life" besides the operation of a plantation, and some of Devereux's activities beyond the bounds of Monte Verdi are next examined.

[87]W. G. Balch to Julien Devereux, March 2, 1849, **ibid.**

[88]Mrs. M. A. Harcourt to Mrs. Sarah Devereux, undated letter, **ibid.** Recipes for "Jonny Cakes," "Gumbo of the West Indies," and other dishes are given in the Record of the Devereux Family. In the J. W. Devereux Scrapbook there is a notation that coffee "is now cultivated extensively in Cuba and other parts of the Spanish Islands. It is now in daily use in Mexico and the Southern and most of the United States. It is met with in most houses in Texas at their dinners and offer it at all times to visitors in place of spiritous liquors & wines. We have it 3 times each day at our table."

[89]Sarah Ann Devereux to Julien S. Devereux, December 27, 1855, Devereux Papers.

CHAPTER VII

Monte Verdi Way of Life

*You refer to my visit to your residence now nearly
three years ago. If to you it was pleasant, it was doubly
so to me. I often recur to it. I enjoyed more real satisfaction during that brief visit than in any portion—or
all—of my trip. The pretty country in which you live;
the lovely scenery with which you are surrounded; your
quiet and unobtrusive but pleasant life, surrounded by
friends and kind neighbors, made me think you the hap-
piest of men.*[1]

MONTE Verdi Plantation had the usual heavy responsibilities
for its owners, but it did provide wealth and comfort and
other compensations. Julien Devereux assumed the position
of "citizen planter" in the true sense of the word, and while residing at Monte Verdi he reared a family, held political offices
in Rusk County, promoted local industry, helped build schools,
traveled, and eventually sat in the state legislature.

Although Devereux wrote to an acquaintance in Alabama
in December of 1852 that, "I have *seen* and indeed I have *felt*
hard times in Texas and I am now barely able to make buckle
and tongue meet . . .,"[2] he probably was not in that bad an
economic condition. During the years at Monte Verdi Devereux
was acquiring more land and slaves; he had a fine carriage,
drank imported wines, and ate the best food that could be purchased in Shreveport and New Orleans. The Devereux carriage
cost $325.00, and a relative in Marshall, inviting the Devereuxs
to visit there in 1849, remarked to Julien that, "It is but a short
trip to one who is as well fixed for traveling as you are."[3]

Devereux's relatives, who were probably in a position to
know, were convinced the Texas planter had been successful.
Brother-in-law Henry Holcombe felt that, "A planter must in

---

[1]R. W. Laughery to Julien S. Devereux, March 26, 1854, Devereux Papers.
[2]Copy of a letter, address missing, December 16, 1852, **ibid.**
[3]W. S. Taylor to Julien S. Devereux, January 25, 1849, **ibid.**

[92]

your country eventually thrive—your expenses are trifling—your lands are the best in the world, and at low prices—you have a fine operative force in slaves—and all things considered together you ought to be content with your lot."[4] Louisiana wrote her brother once that, "While others almost starved" she would "often think how comfortably and independently you are situated in Texas and feel that it is as near true happiness as we can have in this world."[5] The sister felt that Julien's wealth put him in a class so that he had "less cause to complain than any in Texas."[6] Frequently, persons who knew Devereux commented on his wealth, as did a friend in 1852 who wrote, "I am pleased to hear of your worldly prosperity,"[7] and a former Alabama associate noted that, "You have been fortunate and . . . become wealthy. . . . You have thousands."[8]

During the 1850's Devereux paid some debts incurred before he left Alabama, including payment of $555.54 to Henry Holcombe.[9] Devereux kept large sums of "cash on hand" and noted on May 6, 1853, that he had $1571 in bank bills, American gold, foreign gold, and silver.[10] How much wealth Devereux had in Alabama cannot be determined but he claimed land and slaves in Pike County, and did own land in Pensacola, Florida. Devereux never made any claim of being wealthy, but always stressed the hardships of the past." Typical of his own analysis of his worth was his statement to an acquaintance that:

> I have seen hard times in Texas, and [make] *no mistake,* but for several years past my situation has been comfortable and I have reason to believe that from now hence I may improve my condition some, by prudent management, but I fear that *better times* has come too late with me, as I am getting advanced in life and my constitution impared by frequent attacks of sickness.[12]

During the 1850's Rusk County ranked as a leading Texas

[4]Henry P. Holcombe to Julien S. Devereux, November 7, 1845, **ibid.**
[5]Louisiana Holcombe to Julien S. Devereux, March 12, 1853, undated letter, 1855, **ibid.**
[6]Louisiana Holcombe to Julien Devereux, March 12, 1853, **ibid.**
[7]Samuel A. Gates to Julien S. Devereux, March 12, 1853, **ibid.**
[8]Joseph P. Clough to Julien S. Devereux, January 23, 1854, **ibid.**
[9]"G. M. Nichols a/c . . . 8th July, 1851." **ibid.**
[10]Julien S. Devereux's Memorandum and Record Book, 1840-1856.
[11]Copy of a letter, Julien S. Devereux to H. F. Sterns, April 16, 1848, Devereux Papers.
[12]Copy of letter, Julien S. Devereux to Gustave Cook, August 16, 1852, **ibid.**

county in population and wealth and could count among its citizens some of the most important persons on the Texas, as well as the East Texas, scene. Because of his position as a leading Rusk County planter[13] in 1850, Devereux was known throughout the county, and his associates included, in addition to planters, prominent business men, educators, newspaper men, lawyers, and politicians. The list reads like a Texas *Who's Who* for the 1850's.

Devereux was acquainted with well-known residents who had attained military reputations, such as James M. Barton, Mathew D. Ector, Robert W. Smith, and General James Smith; lawyers Frank Welsh Bowdon, James Henry Jones, William Wright Morris, and William Stedman; politicians such as James Winwright Flanagan and David Gage; and a wide range of persons in other fields and professions. James M. Barton, who served as sheriff of Rusk County for about a decade, was a noted participant in the Regulator-Moderator War and Mexican War.[14] Robert W. Smith, participant in the battle of San Jacinto and captain of a company in the battle of the Neches in 1839, when he fired the shot that killed Chief Bowles of the Cherokees, rented land to Julien Devereux when he first arrived in Rusk County in 1845. Another military acquaintance Devereux had was with General James Smith, participant in the Texas Revolution, who settled in 1836 on the site of Henderson and when Rusk County was created in 1843 offered to donate sixty-nine acres of land for the proposed county seat. Smith County was named in honor of James Smith, and when he died on December 25, 1855, he was buried with full military honors with General Thomas J. Rusk officiating.

Of the significant lawyers Devereux knew in the 1850's, none had a wider reputation than Frank Welsh Bowdon. Devereux and Bowdon were both opposed to the Know-Nothing party in Texas, and Bowdon on several occasions debated the merits and demerits of Know-Nothingism with Sam Houston. Bowdon was once described by Henry Clay as "the greatest living orator." Texas Governor Oran M. Roberts is reported to have stated on one occasion that Bowdon was the greatest ora-

---

[13]Only one other Rusk County planter, B. F. Thompson, according to the Census of 1850, was in the category with Devereux.

[14]Detailed biographical sketches of all persons mentioned here may be found in the **Handbook of Texas** and Dorman H. Winfrey, **A History of Rusk County, Texas.**

tor Texas ever had, and John H. Reagan is credited with the statement that Bowdon was the most phenomenal orator he had heard. William Wright Morris, noted Rusk County lawyer who handled much legal work for Devereux, became district judge in 1854, encouraged the development of Rusk County resources, and had a county, Morris, created in 1875, named in his honor. Another Rusk County lawyer Devereux knew was James Henry Jones, member of the United States Congress from 1883 to 1887, and appointee of Governor O .M. Roberts to the Board of Regents of the University of Texas. Devereux served in the legislature with the distinguished attorney from Rusk County, William Stedman, who was elected attorney general of Texas in August, 1863, but because of his anti-sessionist feelings he did not qualify for office.

Julien S. Devereux was acquainted with Rusk County politicians like James Winwright Flanagan, member of the Texas House of Representatives from 1851 to 1852, the Texas Senate from 1855 to 1856, and the United States Senate from 1870 to 1875, and Devereux was a neighbor to David Gage, member of the Ninth Congress of the Republic of Texas and member of the Annexation Convention in 1845.

Editor Mathew Duncan Ector of the Henderson *Democrat* served with Devereux in the legislature and the two men shared a room in Austin during the session. Ector attained the rank of brigadier general in the Confederate Army and Ector County, created in 1874, was named in his honor.

One other notable in the county who was numbered among Devereux's friends was H. D. E. Redwine, one time chief justice of the county and member of the legislature who raised a company of Rusk County men for the Confederate Army.

In adjoining Harrison County Devereux was a close friend of Robert W. Loughery, an influential editor of the *Texas Republican,* published at Marshall. The two were in agreement in opposing the Know-Nothing party in 1855. Devereux's plantation was only a few miles from Nacogdoches County, and in that county he was acquainted with James Harper Starr, secretary of the treasury under Mirabeau B. Lamar; Adolphus Sterne, agent of the provisional government of Texas during the Revolution who raised and equipped one of the companies of "New Orleans Greys;" and Thomas J. Rusk, signer of the Texas Declaration of Independence, important participant in the Texas

[95]

Revolution, United States Senator, and the person for whom Rusk County was named.

Outside his immediate locality Julien Devereux was personally acquainted with or carried on correspondence during the late 1840's and early 1850's with leading Texans such as Stockton P. Donley, district attorney of the Sixth Judicial District in 1853; John T. Mills, candidate for governor on the Democratic ticket in 1849; David Spangler Kaufman, the first man from Texas to be seated in the House of Representatives of the Congress of the United States; and Gideon Lincecum, Indian trader, physician, and naturalist who did valuable work concerning the agricultural ant in Texas.

,Friends and acquaintances with prestige were fine to have, but Julien Devereux's real interest remained in the Monte Verdi Plantation where his family was with him. The Devereux family rejoiced in the birth of a healthy son, Albert, on December 15, 1848. Another son, Julien Sidney Devereux, was born on February 2, 1851. This son is not to be confused with the boy born to Mrs. Barbara Scott Way,[15] who for a time was given the name Julien Sidney and later called only Sidney. Two more sons were born to Julien and Sarah Devereux; William Penn Devereux was born on April 11, 1853, and Charles Devereux was born on August 15, 1855. In addition to the boys there was Antoinette, who had been born in Macon County, Alabama, on May 1, 1840. Julien Devereux was a family man deeply devoted to his father, his wife, and his children. For many years, even back in Alabama, father John William had resided with Julien, and when Julien was absent on business he was concerned that his father would be lonely and that he would not stay warm. Julien would purchase the finest in silks for his "dear wife Sarah," and trips to Henderson and Mount Enterprise called for a memo to get a doll for Antoinette or marbles for the boys.

Antoinette and Sidney occupied a somewhat unusual place in the Devereux household. Antoinette's mother was a sister of Andrew G. Scott, the supervisor who brought Antoinette to Texas in 1841 along with Devereux's possessions and who stayed on and worked with Devereux for several years in Montgomery County. The boy, whose name was shortened from Julien Sidney to Sidney, was born to Andrew Scott's sister, Barbara Scott

---

[15]Mrs. Barbara Scott Way later married Larkin Turner.

Way, probably in January of 1843[16] in Montgomery County. No information is available to indicate that Antoinette and Sidney had the same mother, but there are indications that parents of the two children were sisters, or a sister, of Andrew G. Scott.[17] Julien Devereux took care of Antoinette and Sidney and in a codicil to his will of November 10, 1847, while living in Rusk County, the father provided for "Sidney Julien Way (a boy child the son of Mrs. Barbara Way)," to inherit a slave and requested that the executors "have the said Sidney Julien Way removed from Montgomery County to this County or to some healthy portion of Eastern Texas."[18] Sidney's mother left Montgomery County and by March, 1850, was married to Larkin Turner and was living in Claiborn Parish, Louisiana.[19]

On July 28, 1850, Julien Devereux wrote to David Gage, Rusk County representative at the time, and requested that as a "special favor" Gage

> . . . will have an act of our Legislature passed altering and changing the names of two children that it has fallen to my lot to take care of and provide for (viz) a girl whose present name is Antoinette Devereux Scott I wish changed to "Antoinette Devereux"—the boy whose present name is Sidney Way—I wish changed to "Sidney Devereux." Should you have the act passed, please see that the names are *spelled right in the Law.* It is a matter that I have neglected too long already and you will greatly oblige me by giving it your earliest attention. . . .[20]

During the summer of 1850 Julien Devereux sent overseer William Howerton and Negro Jesse in the carriage to Louisiana to get Sidney. From Monte Verdi Devereux wrote Sidney's mother concerning the boy's arrival that "every one on the place—white & black was glad to see him, and, he appears very well satisfied here, and I have no doubt but he will remain perfectly contented."[21] Sidney and Antoinette enrolled in Forest Hill Academy in the fall, and on September 4, 1850, the State Legislature approved an act, "That the name of Antoniett [sic]

---

[16]Copy of undated letter, Julien S. Devereux to Mrs. B. Larkin, Devereux Papers.
[17]Will of John William Devereux, December 30, 1843, and Will of Julien S. Devereux, May 7, 1852, **ibid.**
[18]Copy of "codicil to Will 10 November 1847," **ibid.**
[19]P. J. Willis to Julien S. Devereux, March 30, 1850, **ibid.**
[20]Julien S. Devereux to David Gage, July 28, 1850, **ibid.**
[21]Julien S. Devereux to Mrs. Barbara Turner, August 8, 1850, **ibid.**

D. Scott be, and the same is hereby changed to Antoniett D. Devereux, and that the name of Sidney Way, be changed to Sidney Devereux."[22]

For some reason Julien Devereux was not satisfied with the first legislative act to change the names of the two children. Perhaps he wanted to be certain Antoinette and Sidney would inherit a share of the property. Representative H. M. Lawson wrote another bill[23] and on January 31, 1852, the following act was approved:

An act changing the names of Antoinette Scott and Sidney Way.

Section 1. Be it enacted by the Legislature of the State of Texas, That the names of Antoinette Scott and Sidney Way, be, and they are hereby changed to Antoinette Devereaux [sic] and Sidney Devereaux.

Sec. 2. That the said Antoinette Devereaux and Sidney Devereaux be, and they are hereby declared capable in law of inheriting the property of their father, Julien S. Devereaux, in the same manner as if they had been born in lawful wedlock; and that this act take effect and be in force from and after its passage.

Approved, January 31, 1852.[24]

Sidney spent part of his time at Monte Verdi and some time with his mother who removed to neighboring Smith County. He became a problem in the school at Forest Hill and had numerous encounters with the teacher.

From time to time Julien Devereux doubted that Sidney was his son. Perhaps such a situation explains the action taken on February 4, 1853, when James W. Flanagan secured passage of a bill in the legislature to repeal the second section of the act of January 31, 1852, which had provided for Sidney and Antoinette to inherit property of their father.[25]

[22]H. P. N. Gammel (comp.), **Laws of Texas, 1822-1897**, III, 795.

[23]H. M. Lawson to Julien S. Devereux, December 25, 1851, Devereux Papers.

[24]Gammel (comp.), **Laws of Texas**, III, 1100.

[25]Ibid., 1362. In his will drawn up on May 7, 1852, Devereux stated: "Contrary to any wish, desire or request of mine the Legislature of the State of Texas at its last session passed the second section of an act entitled 'an act changing the names of Antoinette Scott and Sidney Way' which act was approved January 31, 1852. . . . Now although it has long been my wish and desire that the names of the said Antoinette Scott and Sidney Way should should [sic] be changed as is provided for by the first Section of the above Recited act, yet I never intended nor was it ever my will that they shall inherit my estate in the manner provided in the said second section. I do therefore now and forever hereafter by this my last

Once in 1855, when twelve-year-old Sidney ran away from Monte Verdi, he gave the excuse of bad treatment as his reason for leaving. Julien Devereux was in Austin sitting in the legislature at the time and wrote to Sidney:

When I found out that your mother had taken you off and caused you to act so ungrateful, I then came to the conclusion that she has been imposing on me all the time and that she knows that you are not my son and taking all things together I am now of the opinion that it is very doubtful at least whether or not you are my child and under that belief together with your bad conduct I have made my will over again and annulled the legacy that I had provided for you in it_____as to my giving you any assistance where you are now living, or under my present opinion of who may be your Father it is out of the question to think a moment about it. And if I really thought or Knew that you were connected with me or my family in any way I would be very far from contributing my means or substance to support a Lad that is likely to be brought up about dram shops and gambling houses and dancing like a monkey for the amusement of loafers and vagabonds. . . .[26]

For a time Antoinette attended school at the Mount Enterprise Male and Female Academy but by 1854, when she was approaching fourteen, she was placed in Mrs. Bewley's school in Henderson. Antoinette had become engaged and this received Julien Devereux's opposition. Sarah Ann Devereux was concerned over the situation the engagement had raised and wrote to Antoinette:

If you knew how much distress and anxiety you have caused **your** Dear Papa by what he considers your imprudent and thoughtless engagement, you certainly would be more cautious for the future . . . he has no disposition to interfere with your choice or affections when you arrive at a proper age, and complete your education, but the thoughts of your marrying at this time renders him very unhappy.[27]

will and testament most solemnly protest against the operation and effect of said section of said act and desire that the said section may be repealed by act of said Legislature at its next session, the same having been passed without my knowledge, consent or approbation and in direct violation of my wishes and desires. . . . And it is also my will that should the said Antoinette and Sidney or either of them die without lineal issue of their body or bodies, the property herein bequeathed is not in any way or under any circumstances to descend or to be inherited by any member of their mother's family."

[26]Julien S. Devereux to Sidney Way Devereux, November 12, 1855, Devereux Papers.

[27]Sarah Ann Devereux to Antoinette Devereux, May 28, 1854, **ibid.**

Julien Devereux did not attend Antoinette's examination exercises at Mrs. Bewley's school during the spring of 1854 because he was leaving on a tour for his health. He was unhappy for a time over Antoinette's attitude, and while on tour wrote to Sarah that he had "bought a breast pin for Antoinette if she deserves it=it is a rich affair."[28] He was always interested in his daughter, nevertheless, and provided well for her. His concern caused one Henderson merchant to assure Devereux, "I will have constant care that your Daughter wants for nothing which can be procured for her. . . ."[28a]

By the time plantation operations were underway at Monte Verdi both Antoinette and Sidney were of school age, and this probably accounts for Julien Devereux's early interest in the establishment of a neighborhood school. In the autumn of 1848, J. R. C. Henderson taught "a common English school at the school house near Deveraux's [sic]" where for a charge of "one dollar per scholar per month" spelling, reading, writing, and arithmetic were taught while English, grammar, and geography cost an additional twenty-five cents.[29] Devereux commented once that, "The school was taught by Councellor Henderson and the money regularly planked up which was the first attempt of the kind in Gourd Neck."[30] In 1850 Devereux took the initiative to take subscriptions to raise money in order to erect a brick school known as the Forest Hill Academy.[31] Devereux provided considerable money to erect the school, and the academy was, for a few years, the pride of the residents in southwestern Rusk County. Both Antoinette and Sidney Devereux attended the school.

Julien Devereux was a strong advocate of the industrial growth of Rusk County. He was a founder of the town of Anadarco situated near Monte Verdi and helped secure the post office established there on November 12, 1849.[32]

Many East Texans felt that the Sabine River, which formed the northern boundary of Rusk County at the time, could be made navigable. The planters were anxious to have the inland

---

[28]Julien S. Devereux to Sarah Ann Devereux, June 23, 1854, **ibid.**
[28a]Sam McClarty to Julien S. Devereux, February 25, 1854, **ibid.**
[29]"Councellor Hendersons School Articles," **ibid.**
[30]**Ibid.**
[31]Forest Hill, near Monte Verdi Plantation, was twelve miles from Mt. Enterprise and nine miles from New Salem. Undated letter, "To the Post Master General, Washington City," **ibid.**
[32]Records of the Post Office Department, M.S., Records of Appointments of Postmasters, The National Archives, Washington, D. C.

transportation, and in order to promote this the Sabine Navigation Company was organized in 1850. Devereux served on the first board of directors for the company which made plans to build a steamboat to be called the *General Rusk*, to be captained by Robert S. Patton. On January 25, 1850, Robert W. Smith wrote Devereux that Captain Patton would be on the Sabine on January 26 and would make a stop at Walling's Ferry in northeastern Rusk County. Devereux was requested to inform his neighbors of the arrival of the boat "and encourage all to haul their cotton to the River."[33] In years of drought the waters of the Sabine would become too shallow for navigation, and the dreams of the members of the Sabine Navigation Company were never realized.

Situated so far inland, residents and planters of Rusk County felt railroads would greatly benefit their area. On November 8, 1851, a railroad convention was held in Shreveport, Louisiana, to go on record as endorsing the construction of a railroad "from Vicksburg, or some other point on the Mississippi River, *via* Monroe, Minden, Shreveport and Greenwood, La., and Marshall, Texas, and westward towards El Paso."[34] Such a railroad, to be known as the Vicksburg, Shreveport and Texas Railroad, would have crossed a portion of Rusk County, and Devereux was named to assist in getting his fellow citizens to support such plans which were "greatly needed by a large, fertile and important region of country."[35]

In Rusk County itself there was considerable railroad activity in the 1850's, and during the decade two railroads, the Eastern Texas Railroad and the Galveston, Houston, and Henderson Railroad Company, were chartered. The Eastern Texas Railroad originated as the Henderson and Burkeville Railroad, chartered on February 10, 1852, and was to connect Burkeville, Newton County, with Henderson.[36] Julien Devereux was a commissioner of the road, which was never completed because of the outbreak of the Civil War. Devereux was also interested in the Galveston, Houston, and Henderson Railroad Company,

---

[33]Robert W. Smith to Julien S. Devereux, January 25, 1850, Devereux Papers.
[34]"Texas, Louisiana and Mississippi Railroad Meeting, November 8, 1851," ibid; E. Dale Odom, "The Vicksburg, Shreveport and Texas: The Fortunes of a Scalawag Railroad," **Southwestern Social Science Quarterly,** Vol. XLIV, No. 3, p. 277.
[35]Ibid.
[36]Gammel (comp.), **Laws of Texas,** III, 1145.

chartered on February 7, 1853.[37] This line was to penetrate the timber belt of East Texas to Henderson, but by the time of the Civil War the construction had been completed only the distance between Galveston and Houston.

Much of the time Julien Devereux was in Texas his health was impaired by what he termed "enlarged spleen." While he was in Montgomery County he complained of his trouble some, but during his years in Rusk County his ailment continued to grow worse. He collected remedies for an enlarged spleen such as the one suggested by his sister Louisiana Holcombe, who supplied a simple remedy of "a small dose of Castor oil every day and charcoal water,"[38] and the one suggested by Dr. James B. Vaught which prescribed:

        1 oz (ounce) Peruvian Bark
        1   "   Snake Root
        ½   "   Rhubarb
        ½   "   gum Guiaicum
        1 Dram of Cayenne pepper
Put the above in a quart of good whiskey after standing 24 hours, take a common dram morning, noon and night.[39]

In January of 1850 Devereux made a trip to Nacogdoches to inquire of "Genl Rusks cure for the spleen."[40] By September of that year Devereux wrote to Sam McClarty in Henderson that "my health has been quite feeble all the spring and summer=I have an enlarged spleen that hurts me very much to ride any distance."[41] Each year Devereux's health grew worse and he concluded that the climate of Rusk County was harmful and that he should consider moving to another locality, perhaps out of Texas.[42]

To secure medical attention Devereux was absent from Monte Verdi from March 17 to April 8, 1852, and the next year on June 2, 1853, Devereux took a more extensive "Southern" trip which took him as far east as Pensacola, Florida.[43] Devereux's health did not improve, however, and he made plans to

[37]**Ibid.**, 1410.
[38]Louisiana Holcombe to Julien S. Devereux, August 10, 1847, Devereux Papers.
[39]Monte Verdi, Texas, Plantation Book.
[40]Julien Sidney Devereux Notebook, 1848.
[41]Julien S. Devereux to Sam McClarty, September, 1850, Devereux Papers.
[42]J. W. Lemmons to Julien S. Devereux, July 22, 1852, **ibid.**
[43]Julien S. Devereux's Monte Verdi Plantation Account Book for 1849-1854.

take an extensive tour of health resorts in Kentucky, Virginia, and on to New York, if necessary, to find a medical remedy for his ailment. Extensive plans were made, and Rusk County merchants and residents wrote letters of introduction for Devereux to use in the various states he planned to tour. In these letters Devereux was described as "one of our most respected and valued citizens,"[44] and "a fine speciman of the southern planter and gentleman."[45] Another letter of introduction stated that, "Colonel Devereux is one of the most respected and opulent planters of our neighborhood is a man of cultivated mind and a perfect type of the Southern Gentleman. He is traveling for health and recreation."[46]

Devereux's most extensive tour for medical attention was taken in the early summer of 1854. Devereux traveled with William Howerton, his former overseer, from Henderson to Shreveport and then down Red River to New Orleans. Up the Mississippi the two men took a steamer to Louisville, Kentucky. From Louisville on June 23, 1854, Devereux wrote to his wife that he had been given an examination by "the celebrated surgeon, Doctor Gross" and the physician diagnosed Devereux's trouble as "neuralgea of some of the lower intestines."[47] At Grayson Springs, Kentucky, Julien Devereux wrote Sarah that the mineral waters were not agreeing with him "by any means," that he had no appetite, and that he was worse off than when he came.[48] Devereux apologized to his wife for writing so gloomy a letter but stated he could not do otherwise after being gone three weeks, spending sleepless nights, and being away from his "dear family." Julien wrote his wife concerning Kentucky:

> I am getting about as far from Texas as I care to ever be, but I will try to pursue whatever course that may appear best for me—some times I almost loose heart when I feel as very bad and am almost ready to give up altogether but when I hear and see what cures appear to have been effected I am encouraged to try—I have not seen any country that appears to be so good for farming purposes as Eastern Texas. . . . Louisville certainly is one of the great cities of the southwest—at this season of the year it appears to be almost equal to N.O. [New Orleans] The people all

[44]Samuel McClarty to Bryant R. Young, June 1, 1854. Devereux Papers.
[45]Copy of letter written by John McClarty, June 1, 1854, **ibid.**
[46]Sam'l McClarty to John L. Helm, June 1, 1854, **ibid.**
[47]Julien S. Devereux to Sarah Devereux, June 23, 1854, **ibid.**
[48]Julien S. Devereux to Sarah Devereux, June 28, 1854, **ibid.**

through this country have quite a fresh & healthy look even men whose heads are as white as snow look red and fresh in the face. All old countries however are said to be healthy and this is getting to be quite an old part of the U. S. Rail roads are exerting a great influence here and is giving it the active appearance of a newly settled country. I am told that a naked lot which had a building burned off of it sold the other day for $1,000 a foot fronting 20 ft. on main street making $20,000—I wonder if real estate in Texas will ever bring such prices.[49]

- - -

For what I have seen of the inland part of Kentucky I must confess that I have a very poor opinion of the country and a worse opinion of the people in general—the common people of the country are a very low bred ignorant and disapated set of fellows and their little broken farms almost lost in the grass with fences almost to the ground everywhere and we have scarcely passed a house between the mouth of Salt River and this place [Grayson Springs] but what has a doggery at it and most instances attached to thin log dwellings—Texas is certainly far ahead of this part of Kentucky in improvements and civilization.[50]

Devereux observed that the Kentucky crops "are said to be better than usual, but if our corn at this season of the year in Texas was no longer than their corn here I should say that we could not make bread."[51]

During his tour Julien Devereux was giving thought to building his "mansion house" on his plantation, and he wanted to make plans "towards getting out on the hill" by the time he got home. Devereux commented that he had seen no place since he left Monte Verdi "as pretty as *that same hill*."[52] The particular "hill" Devereux had in mind is located in one of the most scenic parts of Rusk County. It was the site on the Elijah Tolbert survey, where, in 1855, Devereux began building his home which was standing in 1964.

Devereux and Howerton traveled into Alabama and Mississippi but Devereux's health continued to grow worse, and from Decatur, Alabama, he wrote, "I am sorry that I can not say to you that my health is any better than when we left home on the contrary I am certain that it is not as good and if I am

---

[49]Julien S. Devereux to Sarah Devereux, June 23, 1854, ibid.
[50]Julien S. Devereux to Sarah Devereux, June 28, 1854, ibid.
[51]Ibid.
[52]Ibid.

[104]

spar'd to get home I will certainly stay there for the future."[53] Before the end of July, 1854, Devereux had returned to Monte Verdi and was reunited with his wife and family.

The next month an election was held in Rusk County in which Julien Devereux polled 1291 votes for the position of county commissioner, the vote "being the highest vote given for any one candidate for that office."[54] The vote must indicate the rather high esteem that Devereux held among the voters of Rusk County. He could not have spent time in electioneering for the position because of his poor health and the trip he had completed just days before the election was held.

The next year, 1855, Devereux's friends and supporters urged him to become a candidate for the State Legislature. He was a well-known person in Rusk County, had some reputation in state politics, and had been a member of the Alabama legislature in 1832. As early as 1845 Devereux's brother-in-law Henry P. Holcombe had written: "Why do you not go ahead politically? I wish to see you in your Legislature—your experience of the workings of our system would enable you to assist materially in framing a Body of Laws for your State."[55]

Devereux was a staunch Democrat and he was violently opposed to the American or Know-Nothing party which had made its appearance in Texas in 1854 and was an outgrowth of the racial and religious antagonism which swept the United States in the 1850's. In the whole country, but in Texas especially, men joined the Know-Nothings to oppose the influx of foreigners, who tended to be Catholic, radical, often illiterate, and anti-slavery. Although the party pretended to support the slave-holders against the abolitionists, the Know-Nothings had little to offer to Democrat Devereux.

On at least one occasion Devereux declined being a candidate for the legislature in the 1855 election because he felt his "long & protracted chronic disease" disqualified him for being useful.[56] On June 5, 1855, John McClarty wrote Devereux that he was the choice of the local Democratic Convention and that Devereux's "election would be entirely secure in the event of your acceptance of the nomination proferred you."[57]

[53]Julien S. Devereux to Sarah Devereux, July 10, 1854, **ibid.**
[54]Certificate of Election, signed by Chief Justice John C. Miller, August 21, 1854, **ibid.**
[55]Henry P. Holcombe to Julien S. Devereux, November 7, 1845, **ibid.**
[56]Copy of an undated letter sent to M. B. Ector, **ibid.**
[57]John McClarty to Julien S. Devereux, June 5, 1855, **ibid.**

An acquaintance wrote to Devereux imploring him to accept the nomination.

Dear Friend,
    I avail myself of the kindness of Esqr. Bagley to communicate to you the fact that you are one of the nominees of the Democratic Party to Represent Rusk in the Lower House of the next Legislature. I sincerely trust it may suit your feelings to accept the nomination. I hope for the success, & future good of old time honored democratic principles that you *will not decline*. Come! Make this sacrifice & serve us this time. . . .[58]

Devereux accepted the nomination to be a candidate for the House of Representatives, and since he was "not in the habit of public speaking," he issued a broadside, "To the Voters of Rusk County" giving his views on state and national policy. Devereux came out in favor of accepting the "Texas Creditors Bill," a proposal by the United States Congress for a payment and final adjustment of the Texas boundary settlement and reimbursement to Texas of claims for damages and depredations committed by United States Indians in Texas since 1836. Devereux favored "State aid to projects of internal improvements," and he felt that any changes in the State Constitution should be submitted to the people. He made clear that he was a "Democrat of the Jeffersonian school" and would oppose "all parties, whether whig or know nothing, which may conflict with the democratic party, or which seeks to subvert or overthrow it."[59]
    The political contest during the summer of 1855 between the Democrats and the Know-Nothings was a heated one. Rusk County sent four representatives and one senator to the legislature and considerable attention was focused on the county election. Julien Devereux put the Know-Nothing party in the same political group with the old Whig party which had disintegrated in 1852, about the time the Know-Nothings came on the scene. The following excerpts from one of Devereux's written speeches give an idea of the political flavor of the campaign in 1855 in Rusk County.

    An excitable and noisy member of the Whig party of this county not long since remarked "that the Democrats

[58]H. M. Lawson to Julien 'S. Devereux, undated letter, 1855, **ibid.**
[59]"To the Voters of Rusk County," broadside, **ibid.**

and Hard=shell Baptist had as great an aversion to books
and learning as a mad dog had to water or a mink to gun-
powder and that he had known a whole Democratic neighborhood entirely depopulated by the introduction of a dozen
Websters spelling books in their midst." Now is it true that
the Democrats as a party are more ignorant and less informed than the Whigs? Of course not and the expressions
used by the above mentioned Whig is a coarse and unjusti-
fiable slander, and would not be worthy of serious notice for
a moment but for some circumstance which might seem to
justify the imputation the most prominent of which are that
we are accustomed lately to see counties containing, or at
least claiming large Democratic majorities with their offices
of trust and profit filled by men taken from the ranks of
the Whig party, and if the Democrats have men of their own
who are equally honest capable and worthy, why let me ask
is this the case? is it an excess of liberality on their part
or are they in want of proper materials among themselves?
If it is on the score of liberality they differ as widely in
that particular from the whigs as they do in political opinions, for I am yet to know of even one, single, solitary instance, where a decided Whig majority has ever sufficiently
appreciated worth and talents in a Democrat to Elect him
to office over one of their own party no matter how incom-
petent and undeserving the Whig candidate may have been
—So common has the practice become even in this county of
sending Whigs to the Legislature and having our most prof-
itable county offices filled by them, that the political com-
plexion of Rusk County is now suspended in doubt and un-
certainty. A few years past the right to be classed among
the strongest of the Democratic counties of this truly Democratic state was fully conceded to Rusk—such however is
not the case at this time, and in a few short months to
come, it will not surprise me in the least (with the assistance of the Whig organ lately set on foot at our court
house) if we find the county of Rusk bound hand and foot
and delivered over to the Whig party. Such being the
tendency of political affairs in this county at the present
time, let the issue be made and the matter put to the test
at our next general election. If Rusk County has become
a Whig work shop let the tools to be used in it be Whig
tools, which certainly will be the case whenever they satisfy themselves that they have the power.[60]

In the election held on the first Monday in August, Rusk
County sent Julien Devereux to the House of Representatives
along with M. D. Ector, J. H. Parsons, and William Stedman.

---

[60]Handwritten copy of Julien S. Devereux campaign speech, 1855, ibid.

Devereux, Ector, and Parsons were choices on the Democrat ballot, and Stedman was elected on the "Railroad Independent Freemen's Ticket," probably the name for the Know-Nothing party. The final tabulation of votes was as follows:

M. D. Ector 850 votes
J. H. Parsons 849 votes
J. S. Devereux 838 votes
Wm. Stedman 832 votes
J. C. Spinks 824 votes
S. P. Hollingsworth 821 votes
W. B. Holloway 819 votes
Allen Birdwell 799 votes[61]

Devereux, the only candidate elected who resided outside of Henderson, was also the only planter by profession, the other elected members being lawyers.

In the state election, Democrat Elisha M. Pease beat the Know-Nothing candidate D. C. Dickson, and the Know-Nothings elected some twenty representatives and five senators to the legislature.

The Sixth Legislature of Texas met in regular session in Austin from November 5, 1855, to February 4, 1856. Elisha M. Pease was governor at the time and Hardin R. Runnels was lieutenant governor. James W. Flanagan of Rusk County sat in the senate. Hamilton P. Bee was speaker of the house, and the membership included such distinguished Texans as John Henry Brown, historian, editor, and veteran of Indian Wars; James W. Throckmorton, who became president of the Constitutional Convention of 1866 and served as governor in 1866 and 1867; Pleasant W. Kittrell, guiding force for the establishment of the University of Texas; and Ashbel Smith, chargé d'affaires to England and France during the Republic and leader in all movements for the advancement of education in Texas.[62]

Julien Devereux arrived in Austin on October 31 in his private carriage, driven by Ray Neil, and Devereux's body servant, Jesse, came along to attend his master during the session. The route taken from Monte Verdi to Austin was by way of the vicinity of Independence, Washington County, and then to the west. Concerning the trip Devereux wrote to Sarah:

[61]Certificate of Election, signed by John C. Miller, Chief Justice, Rusk County, August 25, 1855, in Election Returns, 1855 (MS), Texas State Library, Austin.

[62]**Members of the Legislature of the State of Texas from 1846 to 1939**, p. 22-26.

This trip has confirmed me more than ever (if possible) in the belief that we are living in the very best portion of Texas. The country all the way from the Neches to the Brazos river is the most forlorn and woe begone looking country I ever have seen. it looks worse than it did when we moved along the road[63] for the reason that what few attempts that have been made to settle that country has been abandoned and the old houses rotting down and the range entirely eat out and growing up in weeds. The people appear to have destroyed themselves in trying to build up little towns. After we crossed the Brazos I found the country in a better state of improvement and a good many large farms on the road in the prairie but no new work either of houses or fences and I am told that a great many of the farms in Washington County are either mortgaged or sold to merchants in Houston & Galveston and that the people all through that country are very much involved.[64]

At the time of Devereux's arrival Austin had been the capital of Texas for less than two decades, having been established as the seat of government in 1839. Because of a Mexican invasion of Texas in March, 1842, while Sam Houston was chief executive, the seat of government was moved from Austin back to Houston and then to Washington-on-the-Brazos. The capital was returned to Austin in 1845 and in 1850, when the population was recorded as 629, a state election designated the site on the Colorado River as the permanent capital. Austin enjoyed considerable growth during the 1850's, and in 1853 the new capitol building was completed. The Governor's Mansion was under construction when Devereux arrived and was completed the following spring.

Devereux wrote lengthy letters to his wife while he was in Austin, and these give a rather good picture of life in Texas' capital city at the time. Devereux took room and board at the home of Colonel K. L. Haralson, and the following excerpt from Devereux's first letter home gives his early impressions of Austin.

I have put up at Col Haralsons private boarding house at the *low rates* of Fifty Dollars a month for myself, and seven dollars for Jesse. The town is litterally cramed & jamed full and boarding very high especially where a room and

---

[63]Devereux is referring to the move from Montgomery County to Rusk County in 1846.
[64]Julien S. Devereux to Sarah Devereux, November 1, 1855, Devereux Papers.

fire place is required. . . . There are any amount of office seekers in Town. I am hourly attacked by some one legged or one arm applicant for some appointment before the Legislature or by some member of the Legislature asking my support for some friend.[65]

Devereux found Austin was not too different a town than he had expected and observed that, "The capitol is a very pretty white rock house situated on a knob of a hill about 300 yards from my boarding house. . . ."[66]

There was spirited activity in Austin during the few days before the Legislature met and Julien Devereux described to his wife some of the goings on that took place on the first day of November:

I returned this evening from the first days meeting at the Democratic barbecue and I wish that I could give you something like a description of the grand and interesting demonstration that was made on the occasion, suffice it to say however that it far excelled my expectations or anything of the kind I have ever seen. . . . The weather suited the occasion exactly being warm and cloudy but without rain every thing conducted with strict propriety & without interruption, the bands of music was the best in the state with severally pieces of canon which were fired in regular intervals through the day, the procession including carriages & other vehicles reached pretty much from the town to the place of meeting a distance of a mile & a half. I have no means of ascertaining the number of persons present but I suppose there must have been over six thousand who partook of the dinner which was very abundant. We joined the procession with our carriage—we had quite a number of speakers a Mr Wilson of St Antonio I think was the best orator among them. we shall have a new supply tomorrow. Col Ector & Rushing made short speeches today and acquitted themselves very well—The torch light and transparent procession is now forming down Town and a ball going on in Capitol—The democrats are wide a wake indeed, and well they may be, for the know nothings are moving heaven & earth to defeat them and they have their shrewdist and most cuning men here and are having their secret meetings every night concocting schemes and plans to defeat Genl Rusk and to sustain Sam Houston who is to meet them here on the 23d of this month[.][67]

[65]Ibid.
[66]Ibid.
[67]Ibid.

In the organization of the legislature Devereux reported that the Know Nothings made a poor showing in securing favored positions. He noted that Caleb Garrison, who later married Antoinette Devereux, was elected engrossing clerk of the senate.[68] Devereux was put on the committees on public printing, education, contingent expenses, privileges and elections, slaves and slavery, and "the select committee on Constitutional Amendments."[69] During the first week of the session Devereux felt:

> From what I can Judge I think the present Legislature is over an average one for intellect and respectability and I have heard the same opinion expressed by old members here. The excitment of the past summer has brought out some of the most talented men in western Texas, and working men at that, and the same may be said in relation to other portions of the State.[70]

Before the end of the month, however, Devereux had changed his mind about the members of the legislature, and on November 29 he wrote to Sarah that, "Most of the members attended the races that are going on here—I have changed my opinion lately as to the business character of our Legislature and I am now sorry to say there is a considerable disposition to idle away time, thereby making this a protracted session for the sake of the per diam pay."[71]

There was still activity among the Know-Nothings who "are agoing to have a grand Pow wow here on the 22d and 23d of this month [November] and will make desperate efforts to sustain Sam Houston who is to be here on the occasion."[72] Sam Houston had been making speeches in East Texas, and Sarah wrote Julien on November 20, that, "Gen. Houston went to Rusk during Court to make a great Know Nothing speech, but Mr. Bowdon whiped him in answer so badly that he left very early next morning."[73] Franklin Welsh Bowdon was the Henderson lawyer and acquaintance of Devereux who was known as "the

---

[68]Julien S. Devereux to Sarah Devereux, November 5, 1855, ibid.

[69]Journal of the House of Representatives of The State of Texas, Sixth Legislature, 15, 22, 45, 92.

[70]Julien S. Devereux to Sarah Devereux, November 9, 1855, Devereux Papers.

[71]Julien Devereux to Sarah Devereux, November 29, 1855, ibid.

[72]Julien Devereux to Sarah Devereux, November 13, 1855, ibid.

[73]Sarah Devereux to Julien Devereux, November 20, 1855, ibid.

one orator who could drive Houston from the rostrum."[74] Bowdon also had the reputation of being a heavy drinker, and Sarah Devereux commented in her letter to her husband that, "Mr. Bowdon has been drinking nearly all the time in court at Rusk."[75]

Among the early legislation considered in November was the election of Thomas J. Rusk as United States Senator by the unanimous vote of members of both houses in a joint session.[76] On November 21, Julien wrote his wife that, "the great men of the country are congregating about Austin. Sam Houston, Commodore Moore, Genl McCloud [Hugh McLeod?] and many other prominent men are here. . . ."[77] Senator Houston, in Austin ostensibly for the Know Nothing meeting, arrived about the same time as did Commodore Edwin Ward Moore. Houston and Moore were bitter enemies as a result of an episode in 1843, when Moore was accused by Houston of disobedience and was suspended from the Texas Navy. The Texas Congress, however, gave to Moore the right to continue his service in the Texas Navy. The arrival of Houston and Moore produced an interesting episode in the House of Representatives on November 22, 1855, when Isaac Parker of Tarrant County introduced a resolution that an invitation be extended to "Gen. Sam Houston, Ex-President of the Late Republic of Texas, to a seat within the Bar of the House."[78] Mathew D. Ector, the Rusk County representative, immediately offered an amendment that Commodore E. W. Moore also be invited. Some confusion prevailed and tempers erupted from the floor. W. B. Ochiltree moved that a vote be taken on the Sam Houston resolution only and this passed by a vote of 82 to 1. Rusk County Representatives Devereux, Ector, and Parsons did not vote while Stedman cast his vote

[74]Dallas **Morning News**, April 21, 1935. Bowdon had a great reputation as a speaker. On one occasion Professor J. C. Miszner, noted graduate of the Leipzig Conservatory who taught music in Henderson, compared a Bowdon speech to "a great symphony orchestra, making me gasp for breath as I listened." Bowdon was said to turn dark in the face when making his best orations.

[75]Sarah Devereux to Julien Devereux, November 20, 1855, Devereux Papers.

[76]**Journal of the House of Representatives of the State of Texas, Sixth Legislature,** 54.

[77]Julien Devereux to Sarah Devereux, November 21, 1855, Devereux Papers. Sam Houston had never returned to Austin after he ordered the removal of the government in 1842. From 1846 until 1859 Houston served as United States Senator.

[78]**Journals of the House of Representatives of the State of Texas, Sixth Legislature,** 89.

for Houston. Ector then reintroduced his bill concerning Moore. After several attempts to table the motion failed, the House by a vote of 48 to 32 approved the resolution.[79]

Devereux made an effort to satisfy the wishes of the constituents of his own area of southwestern Rusk County with a petition to create a new county out of the southern portion of Rusk and northern part of Nacogdoches counties. The persons living in southern Rusk County felt they were too far from the county seat of Henderson. The proposed county would consist of territory twelve miles north of the Rusk-Nacogdoches boundary line and eight miles south of the line, with boundaries of Cherokee County on the west and Panola and Shelby counties on the east. The proposed county was to be called Franklin "after the illustrious and wise statesman and benefactor of mankind, Doctor Benjamin Franklin," and the proposed county seat would be known as Lafayette, "after the patriot and friend of Liberty Marquis De Lafayette."[80] Devereux was the only Rusk County representative from the area which would enjoy benefits if a new county were created, and he was never able to secure support for his proposal.

During his sojourn in Austin, Devereux was frequently homesick for his family and friends at Monte Verdi and after being in Austin less than a month he wrote:

> Dear Sarah I am getting home sick indeed—I dont know when I have ever wanted to see you and my dear little boys so bad as I do now. I want to see everything about our place, and I want to see my good friends & neighbours. tell my dear little boys to be good children and Papa will come home as soon as he can. God bless their little hearts If I am spared to return home I never will leave you all again to be so far from you.[81]

There were many things about Austin Devereux did not like, and the water in the capitol city was not so good as that back home. Some water was brought from the Colorado River, and cisterns were also in use. Devereux wrote that, "The cistern water is all that I can drink & they took a large hog (dead) out of one of the state house cisterns yesterday, but as good

[79]*Ibid.*, 91.
[80]"Petition to the Honorable Members of the Senate and House of Representatives of the State of Texas in session at the city of Austin [1855]," Devereux Papers.
[81]Julien S. Devereux to Sarah Devereux, November 13, 1855, **ibid.**

luck I did not drink any of the water."[82] Food was far from satisfactory:

> Our fare is only tolerable (I mean in the eating way). I have heard much said about the fine beef of this part of the country, but the beef we have on the table is nothing to compare with what we have at home, and our Landlord pays 5 and 6 cents a pound for it at that—I have not seen any fresh butter since I have been here and no cream for our coffee. Our bacon costs 22 cents a pound and old at that.[83]

Grasshoppers were in evidence in large numbers in 1855 when Devereux observed:

> I have seen scarcely any hogs since I crossed the Brazos river, what few hogs that are about the Town are getting fat on grasshoppers for the last 3 or 4 days, the whole atmosphere is full of grasshoppers about an inch long[.] we have to keep the doors and windows shut to keep them out. of an evening I have seen the side of the state house for 10 feet high perfectly black with them they are very much like those that we sometimes see in our yard or garden that fly and quiver in the air, only not quite so large—they appear to be immigrating, and their course south west—the people here do not appear to think anything strange in their appearance.[84]

Devereux's additional comments on Austin in 1855 included the following:

> There is great complaint here of hard times and scarcity of money and except what is paid out by the state there is very little money in this part of the country. Col Boggess[85] purchased a likely young negro fellow at auction for $710—and an ordinary fellow was sold the same day for $450—provisions however is high. corn delivered in Town is worth one dollar a bushel and nubbins at that. I have examined several loads that came into Town and it certainly is very indifferent corn. beef is worth from 5 to 6 cents. old bacon 22 c and mutton 12½, flour $20 per barrel and yet property generally is lower than it is in our county. I have not as yet seen any good mules about town—the mules that came

---

[82]Julien S. Devereux to Sarah Devereux, November 5, 1855, **ibid.**
[83]Julien S. Devereux to Sarah Devereux, November 9, 1855, **ibid.**
[84]**Ibid.**
[85]Giles Sanford Boggess, resident of Rusk County, was assistant door-keeper in the House of Representatives of the Sixth Legislature.

in our carriage are better looking than any I have seen here. cattle are worth from six to eight dollars per head up to two year olds. there is no stocks of cattle however near here as the range is all gone. the price relates to stocks some 40 or 50 miles about here. the more I see and learn about this western country the better I am pleased with Eastern Texas—it is not only the case with me, but every eastern member that I have conversed with is of the same way of thinking—[86]

And on December 10, 1855, he wrote:

Every thing that is eat here except corn is hauled from the sea coast, (and also except some very indifferent beef)— the plank used for building cost $4.75 c per hundred feet and scarce at that and of bad quality—Austin is the most artificial city or town I have seen, I have not seen a bale of cotton since I have been in the place nor any pork hogs —no vegetables of any kind except a few yankee onions that sell at 20 cents a pound. What few turnips and cabbage that was alive in the country have been *swept clean* by the grasshoppers and also what wheat that had been sowed. I dont see what inducement people have to move here & pay high prices for land.[87]

Beside legislative matters, Devereux was concerned with the plantation operations at Monte Verdi and the erection of his mansion house. Julien Devereux was anxious to have news of what was going on at Monte Verdi, and Sarah often wrote about the work that was being done. On December 6, 1855, she remarked that the hands "finished picking cotton today and came out of the field shouting and blowing their horns like there had been a democratic victory."[88] By December 20 some 7160 pounds of pork had been secured "out of the woods." William Howerton, Devereux's former overseer, had helped with the hog killing and remarked that, "There is more wild hogs than I have ever seen."[89] Christmas week usually meant no work on most plantations, and on December 28, Sarah wrote that, "The black ones have all been very healthy and enjoy Chrismas [sic] as much as ever as cold as it is."[90]

Texas experienced a drought in 1855 and conditions led

[86]Julien Devereux to Sarah Devereux, November 19, 1855, Devereux Papers.
[87]Julien Devereux to Sarah Devereux, December 10, 1855, **ibid.**
[88]Sarah Devereux to Julien Devereux, December 6, 1855, **ibid.**
[89]William Howerton to Julien Devereux, December 16, 1855, **ibid.**
[90]Sarah Devereux to Julien Devereux, December 28, 1855, **ibid.**

Devereux to comment that "next to the health of my family and my negroes the dread of fire gives me more uneasiness."[91] It was fortunate for Devereux that he had his father-in-law, John Landrum, living near Monte Verdi who could be available when Sarah needed assistance and advice.

Most planters agreed that a thorough breaking of the land must take place in December or January so that the earth could benefit from winter rains and freezes. Devereux, an advocate of deep ploughing, wrote to his wife that:

> Since I left home I am more than ever confirmed in early & *deep* ploughing in preparing for another crop. I see that the best planters on the way are persuing that course. The Reed Field & the Talley Field I am certain requires early and *very deep ploughing*. The subject of *deep* ploughing in old land has become a kind of hobby with me[.] a plenty of team should be used or the animals would be injured. in the heavy lands I see they use from three to five yoke of oxen to one plough.[92]

Like many successful planters Julien Devereux decided to erect a mansion house on his plantation. The home was to be a large two-story structure situated on the highest elevation of Monte Verdi land. Devereux probably had the idea to build his permanent residence as early the summer of 1854 when he was making one of his tours for his health because at that time he mentioned that he wanted to locate a home "out on the hill."[93] On August 14, 1854, M. D. Ector wrote Devereux that, "I understand that you intend building a house,"[94] and William Stedman wrote Devereux a letter in the fall suggesting a Mr. Lackey for the brick work because "he has the character of being a first rate workman & the best indeed in our county."[95] Large quantities of lumber, brick, paint, and other materials were purchased in 1855, and work was well underway when Devereux took his seat in the legislature in November. In his first letter written from Austin, Devereux told his wife that he had instructed the carriage driver, Neil, "to dig up some small muskeat [mesquite] bushes, live oaks, wild peach, cotton wood, sicamore etc on his

---

[91]Julien Devereux to Sarah Devereux, November 5, 1855, **ibid.**
[92]Julien Devereux to Sarah Devereux, November 1, 1855, **ibid.**
[93]Julien S. Devereux to Sarah Devereux, June 28, 1854, **ibid.** The "hill" was situated on the Elijah Tolbert survey.
[94]M. D. Ector to Julien S. Devereux, August 14, 1854, **ibid.**
[95]William Stedman to Julien S. Devereux, October 2, 1854, **ibid.**

return and . . . you can put them out carefully in front of our new house."[96] Devereux stressed that in building the new home they "should be very cautious on the subject of debt and with the exception of the windows and painting the roof, we had best confine our operations for the present to the lower story."[97]

Because the house Sarah and the children occupied was "too open and cold to winter in,"[98] Devereux was particularly anxious for the work on the lower floor of the new house to be completed before the coldest weather arrived, so Sarah and the children could move in. At times complications developed concerning the work and the builders, and once Devereux wrote that, "Mr Lynch knowd very well that I never employed them to do anything else than *lay the floor of the dining room*. . . . If they are willing to settle according to their original offer your Papa can pay them off, but if they undertake to act mean about the matter let the whole matter rest until I get home."[99] Sarah Devereux kept her husband informed on the details of the work on the mansion house and in her letter on December 4 she said that:

> I have had the large doors brought up so We can now shut up the passage, which makes it much more comfortable than it was before. Linch and Bonds have at last finished the dining room I yet dont know their price I expect from what I have heard Howerton and others say it will not be less than two hundred dollars. the other workmen will finish the room joining in a few days and If I find the old house getting too uncomfortable we can very easily go into that part of the new house but shall prefer remaining in the old house as long as we can or at least while they are at work.[100]

Bond and Lynch submitted their bill for work on the dining room the following day, and the "whole amount" totaled $292.02.[101] The flooring covered an area of twenty-two feet by sixteen feet and came to about a hundred dollars more than Sarah had estimated.

The exact date has not been determined when Sarah and the children moved into the mansion house, but on December 29 Sarah wrote that, "I think we shall move our sleeping into the

---

[96]Julien Devereux to Sarah Devereux, November 1, 1855, **ibid.**
[97]**Ibid.**
[98]Julien Devereux to Sarah Devereux, November 13, 1855, **ibid.**
[99]Julien Devereux to Sarah Devereux, November 19, 1855, **ibid.**
[100]Sarah Devereux to Julien Devereux, December 4, 1855, **ibid.**
[101]"Copy of Bill made out by Lynch & Bond," December 5, 1855, **ibid.**

new house as two rooms are finished and locks on the doors."[102] Most probably the family was in the new quarters by January 4, 1856, when Sarah wrote that one room of the old house had been moved up to the hill and would be used for the kitchen. The room used had been "neatly put" and "it is a better one than they could have made of new logs and much quicker done."[103]

Among the most welcomed letters Julien Devereux received in Austin were those with the news concerning Sarah and the children, and Julien wrote Sarah, "You can scarcely imagine how much pleasure it gives me to receive your letters and to hear that you and my dear children are well and to read about what they say and do. One line from you telling me what they talk about and their little innocent prattle and plans is valued more highly by me than the most interesting speech from the best orator in Austin."[104] The following lines from Sarah must have meant much to Julien:

> Albert is very anxious I should write that he learns his Book every day. and has caught several rabbits around the cowpen and garden has them nicely cooked and all the family has to partake of the rabbit I wish you could see them all come in sometimes and look me right in the face and say Ma lets go to Austin with as much confidence as if we could fix up and go to Austin as easy as to their grand Mas they tell me that Pa said we could go they take a trip to Austin almost every day Julien has to have a bundle of provisions tied up in a paper and goes out and gets the children and little negros and eats out doors like they were camped out[105]

> \-   -   -

> I am up to night after the children have all gone to sleep—and have read your letters over and over again and could sit up all night and read them if they were long enough.[106]

Julien Devereux's health was such that he probably shortened his life by serving the one term in the legislature. His "enlarged spleen" continued to give him trouble; he was in pain most of the time he was in Austin and his condition grew worse each week. In his first letter home Devereux stated that if he

---

[102] Sarah Devereux to Julien Devereux, December 29, 1855, **ibid.**
[103] Sarah Devereux to Julien Devereux, January 4, 1856, **ibid.**
[104] Julien Devereux to Sarah Devereux, November 19, 1855, **ibid.**
[105] Sarah Devereux to Julien Devereux, December 4, 1855, **ibid.**
[106] Sarah Devereux to Julien Devereux, December 8, 1855, **ibid.**

lived through the session it would be his "last voluntary exile from home and family."[107] Julien was homesick most of the time for Sarah and the boys and he once remarked to Sarah, "My seat in the Legislature poorly repays me for my absence from you and our little boys."[108] Holidays were difficult days to be away from the family. Governor E. M. Pease proclaimed November 29 as Thanksgiving Day, and Devereux attended "the Episcopalian church" and heard a "most able and eloquent sermon preached by Edward Fontaine."[109] Christmas of 1855 at Monte Verdi, according to Sarah Devereux, was "as cold as it is possible for it to be."[110] Sarah described how the boys hung their stockings on the chimney mantle on Christmas eve, and since she had no cakes or candy to put in the stockings she had put a dime in each. This dime, Sarah told the boys, was the work of the "good little man." Young Julien was concerned about how "the little man" could get in the house, and, "After Julien had gone to bed he raised up and looked at the fire place. I recon he thought it was to hot. he layed down and told Phebee[111] to open the window so he [the "good little man"] [could] come there and put something in his stocking."[112]

After two months' absence from Monte Verdi, Sarah wrote Julien that, "If we could know the day that you would reach home the whole plantation would be a half a days journey to meet you for there never was a set of people that want to see any body as much as we all want to see you and Jesse. . . ."[113] During the first week of the new year Sarah wrote to her husband, "Oh how we wish you was here to be with us it dont seem right to go about the plantation when you are not here."[114]

Julien Devereux's health continued to grow worse. His chills became more frequent, he was unable to sleep, and he was in pain much of the time. While Devereux's condition was becoming more serious he received a letter from his New Salem neighbor, H. F. Nelson, which may have caused Devereux to reflect on things at some length. Nelson wrote, "You know something

[107]Julien Devereux to Sarah Devereux, November 1, 1855, **ibid.**
[108]Julien Devereux to Sarah Devereux, November 19, 1855, **ibid.**
[109]Julien Devereux to Sarah Devereux, November 29, 1855, **ibid.**
[110]Sarah Devereux to Julien Devereux, December 29, 1855, **ibid.**
[111]Phebee, also spelled Phoebe, was a slave.
[112]Sarah Devereux to Julien Devereux, December 29, 1855, Devereux Papers.
[113]Sarah Devereux to Julien Devereux, December 27, 1855, **ibid.**
[114]Sarah Devereux to Julien Devereux, January 4, 1856, **ibid.**

of a political life . . . of the unthankfulness of public sentiment after a man has worn himself out forsaken his fireside and all the tender associations that is most dear to Father & Husband. . . ."[115] As hard as he tried, Julien Devereux could not last until the session ended on February 4, 1856. On January 9 he wrote to Sarah that he had requested to be excused from attending sessions on January 20, and that he would return home when the carriage arrived. In the meantime he was "thinking about nothing else now but home."[116] The Democratic State Convention met in Austin on January 16, and Devereux was to represent Rusk County along with Giles S. Boggess, Jr., M. D. Ector, G. S. Boggess, Sr., J. H. Parsons, and C. J. Garrison. No doubt the poor condition of Devereux's health at the time prohibited his attendance.

Julien Devereux returned to his Monte Verdi plantation before the end of January, 1856, and resided for the first time in the new mansion house, still uncompleted. For the next three months he lived there but was so ill that he could not enjoy the fruits of his years of labor or supervise the completion of his dream. On May 1, 1856, at the age of fifty, Julien Devereux died. His remains are beside those of his father in the family burial plot. The news of his death was carried on the front pages of many newspapers in the state, and the editor of the Henderson *Democrat,* M. D. Ector, who had served with Devereux in the State Legislature, wrote the following:

> Late on yesterday evening the melancholy news reached us of the death of the Hon. Julien S. Devereux, of this county. He died at his residence . . . from an inflamation of the spleen. His death has cast a gloom over the entire community. For several days we had learned that he was considered to be dangerously ill, and in common with the whole circle of his acquaintance, we embraced every opportunity to learn his exact situation. . . . From the State of Alabama he removed to Texas at an early day and before his death was one of the oldest Texans (using a figure often used amongst us) in the county.
>
> - - -
>
> At the solicitation of many of his friends, last year he consented to become a candidate for a seat in the Legislature, and was elected. On account of the state of his health and a disposition to prefer the quiet of home to the busy

[115]H. F. Nelson to Julien Devereux, January 11, 1856, **ibid.**
[116]Julien Devereux to Sarah Devereux, January 9, 1856, **ibid.**

bustle of a public life; it was with considerable reluctance he would consent to let his name go before the public. During the session of the Legislature we had the pleasure of rooming with him, and thus had a better opportunity to appreciate his true worth, his many social qualities and that true refinement of feeling which is so characteristic of a gentleman; as a legislator, few men in that body had more influence, possessing a clear and penetrating mind, a strong and sound judgment, a calm and even temper a deliberative and discriminating mind, a constant and persevering resolution, and a modest and gentlemanly deportment; together with his incorruptible honesty, he was admirably qualified to make a useful member to his constituents. Although by nature and education qualified to grace almost any prominent position to which he might have been elevated, still, public life was not most congenial to his taste. Far more did he prefer to be engaged in the more retired and not less honorable employment of occupying his time on his farm. It was around his own fireside with his household about him, and in the circle of his immediate neighbors and friends, that the gentler current of his nature ran.—'Twas here that the generous and more devoted qualities of the man could find scope for the exercise of the finer feelings of his heart. Those alone who have partaken of his hospitable board,—who have witnessed the affectionate regard manifested at all times by him for the loved ones of home, and the kind consideration shown towards his servants, could form a just conception of the goodness of the man. He possessed a large amount of the goods of this world, and managed his pecuniary matters very well, still he was ever ready to give of his worldly goods to those less fortunate than himself; besides being liberal to the poor,—the various institutions of learning, and the religious denominations throughout the section in which he lived, were alike the recipients of his bounty. What he gave, he gave without any ostentation.—He was ever condescending to his equals, kind to his inferiors, and tender to the objects of his affection. Such was the man whose death the community now mourns.

In his death his wife has lost an affectionate husband, his children a kind parent, his servants a considerate and indulgent master, his neighbors a public benefactor, and Rusk county a faithful public servant. Peace to his memory; and may the sunlight of the hope of a blissful reunion, radiate the recesses of the widowed heart now so sadly affflicted by this melancholy dispensation of Providence.[117]

To pay the proper respect to Julien S. Devereux's death "a

----

[117]Henderson **Democrat,** May 3, 1856.

meeting of a portion of the people of Rusk County, Texas," was held in Henderson on Saturday morning May 3, and the following proceedings were drawn up:

Obituary.

At a meeting of a portion of the people of Rusk county, Texas, held in the town of Henderson on Saturday morning May 3rd 1856, the following proceedings were had.

On motion of Dr. A. B. Graham, J. H. Parsons, was called to the chair, and on motion of Bennett Boggess, James R. Armstrong, was appointed Secretary.

The Chairman stated that the melancholy intelligence of the death of the Hon. Julien S. Devereux, had just been received; and that this meeting of the people, was for the purpose of paying a last tribute of respect to his memory, as a faithful and efficient public servant.

On motion of M. D. Ector, the chair appointed a Committee of five, to draft a preamble and resolutions, expressive of the sense of the meeting as to the life and character of the deceased. The committee consisted of M. D. Ector, M. D. Graham, Thos. M. Likens, B. F. McDonough and Thos. R. Pitner.

The committee reported the following preamble and resolutions, which were unanimously adopted by the meeting.

Whereas, the melancholy and afflictive intelligence has reached us of the death of Col. Julian S. Devereux,—a prominent citizen of our county, and one of our Representatives, in the popular branch of our State Legislature. And whereas the deceased has occupied high positions of confidence and public trust, both in this State, and the State from which he emigrated and has always brought to the discharge of his duties of both a private and public nature, an honest sincerity, a fervent zeal, and an enlightened understanding. And whereas in the dark hours of the Republic,—"the times which tried mens souls,"—he proved a true legal, and unwavering supporter and friend of Texas; that since the establishment of peace, and the organization of the Republic into a State, under the Stars and Stripes of the Union, he has contributed his energies and influence to the promotion of her advancing prosperity and power. And whereas it is due and but a just tribute of the respect to the private moral, and public worth of the deceased, that we should make some public record the estimate, which we place upon his many virtues.

Be it therefore Resolved. That we a portion of the people of Rusk Co. have heard with a sincere and unaffected regret, of the Death of our friend and representative Col. Julian S. Devereux.

Resolved. That in the death of the deceased, his family have lost an affectionate and indulgent husband and father, —the community in which he resided a kind and accommodating neighbor,—society, one of its most prominent and influencial [sic] members; the county an intelligent and faithful representative, and the State, a "tried and trusty" citizen.

Resolved. That we respectfully tender to his heart stricken, and bereaved family, our sincerest sympathy and confidence, in the crushing affliction and irreparable loss, which they have sustained.

Resolved, That the Secretary forward a copy of the proceedings of this meeting, to the family of the deceased, and that the town papers be requested to publish the same. The Austin papers, the Montgomery Ala., papers, and the Georgia Federal Union are requested to copy.

  M. D. Ector,
  T. M. Likens,
  B. F. McDonough,   Committee.
  T. R. Pitner,
  M. D. Graham.
The meeting then adjourned
      J. H. Parsons, Chm'n.
  James R. Armstrong.   Sec'y.[118]

In the adjourned session of the House of Representatives at Austin on July 12, 1856, resolutions were drawn up with respect to the death of Julien Devereux. The former member of the legislature was described as "simple and unostentatious in all his habits—firm and undiviating in the cause of right. . . ."[119] Representative William Stedman from Rusk County, the Know-Nothing candidate who served in the legislature with Devereux, entered the following comments into the resolutions:

> I do not hesitate to say that a purer-hearted gentleman, a more liberal and patriotic citizen, a safer and more reliable public servant I never knew. It was my fortune to have ever differed widely from him in political sentiment; but he was one of the few that could think and allow others to think, and he never suffered such differences to interfere with or disturb his social relations. Previous to his emigration to Texas, and since his residence here, he was frequently called to positions of honor and responsibility, but never, I believe, at his own seeking. He was emphatically a man

---

[118]Newspaper clipping, Mrs. Julien S. Devereux Scrapbook, Devereux Papers.
[119]Official Journal of the House of Representatives of the State of Texas at the Adjourned Session, Sixth Legislature, 56.

whom the office sought, and was in every instance, at least since my acquaintance with him, literally dragged from the quiet and repose of private life into the public service.[120]

In the role of plantation planter, local citizen, and public servant Julien Devereux in ten years' time had left his area a better one than he had found it. The prosperity Rusk County enjoyed in the 1850's was, in large part, because of successful planters like Devereux. Of importance also to the county and its residents was the time Devereux devoted to bringing in industry and erecting schools; the services he rendered as justice of the peace, county commissioner, and legislator; the good neighbor he was in times of sickness; and the able provider he was for his wife, children, and slaves, as well as for the less fortunate in his midst.

One other contribution Devereux made was the erection of his mansion house, still standing today in Rusk County after more than a century "on that same beautiful hill." A main reason Julien Devereux has earned a permanent place in Texas history has been his Monte Verdi Mansion House. This beautiful monument is examined next.

---

[120]Newspaper clipping, Mrs. Julien S. Devereux Scrapbook, Devereux Papers.

CHAPTER VIII

Monte Verdi Epilogue

*I hope however that something will have been
done towards getting out on the hill by the time I
get home. I have been no place since I left that is
as pretty as that same hill. . . .*[1]

At Julien Devereux's death on May 1, 1856, Sarah was left
with the responsibility to rear four small boys. Albert was
eight years old, Julien was five, William Penn was three, and
Charles was only nine months. On May 15, two weeks after
Julien Devereux died, his daughter, Antoinette, was married to
Caleb Jackson Garrison, a Henderson mercantile operator who
had served as engrossing clerk of the senate of the Sixth Texas
Legislature at the time Devereux sat in the house of representatives. Caleb Garrison was able to assist Sarah Devereux from
time to time with the management of Monte Verdi Plantation
during the difficult years following her husband's death.

Julien Devereux's will was probated on May 26, 1856, and
an inventory filed on July 10.[2] He had provided well for his
wife and children and left the following possessions:

        10,721 acres of land
            80 slaves
             6 head horses
            15 head mules
            15 yoke oxen
           300 head cattle
           300 head hog
           230 head sheep
            16 head goats
             4 road wagons
             1 two horse wagon

[1]Julien S. Devereux to Sarah Devereux, June 28, 1854, Devereux Papers.
[2]Will of Julien S. Devereux, Vol. G., Probate Records, Rusk County,
Texas, M.S., 345; 356, County Clerk's Office, Henderson, Texas. A copy
of the will is also in the Devereux Papers, and is included in the Appendix.

```
        1 pleasure carriage
        2 gin stands
        1 horse mill
        1 set black smith tools
       38 ploughs
       21 pair blow gear
       25 weeding hoes
       14 grabing [grubbing] hoes
       18 chopping axes
        2 broad axes
       12 log chains
        8 iron wedges
        4 bed steads
        6 feather beds & furniture
        6 cotton mattresses
        1 dozen chairs
        1 bureau
        1 press (clothes)
        1 safe or cupboard
        1 lot of books
        1 double barrel gun
        2 rifle guns
        2 pistols
        1 repeter &1 durenger [derringer]
        6 bake ovens
        2 wash pots
        2 cook pots
        1 brass kettle
$1,912.40 total money³
```

Devereux made ample provision for Sarah and his boys as well as for Antoinette and Sidney, who were given certain slaves and "one horse saddle and bridle, one bed stead and firniture [sic] and two cows and calves."⁴ Maintenance and education were also provided for Antoinette and Sidney.

None of Devereux's slaves were to be sold because "they are family slaves and it is my will that they so remain after my death."⁵ The two old slaves, Scott and Tabby, were not forgotten:

> In consideration of the long and faithfully services of the two old negroes slaves Scott and Tabby . . . it is my will and desire that from and after my death, they be exempted from compulsory personal labor further than to give such attention as they may be able in nursing and taking care of my children after my death; and I further will and desire

³Ibid.
⁴Ibid.
⁵Ibid.

that the said Scott and Tabby shall be humanely treated and well provided for by my executors.[6]

Sarah's burden of taking care of four small boys was relieved some when she employed Mrs. M. A. Harcourt of Austin as governess in the autumn of 1856. Mrs. Harcourt, who became a close friend to Sarah and was devoted to the Devereux children, was described as "a pleasant intelligent and agreeable companion and a lady of high standing and great moral worth."[7]

Julien Devereux had waited almost a decade from the time he arrived in Rusk County until he began construction of his permanent residence. As a wise planter he had deferred construction until more essential things had been accomplished,[8] and his fine home, like others of the period, "when it came at all, came late and never in great abundance."[9] There is no available information to indicate from what source Devereux drew plans for his home. One early plantation home, Rosedown, built near St. Francisville, Louisiana,[10] after 1835 by Daniel Turnbull, has a likeness which appears in the early Monte Verdi photographs. Perhaps Julien Devereux saw this home, or some other such plantation, on one of his Southern tours and decided on the style for his own mansion house.

During the early summer of 1856 Sarah Devereux probably began the work to finish the mansion house. On June 17, John McClarty, merchant and longtime friend of the Devereuxs, wrote to Mrs. Devereux that, "the bearer of this letter *Mr. Jackson* writes you for the purpose of ascertaining whether it is your intention to finish your house or not the present year and if so the possibility of his getting work to do." Jackson "would not stop until the work is completed."[11] William Stedman, who served with Julien Devereux in the legislature, wrote to Sarah Devereux to introduce a Mr. Howard for the "purpose of building your house."[12] The completion date of work on Monte Verdi is not stated, but on May 9, 1857, Sarah Devereux paid M. C.

---

[6]Ibid.

[7]Israel Worsham to Mrs. Julien S. Devereux, August 20, 1856, Devereux Papers.

[8]Ulrich Bonnell Phillips, **Life and Labor in the Old South**, 232.

[9]Francis Pendleton Gaines, **The Southern Plantation, A Study in the Development and the Accuracy of a Tradition**, 169.

[10]Harnett T. Kane, **Plantation Parade, The Grand Manner in Louisiana**, 154-155.

[11]John McClarty to Mrs. Julien S. Devereux, June 17, 1856, Devereux Papers.

[12]William Stedman to Mrs. Julien S. Devereux, June 20, 1856, **ibid.**

Jackson "four hundred dollars in parte payment for work done on hur hous [sic] this the 9 of May 1857."[13]

When completed Monte Verdi probably ranked among the finest of the plantation homes in East Texas. The house, an imposing structure with tall columns, was in many ways what is generally imagined as the "typical" home of the successful planter in the ante-bellum Old South. Some statistics on the home will give an idea of its size. The front porch was 52'5" long and 9' 10" wide. The entry room had two doors leading to the two front rooms and a stairway to the second floor. The first floor rooms measured 19' by 19' with a fireplace and four large windows in each room. The fireplaces measured 6' 10" wide and 4' 9" high, and the windows were 4' 11" wide and 10' 6" high. The dining room on the northwest of the house measured 15' by 21' and contained cabinets, pantries, and a fireplace. An L-shaped porch was on the back of the house.

The stairway was 3'4" wide with a distance of 14' to the first landing. The first landing was 10' 11" long and 3' 4" wide. The distance from the first landing to the second landing was 6' 11." A hall at the top of the landing connected the two upstairs bedrooms, measuring 19' by 19', which with two fireplaces, were identical to the downstairs rooms. The kitchen was some fifty feet west of the house. About one hundred yards to the north and northwest of the house were located the slave quarters.

Sarah Devereux had some contact with Julien's relatives in Alabama, and Sarah and her sister-in-law, Louisiana Holcombe corresponded frequently. On January 29, 1857, Louisiana mentioned that her father would be proud of Sarah's four Devereux boys "as he seemed to fear the name would run out."[14] If the boys grew to manhood "there would be the old names represented"—Albert, Julien, William, and Charles.[15] Louisiana wrote that she had never seen Sidney but that she hoped "he may be a worthy and dutiful son and do well, and aid you as an own son[.]"[16]

T. Y. Logan was the Monte Verdi overseer in 1857, and the

---

[13]Receipt from M. C. Jackson to Mrs. Sarah Ann Devereux, May 9, 1857, **ibid.**

[14]Louisiana A. Holcombe to Mrs. Sarah Devereux, January 29, 1857, **ibid.**

[15]**Ibid.** Albert was named for his uncle, Julien was named for his father, William was named for grandfather John William, and Charles was named for his great grandfather.

[16]**Ibid.**

next year, 1858, William Howerton was back on the plantation. During that year Sarah Devereux reported the following property for purposes of taxation:

61 slaves valued at	$30,000
6952 acres valued at 2½ dollars per acre	$22,825
22 head of horses & mules valued at	1,800
300 head of cattle valued	1,500
100 head of hogs valued at	100
8 yoke of work oxen valued at	320
150 head of sheep valued at	300
30 head of goats valued	45
2 ox waggons valued at	200
1 Pleasure carriage valued at	200
Household & kitchen Firniture	256
	$57,546[17]

Sarah Devereux probably spent most of her time attempting to manage Monte Verdi. She did visit her old friends in Montgomery County, and for a time she lived in Henderson and took music lessons from the noted teacher, J. C. Miszner, a student of Franz Liszt and graduate of the Leipzig Conservatory of Music.

By 1860, the year before the outbreak of the Civil War, Rusk County had developed in population and wealth to rank as one of Texas' most important counties. Rusk County had the largest population in Texas in 1860 with 15,803 persons listed,[18] and the census for that year revealed a substantial amount of wealth among the inhabitants.

Several significant events took place in 1860 which most probably had adverse effects on Sarah Devereux and Monte Verdi Plantation. At Tyler, Texas, in April of 1860, the Supreme Court of Texas heard the case of L. D. Sanders *vs.* Sarah A. Devereux.[19] In the case, on the basis of a contract entered into between Sanders and Devereux slaves, Mrs. Devereux attempted to make Sanders take responsibility for 20,158 pounds of cotton which had been produced on Devereux land but was destroyed by fire before it was delivered to Sanders. The Su-

---

[17]"A List of Taxable Property given in by S. A. Devereux for the year AD 1858," ibid.
[18]Population of the United States in 1860, pp. 503-504.
[19]George W. Paschal, Reports of Cases Argued and Decided in the Supreme Court of the State of Texas during the Conclusion of the Tyler Session, 1860, and the Whole of the Austin Session, 1860 . . ., pp. 15-26.

preme Court ruled against Mrs. Devereux on the grounds that the contract between the slaves and Sanders was void, and also because the property right in the cotton was in the estate of her husband and his executors.[20]

Two catastrophies in 1860—a fire in the county seat of Henderson and a prolonged drought—caused real hardships among Rusk County residents, and no doubt the effects were felt on Monte Verdi Plantation. On Sunday night, August 5, a few days after the census had been completed in Henderson, the town burned. It was believed that the fire was caused by an incendiary, because it was not the first fire to take place in Texas that year.[21] The damage in Henderson was severe, the total loss being placed at $220,000, of which $8,500 was insured, leaving a net loss of $211,500. Forty-three buildings were destroyed,[22] as were two Henderson newspapers, the *Texas New Era* and the *Star-Spangled Banner*. Best accounts indicate that only one business house was left standing, and all supplies and provisions for the area were destroyed, including $50,000 worth of goods which burned in the street after being removed from the stores.[23]

The August fire came at a time of severe drought; it was stated that no rain had fallen in Rusk County since February, and that "it was the hottest summer ever known in Texas, the temperature in July running up to 112 degrees in the shade."[24] One account of the drought conditions stated that, "The crops in this section simply 'are not,' and unless the Red River is navigable by the last of December, affording means to import provisions, there must be much suffering."[25] No doubt Monte Verdi crops were severely damaged during the drought.

It is not known what results the burning of Henderson and the great drought in 1860 had on Rusk County's contribution in supplies and material to the Confederacy when the Civil War broke out the following year. The county did not have many factories, and Rusk probably was not among those leading in

---

[20]*Ibid.*, 26.

[21]For an account of the fires in Dallas and other Texas towns see William W. White, "The Texas Slave Insurrection of 1860," **Southwestern Historical Quarterly**, LII, 259-285.

[22]**State Gazette** (Austin), September 1, 1860, quoting **East Texas Times** (Henderson), date not given.

[23]**Evening Picayune** (New Orleans), August 20, 1860, quoting Galveston **News,** August 16, 1860.

[24]S. B. Barron, **The Lone Star Defenders**, 16.

[25]**State Gazette** (Austin), September 15, 1860.

material contributions. It is possible, however, that the county ranked among the first in Texas in the contribution of men for the fighting forces, for the county, according to tradition,[26] is supposed to have furnished more soldiers for the Confederate Army than any other county in the state. Records in the Texas State Archives indicate that at least twelve companies were raised in Rusk County.

Sarah Devereux's own sons were too young for Confederate military service, but Sidney Devereux, at the age of twenty, was one of the first to volunteer in Rusk County. He joined Milton M. Boggess' Company, First Texas Volunteers (Cavalry), which was mustered into service on April 6, 1861,[27] six days before the firing at Fort Sumter.

On the eve of the Civil War Sarah Devereux was most probably in a highly solvent financial condition. The census of 1860 listed thirty-three-year-old Sarah with real estate valued at $70,000, the second highest figure recorded in Rusk County, and she had a personal estate of $66,000.[28] With the outbreak of the Civil War, Sarah Devereux faced real hardships in running the huge plantation. Taxes increased each year during the war. In 1862 the Confederate tax on Monte Verdi was $304.80[29] compared with $147.67 for 1861.[30] Sarah Devereux must have been hard pressed for money, because the 1861 tax was not paid until August 18 and September 1, 1862,[31] and the taxes for 1862 were not paid until January 20, 1864.[32]

The year of 1863 was a critical one for the Confederacy and conditions in Rusk County were no exception. During the year the commissioners' court voted to aid the war effort by deliver-

---

[26]Dallas **Morning News,** August 30, 19('-), clipping in Mrs. J. E. Watkins' scrapbook on Rusk County.

[27]Muster Roll for Rusk County, April 6, 1861, Archives, Texas State Library, Austin, Texas. Sidney probably died sometime in the 1890's and was buried in an unmarked grave in the McKnight Seminary Cemetery, located about a half mile north of Highway 204 between Cushing and Sacul, Nacogdoches County. At the time of his death, Sidney's body was to be taken across the Angelina River for burial and a grave was dug. A torrential rain came, and the Angelina rose so high that the river could not be crossed. A second grave, in the McKnight Seminary Cemetery, was dug. Old timers point out that, "It took two graves to bury Sidney." Archie Buckner to D. W., July 28, 1961.

[28]Eighth United States Census (1860), Population Schedule (Microfilm), University of Texas Library, Austin.

[29]"Confederate Tax Due for Year, 1862," Devereux Papers.

[30]"Taxes for the Year 1861," **ibid.**

[31]**Ibid.**

[32]"Confederate Tax Due for Year, 1862," **ibid.**

ing the iron cage of the county jail to the Confederate government at 65¢ a pound.[33] J. M. Dodson, editor of the Henderson *Times,* on April 28, urged persons not to use grain for whiskey. He pleaded:

> In the name of patriotism, in the name of the families of the poor soldiers . . . we entreat the people to put a stop to the manufacture and sale of whiskey (save for medical purposes), until our country passes through the dreadful ordeal she is now exposed to.[34]

On November 21, the Henderson *Times* carried the following item on the front page:

NOTICE!
Headquarters, Rusk Co., Texas

November 9th, 1863.
To the Slave-Holders of Rusk County:—
The Government of the Confederate Stat[es] now requires of you one third of the ablebodied negro men between the ages of 18 and 50, to be employed immediately, and having been appointed principal agent of this County, I hope the patriotic Slave holders will comply cheerfully and faithfully with their country's demands.
The negroes will be placed in camps, near the centre of the county, until further orders from the Headquarters of this Bureau.
You will be notified by the county agents or sub county agents, what time to report your negroes and obtain receipts for them.

W. L. McMurray, County Agent.[35]

Monte Verdi Plantation felt the effect of Confederate reverses in 1863 and was especially hard hit when the Confederate Congress levied a "tax in kind." This tax was devised as a means of provisioning the Confederate Army without further issue of money which would have made the existing inflation more unbearable. The tax was levied solely on the land holders and required that they give to the government one tenth of their produce for one year. The Secretary of the Treasury was responsible for the cotton, tobacco, and wool, which he used to guarantee Confederate bonds, while the Secretary of War, through the Quartermaster Corps, collected the edible products,

[33]Myrtis and Pax Watkins, **In Old Rusk County,** unpaged.
[34]Henderson **Times,** April 28, 1863.
[35]**Ibid.,** November 21, 1863.

[132]

such as corn, fodder, potatoes, peas, wheat, and the like, for distribution to the armies.[36]

Huge requisitions were made on the produce at Monte Verdi such as on February 7, 1864, when Mrs. Devereux turned over to the Confederate Government at the New Salem depot 533 bushels of corn, 2433 pounds of fodder, 617 pounds of oats, and 2½ bushels of potatoes "on her tax in kind upon produce for the year 1863."[37] The following month on March 14 Sarah Devereux turned over articles "necessary for the public service" consisting of "100 bushels of corn at $2 per bushel and 5675 pounds of fodder at 2¢ a pound."[38] Officer A. P. Corley, who took the produce, noted, "I have not paid this acct for want of funds."[39]

Caleb Jackson Garrison, Antoinette's husband, went into the Confederate Army and this created additional problems in plantation management for Sarah. For a time Garrison was a member of Company K, Fourteenth Texas Infantry, Mathew Duncan Ector's Brigade, Army of Tennessee.[40] From Shelbyville, Tennessee, on March 30, 1863, Garrison wrote, probably to Sarah Devereux, the following:

> I write by Dr Graham,—but can say little things are much the same as they were when I wrote you before—my health is not very good at this time, though I hope I will be better soon—we are still encamped here and likely will remain here for some time to come—I do not think that the Federals will advance upon us soon, and of course we are making no steps to advance upon them—and this being the case there is not much probability of an early fight. I am unable to form any conjectures as to what old Rosencranz, [William S. Rosencrans] means by not making a forward movement, unless his men are unwilling to fight us again— The more we ascertain of the Murfreesboro fight, the worse

[36]E. Merton Coulter, **Confederate States of America, 1861-1865**, pp. 178-180. Although the tax could have been beneficial in the supply of food to the undernourished men in the field, the opportunities for graft and corruption marred its effectiveness and it has been estimated that of the $145,-000,000 worth of supplies collected, only $40,000,000 ever reached their destination.

[37]Receipt, N. G. Bagby, agent for Captain E .M. Bacon, February 7, 1864, Devereux Papers.

[38]Receipt for Requisitioned Goods, A. P. Corley, Capt., Ass't Quartermaster, C. S. A., April 10, 1864, **ibid.**

[39]**Ibid.**

[40]L. E. Daniell, **Personnel of the Texas State Government**, 76. Antoinette Devereux Garrison died on August 29, 1872, and she and Caleb were parents of the following children: Julien, Abbie, Homer, and Arthur.

[133]

we learn we whipped them—and when we fight again we will whip him worse—Things are seemingly at a perfect stand still all over the Confederacy—but when this thing will stop no one can tell—but I think this spring some time —Our army is in fine fix and well rested and fed—and are getting verry restless now about a fight. All of your acquaintances are well—Brother Smith, is here now on a visit to see us—he left home on the 19th and will leave this evening for home—Antoinette has a girl, it was born on the 18th and was doing very well.—The children are doing well—Zed received your letters written on the 27th of Feby. I have heard nothing from you only through the channel of others since I left—you stated in your letter to Zed that you wanted me to advise you in refference to the sale of your cotton I can only say, that I am not willing to sell my cotton yet, and were I in your place, I should hold the ballance of my cotton for a higher price. You spoke of some of your home troubles but did not say anything of their nature—what on earth can be the matter—How is your overseer getting along—and how much corn have you sold and how much can you sell—How does wheat oats, Rye and Barley look—who have married, and who are going to marry—who have gone to the war and who are going—and every thing that has taken place since I left=write every thing leaving nothing out—All the boys are getting letters from Texas by mail but myself—Well I suppose its all right —Ann and Mariah could write once a week I should think Tell Mintz to push every thing and make a good crop for me to come home to this fall

Yours truly
C. J. Garrison.[41]

On one occasion Garrison wrote in a letter that, "You [Sarah Devereux?] ought not to complain of living hard, and I am satisfied you would not if you could only see the patience and endurance of our soldiers, with the little complaining they receive the rations of bread and meat."[42]

To exist and to manage a plantation the size of Monte Verdi during the Civil War must have been a real struggle for Sarah Devereux. Tremendous supplies were needed for the working force of slaves, and shortages of all kinds became acute. Taxes continued to increase, as the state and county taxes for 1864 came to $935.65.[43]

Word concerning the collapse of the Confederacy was re-

---

[41]C. J. Garrison, address missing, March 30, 1863, Devereux Papers.
[42]C. J. Garrison, address and date missing, **ibid.**
[43]Rusk County, Texas, Tax Receipt for the Year, 1864, **ibid.**

ceived in Rusk County on April 12, 1865, when Robert Bruce Richardson, a Henderson resident, wrote the following lines in his diary: *"Oh, God! Lee has surrendered! We are lost."* The following month, on May 29, Richardson noted the Confederate Army had disbanded, and "We are a conquered people."[44]

Somehow Sarah Devereux had been able to hold on to Monte Verdi during the war. The burden of operating a plantation and rearing four small boys would have been a heavy task for any person, but with the addition of wartime difficulties it must have been almost insurmountable for a widow. No doubt, the tremendous responsibilities accounted for Sarah's gray hair. Perhaps she drew strength from her religion, for as a Methodist she has been described as a "consistant Christian."[45] One person, who remembers Sarah Devereux, has recalled that she was a lovable and "very sweet tempered person" with a deep devotion to her four sons.[46]

Following the surrender of Confederate forces, Rusk County went through a period of Reconstruction similar to that of other Texas counties. Monte Verdi slaves were set free when General Gordon Granger on June 19, 1865, issued his emancipation proclamation in Texas.[47] Post war conditions were unsettled, and the future was not bright for a widow. On April 1, 1869, Sarah Devereux married James Freeborn Garrison, brother of Caleb Jackson Garrison, who had married Antoinette Devereux in 1856. The marriage, unfortunately, was not a happy one, and Sarah left the following handwritten account:

When I and J. F. Garrison were married Apr 1st-69 I owned all the property[.] there was our home & furniture of 1300 acrs. He had nothing. unless it was a horse. I had a home, and a good farm. (1300) Thirteen hundred acres of Land. Some horses & mules cattle hoggs, and everything belonging to a farm. And all housekeeping arrangements. I owed no debts. I think about the second year, (I married) after I sold a house and Lot in Henderson which belong to myself and my four children. For 1000 thousand dollars in two payments. The first 500 hundred dollars was equally divided one hundred (100) dollars to each of us. I having the care of Williams & Charlies with mine which amounted

[44]Robert Bruce Richardson Diary, in possession of Miss Virginia Richardson, Henderson, Texas.
[45]Mrs. C. E. Carlock to D. W., August 11, 1961.
[46]Interview, Mrs. J. F. Thompson to D. W., August 15, 1961.
[47]Galveston **Tri-Weekly News**, June 30, 1865; July 5, 1865.

to three hundred (300) dollars. (all of which) Jim used.
the next payment. He used mine and Charlies makeing
what he used of that property (500). five hundred dollars.
I think it was in 1873. I was induced greatly by his influence to sell my home. and I will say here. That he said
to me just a few days before I left Timpson that he did it
to get everything in his own hands. so he could controul
it all. My home was sold to C. J. Garrison for $7500) Sev-
en thousand five hundred dollars[.] some how in there two
or three years. (He having the management of everything)
Debts had acumulated. to (2500) Twenty five hundred
dollars. (Our debts as he calls them. It think it was most-
ly Saloon debts. and to pay him out of Scrapes & difficulties he would get into, when he would be in his drinking
carousals.) All this time the place was makeing tolerable
good crops. Corn and from 15 to 30 Bales of Cotton. The
2500 hundred dollars was paid out of the proceeds of my
place. The ballance was C. J. Garrisons notes for the place.
and a tract of Land in Wise County which was afterwards
Sold to J. S. Devereux my son. In part payment for the
tract of land now belonging to me Justly. Being paid for
with this Wise County Land. and note given by C. J. Garrison for my original home. The amount paid J S Devereux
was three (3000) thousand dollars Afterwards Jim Sold a
part of the Land bought from J.S.D. to Mays & Swink for
1000 thousand dollars. There is other things I cant think
of or write now. One thing though is a lot of cattle he
sold in Van Zant County belonging to the Estate

S. A. Garrison[48]

Sarah sometimes heard from her old friend, Mrs. M. A.
Harcourt, who wrote on April 22, 1872, during the Reconstruction era:

Spring Ridge
Caddo Parish [Louisiana]

Dear Friend,
Looking over my "old letters," I find one, that I prized
highly, and had laid it with my other treasures, reading it
over, it carried me back to our dear sunnie faced, blue eyed
friends whome I loved so well, those when happy days, before the hateful Yankee poluted our once happy homes it
seems since they have come among us, and have located
themselves in our beautiful South, that their *stinking*, poi-
sonous breaths turn to ice, and freeze every thing it touches,
this has been the most severe Winter we have ever had at

---

[48]Sarah Ann Devereux Garrison, undated memorandum, Devereux Papers.

the South and I attributed it to the sojourn of the Yank's among us, Oh my Friend, when I think of the degradation of a surrender of our country to the Yankee's, I *hate* too much, to think of despiseing them, to have to submit to Yankee domination, is more than my proud Southern blood can bear at times, God only enable us to bear it with Christian fortitude but I may be tireing you, and will stop. My relatives are all on the other side of the question, and often tell me, I must stoop too, and kiss the rod with which I'm beaten. . . .[49]

Sarah Ann Devereux Garrison died on April 25, 1900, five days before her seventy-fourth birthday, in Jacksonville, Texas, at the home of her son, William P. Devereux, with whom she had been residing for several years. She left an estate with a "probate value of six hundred dollars."[50] The land owned by Julien S. Devereux, consisting at one time of more than ten thousand acres, was sold off little by little. The Devereux sons left the home place. Albert, the oldest boy, married Elizabeth A. Stamps on February 11, 1869, moved to Wise County and raised a family.[51] He died in Decatur on March 7, 1918. Julien Sidney Devereux moved to Odessa and served for a number of years as Ector County District Clerk. He died on June 8, 1896, and was never married. William Penn Devereux, who preserved the family papers, was married three times; to Mary Bolton, Jennie Miller Douglas, and Mary Perkins. He lived for several years in Cherokee County and died in Minden, Louisiana, on December 6, 1928. Charles Devereux became a doctor, and at the time of his death on September 30, 1884, he was living in Montgomery County with his wife and two children.[52]

The Monte Verdi Mansion House passed from ownership of members of the Devereux family and changed hands numerous times. By 1958 the house was owned by J. J. Sinclair of Minden, Texas. It was unoccupied for a number of years and was rapidly going to ruin. Bricks had fallen from the chimney, window panes were out, boards had fallen from the outside walls, wind

---

[49]Mrs. M. A. Harcourt to Mrs. Sarah Ann Garrison, April 22, 1872, **ibid.**
[50]Probate Record, Filed May 10, 1906, County Clerk's Office, Henderson, Texas.
[51]Cliff D. Cates, **Pioneer History of Wise County,** 339-340; B. B. Paddock, **A Twentieth Century History and Biographical Record of North and West Texas,** II, 58.
[52]Newspaper clipping, Mrs. Sarah Ann Devereux Scrapbook, Devereux Papers.

blew rain into all the rooms, one column of the front porch had fallen, and the front porch was almost completely in ruins. Monte Verdi, after the winter of 1958-1959, was almost a total loss.

Then an event, almost miraculous, came about. The dilapidated Monte Verdi Mansion House came to the attention of Mr. and Mrs. Emmett Lowry of Texas City. With a true sense of historical appreciation the Lowrys bought Monte Verdi and began the laborious task of restoration. They had a priceless, but neglected, piece of Texas history treasure on which to work. This is their account of what took place:

We finally located Monte Verdi in November, 1958, the evening of a cold, bright day. The remoteness of the house gave it a fascination it would not have had in a group of houses. The front porch, collapsed, offered no help in entering. We finally pushed the guarding wisteria vine from the back door and entered. Hay in the parlor, the rail half gone from the stair, dead birds, names written on the painted walls as far back as the 1880's, banging doors and rattling windows, and we fell in love with it.

We went back to buy it in February of 1959.

The illustration of Monte Verdi 1900-1910 is probably the way the house looked originally. There were double galleries across the front, each supported by six plain doric columns, making twelve columns, in all. Each gallery was outlined by a wooden handrail.

The house has two large rooms upstairs divided by a hall landing. There are three large rooms downstairs with a large hall dividing the two on the front. Double doors open from this hall to the back porch and a single door with side panel lights opens the hall to the front. The third room is the one-story part of the house. It is our opinion that the original owner intended to enlarge the house later by building a room over this one, since the window pattern of the south west was not carried out over this room on the north west. The house's most endearing quality is its extremely well-built, but almost severe simplicity.

It is interesting to note that here, as in so many houses of this period, each room shows a different style of woodwork around the windows and doors. The mantel in the living room and the panels above it are especially beautiful and sincerely appreciated by the present owners who spent one summer and fall scraping coats and coats of ancient paint from them!

Two things saved the house during its long abandonment. The roof was covered with corrugated iron somewhere down the years. This kept the interior from being water-soaked beyond repair. When this roof was torn away we found badly worn shingles in the attic buried under several inches of dirt. Secondly, the house sits on a brick chain wall foundation. This is continuous under all outside walls and interior partitions. The brick are in turn placed on a two foot square pad of iron rock, which is plentiful on the plantation.

The floors appeared to be in very poor condition but the boards were two inches thick, the top being hand-planed and the bottom hand-hewn. Each board was a different width, so it was necessary to mark them as we took them up in order to fit them back together. We ran them through a planer to a thickness of one inch, turned them bottom side up and re-laid them over a sub floor where previously there had been none. The beauty of the old, deep golden pine has more than paid for this labor. We lost only two rooms flooring in the house.

The pine sills of the house, placed upon the brick chain wall, were in perfect condition with the exception of the two front corners. Here the fallen front porch and broken windows had allowed the rains inside the walls, and necessitated replacing the rotted wood. The entire frame of the house is morticed, tenoned and pegged from the sills to the entablature.

On each window frame there remained four half hinges, hand-forged, to hold shutters of which no trace could be found. We have been able to rework thirteen old pairs so far to replace these. Here, I would like to explain that we constantly haunt sites where old houses of the period of Monte Verdi are being "wrecked for progress" to buy old materials to replace those long lost on our house. We were fortunate in securing our six beautiful full-length columns, upper gallery rail and ballisters in such manner.

The hand-planed siding and trim on the front was in excellent condition, having protection from the 12 foot overhanging roof that ran the entire 52 foot width of the house. The west or back of the house showed the greatest amount of wear. The soft part of the grain in most of the siding had eroded almost a half inch.

The house had to be wired for electricity and plumbing installed. It had neither. We found the original well in excellent condition with the hand made brick lining in tact. We installed an electric pump and it serves the house well.

Our two main chimneys reach almost 35 feet into the air and serve four fire places. A shorter one serves the fireplace in the dining room. The house was heated originally by these five fire places. Besides the panelled mantel, four colonial mantels grace the bedrooms and parlor.

The two upstairs rooms have been prepared with repro-
ductions of old patterns. The rest of the house is painted
a soft, restoration green. The stair rail was replaced by a
curving, colonial rail, the original being gone.

The foundation of the old kitchen rests about 50 feet
from the main house. With the exception of one huge old
cedar and a ragged mulberry, no trees remained. Close to
the house, but a hundred yards to the north, a row of huge
oaks lead to the springs and toward the old slave quarters,
where hand made brick may still be found. We have been
slow in replanting as protecting the house without delay
was necessary.

The view from Monte Verdi is beautiful on all sides and
one can understand immediately why this site was selected
by the Devereuxs. The front of the house faces east, the
rear the west. It is possible to find a comfortable temperature all day by changing from one spot to another as the
sun moves.

The house is so dear to us we would love to call it our
permanent residence. There is work to be done all the time.
However, if we are never to live there permanently, we have
realized the dream of so many people—to save or restore
an old house.[53]

Persons who visit the Monte Verdi Mansion House can rea-
dily understand, as Mrs. Lowry mentioned, why Julien Devereux
chose this particular site for a home. The hill is beautiful and
views from it in all directions are breathtaking. In one direction
there is the distant haze of the Angelina River bottoms; in another, one can see Henderson, some twenty miles away. From
the Monte Verdi Mansion House the view in all directions, including some of the most striking parts of Rusk County, is one
of supreme beauty at any time of the year.

The house today serves as a fine monument to Julien Sidney
Devereux and the members of his family who moved into the
area at an early period and within a decade they had established at Monte Verdi one of the largest and most successful of
the East Texas plantations. The historical importance of the
house was recognized on October 6, 1962, when the Texas Historical Survey Committee awarded a medallion marker. Today,
after more than a century, only the house and some ninety acres
of the land serve to recall a by-gone era in Texas and Southern
history. Persons who visit the restored Monte Verdi Mansion

[53]Mrs. Emmett Lowry to D. W., July 7, 1961. Letter in possession of
writer.

House currently and observe the view agree with what Julien
Devereux wrote to Sarah back in 1854: "I have seen no place
. . . that is as pretty as *that same hill*."[54]

---

[54]Julien S. Devereux to Sarah Devereux, June 28, 1854, Devereux Papers.

Will of Julien Devereux

I, Julien Sidney Devereux of the County of Rusk and State of Texas, being of sound mind do make this my last will and testament, hereby revoking all others.

1st: It is my will that after my decease my remains be interred in a suitable and Christian like manner in the burying ground adjacent to the Baptist Church in the neighborhood of the town of Anadarco; a tomb of stone or brick to be erected over my remains with a suitable head piece of stone on which to be engraved the date of my birth and death.

2nd: I give and bequeath unto my beloved wife, Sarah Ann Devereux the following named slaves, to-wit: (1) Bill, a boy about twenty years old; (2) Tabby, a girl about sixteen years old and her male child, Franklin, about two months old; (3) Judy a woman about twenty four years old and her three sons, to-wit: Peter the eldest and George and Isaac (twins) about four years old; also her twin daughters, Kizzy and Emelissa, about two years old and such household and kitchen furniture as I may own at my death. I also give my said wife one-third part of whatever stock of cattle and hogs and the one-fourth part of whatever stock of mules and horses I may own at my death and the one-fourth part of such farming utensils as I may own at my death.

3. I give and bequeath to my natural daughter, Antoinett [sic] Devereux, the following slaves, to-wit: (1) Jim, a man about twenty one years of age; (2) Rhoda a woman about eighteen years old and her two children, to-wit: Cynthia say two years old, and the female infant she now has about eight months old named_____. I also give to Antoinett one horse saddle and bridle, one bed bedstead and firniture [sic] and two cows and calves. I also give said Antoinett her maintainance and education as hereinafter provided. And should the said Antoinett die leaving no direct lineal heirs of her body begotten, then it is my will that said slaves and their increase shall revert

to my child or children by my said wife, Sarah Ann to be equally divided among them or their lineal heirs. And should said slaves die or any one or more of them before the said Antoinett shall arrive at the age of twenty one years or before she may marry, then it is my will that she shall receive and have other slaves to be taken out of those hereinafter bequeathed to my children by my wife of equal value with such as may so die to be set apart to her by my executors.

4. I will and bequeath to my natural son, Sidney Devereux two slaves, to-wit: Joe, a boy about nineteen years old and Joanna a girl about twelve years old, together with their increase. And I also bequeath to the said Sidney one horse saddle and bridle; one bed bedstead and furniture and two cows and calves. And I also give the said Sidney his maintainance and education, as hereinafter provided. And should the said Sidney died [sic] leaving no child or children or the descendants of child or children, then it is my will and desire that said slaves shall revert to my children by my wife, Sarah Ann or their lineal heirs to be equally divided between them. And should one or both of said slaves die before the said Sidney shall arrive at the age of twenty one years, then it is my will that he shall have and receive other slave or slaves in lieu thereof in like manner as hereinbefore provided, Antoinett Devereux.

5. I hereby will and bequeath the residue of my property, real, personal and mixed, choses in action, effects and rights of whatever description (among which I estimate fifty six slaves) to my two sons, Albert and Julien Devereux by my present wife, together and in common with such other child or children as she may hereafter have by me to be equally divided between my said two sons and such other child or children as may so be born. If there shall be but one of said sons living at my death and no other child born, then he is to have all the property herein bequeathed to both; if both of said sons are living at my death and no other child born then said property to be divided between them if there shall be at my death, said two sons and one or more other child or children of my present wife living or posthumous, then it is my desire that said property shall be equally divided between all of said children. And for greater certainty, I here give the names of the slaves mentioned and intended to pass to said children by this my 5th bequest to the best of my recollection, to-wit: 1. Scott, 2 Jack

Shaw. 3. Henry 4. Lucius, 5. Martin, 6 Lewis. 7 Jesse. 8, July, 9. Daniel, 10. Stephen. 11. Leven. 12. Randal. 13. Juby. 14. Little Jack 15, Amos, 16. Charles, 17. Ham. 18. Tom. 19. Anthony. 20. Walton 21. Richmond. 22 Green. 23, Arthur, 24 Sam. 25. Little Jesse, 26. Nelson. 27. Dennis. 28. Mason, 29. Harrison, 30. Aron. 31. Anderson, 32. Robert. 33. (old) Tabby. 34. Mary. 35. Henry Mariah. 36. Lev Mariah. 37. Katy. 38. Martha. 39. Amey, 40. Matilda. 41. Eliza. 42, Dianah, 43, Mahala, 44 Sarah, 45 Jane, 46, Phebe, 47 Jinny 48. Almina; 49. Jincy, 50 Louisa. 51 Peniah, 52 Charlotte, 53. Little Amey, 54 Katys child not named and 55. and 56 (two others) names not recollected, together with all the increase of said slaves. This my 5th bequest is made charged with and subject to the following restrictions, uses and conditions, to-wit: That my present wife, Sarah Ann remain on the plantation where we now reside and under the supervisions of my executors as hereinafter directed carry on the plantation for the maintainance of herself and her children and the two natural children, Antoinett and Sidney and for the education of her own children as well as the said Antoinett and Sidney and that she may be able to do so, it is my will that she have the use of the said plantation, negroes, stock, mules, farming utensils and other articles properly appertaining to a plantation during her natural life or widowhood with this exception, that as my children if sons, severally attain to the age of twenty one or if daughters when they shall severally marry, the legacies and property bequeathed to them by this will is to be delivered over to them respectfully provided that my present residence and land to the extent of two hundred acres including the same shall not be sold during the life time of my said wife. And should my said wife, Sarah Ann again marry, it is my will that then there be a complete separation of her property and interest in all things of a pecuniary character from those of my children.

6. I devise and bequeath to my said wife and her children all the real estate which I may own and possess at my death to be equally divided between them, that is to say, If I shall have one or more child or children by her she is to have a childs part of said real estate in value equal to the part or share of said child or children to be laid off so as to include our present residence. My residence as I desire here to explain consists of the mansion house and the other buildings and four thousand acres

of land, more or less, attached thereto in different surveys, known as the William F. Allison tract and others lying on one body. The division of said land here contemplated to be fairly and equitably made by my executors.

7. In the event I leave no child or children by my present wife living or posthumous at my death, then I will and bequeath the property and its increase (herein before devised to such child or children) to my said wife and the said Antoinett and Sidney Devereux to be equally divided between them, that is to say said property is to be equally divided between my said wife, the said Antoinett and the said Sidney or their direct lineal descendants provided I leave no child or children in being or posthumous by my said wife or the direct lineal heirs of such child or children by my said wife. Said division to be made between my said wife and the said Antoinett and the said Sidney in three equal parts share and share alike. 8. In consideration of the long and faithfully services of the two old negroes slaves Scott and Tabby hereinbefore bequeathed to my sons, Albert and Julien, it is my will and desire that from and after my death, they be exempted from compulsory personal labor further than to give such attention as they may be able in nursing and taking care of my children after my death; and I further will and desire that the said Scott and Tabby shall be humanely treated and well provided for by my executors.

9. It is my will and desire that all my just debts be paid before distribution of my estate takes place and in providing for the maintainance of my children, I estimate the profits of my plantation as being sufficient for those purposes and pay my just debts. If however, the fund arising from my plantation is insufficient for all the contemplated purposes and it is deemed necessary by my executors to sell any portion of my estate for the payment of my debts, it is my desire that none of my slaves shall be sold, they are family slaves and it is my will that they so remain after my death. I hereby designate as property to be sold for the payment of my debts if necessary, two tracts of land, to-wit: Eleven hundred and seven acres, the head right survey of Col. Robert W. Smith and eight hundred and eighty acres, known as the place I purchased of Doctor Elijah Dodson, or so much thereof as my executors may deem sufficient.

10. Contrary to any wish, desire or request of mine the Legislature of the State of Texas at its last session passed the

[145]

second section of an act entitled "an act changing the names of Antoinett Scott and Sidney Way" which act was approved January 31, 1852. Said second section is in the words "that that [sic] the said Antoinett Devereux and Sidney Devereux be and they are hereby declared capable in law of inheriting the property of their father, Julien S. Devereux in the same manner as if they had been born in lawful wedlock and that this act take effect and be in force from and after its passage." Now although it has long been my wish and desire that the names of the said Antoinett Scott and Sidney Way should should [sic] be changed as is provided for by the first Section of the above recited act, yet I never intended nor was it ever my will that they shall inherit my estate in the manner provided in the said second section. I do therefore now and forever hereafter by this my last will and testament most solemnly protest against the operation and effect of said second section of said act and desire that said section may be repealed by act of said Legislature at its next session, the same having been passed without my knowledge, consent or approbation and in direct violation of my wishes and desires. It is my will that the said Antoinett and Sidney be provided for and receive portions of my estate after my death only in such manner as in this my last will and testament set forth and stated and in no other way.

11. As I have before intimated it is my will that a sufficient amount independent of the bequests herein made be set apart and devoted to the maintainance and education of Antoinett Devereux and Sidney Devereux and my two sons, Albert and Julien and such other children of mine as may hereafter be born. And it is also my will that should the said Antoinett and Sidney or either of them die without lineal issue of their body or bodies the property herein bequeathed is not in any way or under any circumstances to descend to or be inherited by any member of their mothers family.

12. My will is that my friend Doctor Peterson T. Richardson be guardian of the person and property of natural daughter, Antoinett Devereux to superintend and direct her education and take care of her and should my said wife, deem it proper for Antoinett to leave her, 'I desire Mrs. Doctor Richardson to take her and raise her. And it is my will and desire that my esteemed friend, Col. William Wright Morris be the guardian of my natural son, Sidney Devereux as well as of his person as his prop-

erty. And I desire that said Morris will consider the said Sidney wholly in his care and under his charge and not permit him to ramble or wander off so as to become identified with his mothers people. That he will superintend the education and moral culture of the said Sidney and in an especial manner, prepare his mind for the study of the law by giving a proper direction to his education.

13. It is my will that none of my slaves be sold. With one exception, they are all family negroes and it is my desire that they all so remain under the contemplated distribution fixed by this will that they may be humanely treated and well taken care of by those who may succeed me in the ownership of them.

14. I do hereby appoint my wife, Sarah Ann Devereux [,] John Landrum, Col. William Wright Morris, Doctor Peterson T. Richardson, Doctor William M. Ross of Rusk County and Doctor James H. Starr of Nacogdoches County, Texas, (my trustworthy friends) my executrix and executors of this my last will and testament, to execute and carry out all the terms and provisions of the same. And it is my will that they or either one of them shall not be required to give bond and security as a condition to entering on the discharge of the duties hereby imposed. It is also expressly my will and direction that no other action shall be had in the County Court in relation to the settlement of the estate herein disposed of than the probation and registration of the will and testament and a return of an inventory of said estate.

It is my desire and will that my wife, Sarah Ann assisted by the counsel and advice of anyone or more of my other executors as she may choose will take upon herself the supervision of my plantation for the purposes expressed in this will. That aided by my other executors she will attend to the hiring of overseers, the sale of produce, the investing of the proceeds of the plantation. That with the aid of said executors she will plan improvements of my plantation, preserve and take care of property and above all she will attend strictly and carefully to the education of my two sons, Albert and Julien and such other children as she may have by me. I hereby appoint the said Sarah Ann Devereux guardian of the persons and property of my said sons, Albert and Julien and such other child or children as she may have by me and in case she should die then it is my will that Doctor Peterson T. Richardson will take the guardianship of said two sons and such other children as she may have as aforesaid.

Given under my hand and seal using a scroll for a seal and I do declare that the foregoing twelve and a half pages contain my last will and testament executed at the town of Henderson, on this the 7th day of May, A. D. 1852.

JULIEN SIDNEY DEVEREUX (SEAL)

The foregoing will of twelve and a half pages signed, sealed and published in our presence and in the presence of each other.

James R. Armstrong
Thomas R. Pitner
John P. Grigsby.

THE STATE OF TEXAS ()
COUNTY OF RUSK ()

BEFORE ME, the undersigned authority, this day personally appeared Thomas R. Pitner and John P. Grigsby, all to me well known and after being duly sworn on oath says that they saw Julien Sidney Devereux sign the above foregoing instrument of writing and declared the same to be his last will and testament and that they signed as witnesses at the request of the said Julien Sidney Devereux in the presence of him, the said Devereux and each other and that they believe the said testator was at that time of sound mind and capable of making a will.

Thomas R. Pitner
John P. Grigsby

Sworn to in open court this the 26th day of May, A.D. 1856.

John C. Miller, Chief Justice

CODICIL

I, Julien Sidney Devereux of the County of Rusk and State of Texas, do make ordain, publish and declare this to be a codicil to the last will and testament by me made and published on the 7th day of May, 1852 in manner and form as follows, to-wit:

1. I hereby revoke and annul so much of the first clause of my said will as bequeathed to my wife, Sarah Ann the following negro slaves, to-wit: Judy, Peter, George, Isaac Kizzy and Emelissa and in lieu of said slaves, I give and bequeath to my said wife, Sarah Ann the following negro slaves and their future increase, to-wit: Levin, about 24 years old and his wife Penina [Peniah] about 22 years old and her infant child Cyrus about 3 months old. Lewis about 38 years old and his wife, Maria

[148]

About 39 years old, Green about 14 years old and Jincy about 7 years old.

2. I also hereby revoke and annul so much of my aforesaid will as gives to my natural daughter, Antoinett, the following negro slaves, to-wit: Rhoda and her children and I direct that the slave Rhoda and all the children she now has or may hereafter have be transferred to the residuum of my estate and take the direction which my said will gives to that and in lieu of said slave Rhoda and her children I hereby give and bequeath to my said daughter, Antoinett the following slaves, to-wit: Judy, now about 29 years old, her son Peter, now about 11 years old, her twin sons, George and Isaac now about 8 years old, her twin daughters Kizzy and Emelissa now about 6 years old and her son, Allen about 2 years old and their future increase and whereas, I have a claim to four hundred and ninety seven acres of land in the land known as the Jose Maria Martinez league adjoining the lands of Dr. P. T. Richardson, now if I succeed in my life time in securing a good title to said 497 acres of land, I give and devise the same to my said daughter, Antoinett and her heirs forever and in the event I do not secure a good title to said land I give and bequeath to my said daughter, Antoinett instead thereof, the sum of One thousand dollars to be paid to her by my executors out of the proceeds and profits of my farm in two equal annual installments, the first to be paid at the expiration of twelve months after she attains the age of twenty one years or marries and the other at the end of twelve months thereafter provided the said proceeds and profits be sufficient for that purpose after paying the usual current expenses of the support of my family and the education of my children, if not, the said sum must be paid to her as soon after they fall due as above as the said proceeds and profits are sufficient for the purpose. I desire here to explain that the reason why I take the negro slave Judy and her children from my wife and give them to my daughter, Antoinett is this, my policy and object is that the family of my slaves be kept together and that no member of any of said families be separated from the others and the said slaves having since my said will was executed intermarried with the slave Jim, whom my said will gives to my said daughter, Antoinett, I therefore make the foregoing change to effectuate my said policy and object.

3. By the third clause of my said will I have provided as

follows, to-wit: "and should said slaves die or any one or more of them before the said Antoinette shall arrive at the age of twenty one years or before she may marry, then it is my will that she shall receive and have other slaves to be taken out of those hereinafter bequeathed to my children by my wife of equal value with such as may so die to be set apart to her by my executors."

And by the fourth clause of my said will a similar provision is made for the benefit of my natural son, Sidney Devereux and whereas the said provisions tend to frustrate and defeat the policy which I have adopted with regard to my slaves as declared in the second clause of this codicil, to my said will I therefore hereby revoke annul and declare void the aforesaid provisions of the said third and fourth clause of my said will.

4. It is my will and desire and intention that the property by this codicil given to my daughter Antoinett be subject to all the conditions, restrictions and limitations provided and declared in my said will with respect to the property therein bequeathed to her.

5. By the fourth clause of my said will is the following provisions to-wit: "And I also give the said Sidney his education and maintainance as hereinafter provided." And by the twelfth clause the said Sidney is committed to the guardianship of Col. (now Judge) William Wright Morris, to whom I have in said 12th clause given full directions with regard to the training and education of the said Sidney. My object with regard to Sidney was and is to have his moral and intellectual culture carefully attended to, and that he be prepared to take and retain a respectable and useful position in society to that end I desire to have the control and direction of his education during my life and that after my death it should be committed to the care and supervision of some person in whose fidelity and capacity I have entire confidence, but whereas my said natural son, Sidney has been removed beyond my power and control to some place to me unknown and is in all probability in the charge and subject to the direction of his mother or maternal relatives and whereas those persons are wholly incapacitated, in my opinion to secure for him the benefit and advantages which I design he should have, therefore in the event that I fail to regain the charge and control of my said son Sidney so that his education may be directed by myself or those upon whom the trust may devolve

after my death, I revoke and annul so much of the said fourth and twelfth clauses of my said will as provides for the maintainance and education of my said natural son, Sidney as well as all other parts of my said will upon the subject. My intention being only to maintain and educate him in case it be done in a proper manner under my own direction and according to my own views.

6. By the Fourteenth clause of my said will it is provided that my executors nor either of them be required to give bond and security as a condition to entering upon the discharge of their duties. I hereby qualify the said provision as follows, to-wit: My will is that my executors nor either of them be required to give bond and security for the faithful performance of their trusts unless they or some one of them shall be guilty of negligence mismanagement or other misconduct in which event, it is my desire that the County Court require bond and security of those so guilty upon the application of my wife or any one or more of my children or the guardian or guardians or any one or more of them.

7. In the sixth clause of my said will there is some ambiguity in the explanation given of my residence and I will here further explain that I mean by my residence the mansion house and other buildings used and occupied by me as such at the time of my death, situated upon that portion of my land known as the William F. Allison tract etc.

8. I hereby revoke and annul so much of the twelfth clause of my said will as commits the guardianship of my natural daughter, Antoinette Devereux to Dr. P. T. Richardson and the care of her in a certain event to Mrs. Dr. Richardson, and I hereby will and direct that my said daughter, Antoinette be subject to the care and control of my beloved wife, Sarah Ann who may assume the guardianship of my said daughter or have it entrusted to some other suitable and trustworthy person whichever my said wife may deem most prudent. I also hereby revoke so much of the fourteenth clause of my said will as appoints the said Dr. P. T. Richardson guardion of my sons, Julien and Albert and such other children as my wife may thereafter have by me after the death of my wife.

9. The ages of the negroes bequeathed by the fourth clause of my said will to my natural son, Sidney are erroneously stated and I here correct them as follows, to-wit: Joe is now about 24

years old and Joanna is about 17 years old.

10. Since my said will was executed my wife, Sarah Ann has given birth to another son, to whom we have given the name of William Penn and I hereby declare him entitled to share equally of my property with my sons, Albert and Julien to receive all the benefits conferred by my said will upon said Albert and Julien and to be subject to all the directions and provisions therein contained respecting them.

11. I hereby revoke that portion of the first clause of my said will which directs my remains to be interred in the burying ground adjacent to the Baptist Church etc and it is my will and desire that my beloved wife, Sarah Ann select a suitable place for the deposit of my remains that she have the bodies of my beloved father and little son removed thither that she procure the erection of suitable tombs over our graves and that she cause apprpopriate inscriptions to be placed thereon.

12. In addition to the executors named in my said will I nominate and appoint my esteemed and trustworthy friend, Dr. A. P. Galloway as one of my executors and I here declare it is my will and intention that my beloved wife, Sarah Ann qualify as executrix of my will and that she exercise her discretion in selecting from among all the individuals I have nominated as my executors such one or more of them as she may desire to have associated with her in the active duties of the executorship and that the person or persons so selected by her qualify as executor or executors and act cojointly with her in the execution and performance of the trusts imposed by my said will and this Codicil.

The foregoing alterations of and additions to my said will I have made under the influence of satisfactory reason moving me thereto and it is my desire and intention that my said will remain in full force in every particular excepting only those that are revoked amended added to, qualified or restricted by this codicil.

In witness whereof I do hereunto subscribe my name and affix a scroll for seal and I do declare the foregoing six pages to contain a codicil to and part of my last will and testament executed and published at Henderson on 7th day of May, 1852. Done at Monte Verdi my place of residence on the 27th day of April, A. D. 1854.

Julien Sidney Devereux (Seal)

The word "may" on the 5th page
interlined before execution.

The contents of the foregoing six pages were signed, sealed published and declared by Julien Sidney Devereux to be a codicil to and a part of his last will and testament in our presence who at his request and in his presence and in the presence of each other do subscribe our names as witnesses thereo.

M. H. Wadsworth
Wm Howerton
John W. McKnight

I will here remark by way of explanation that the exlusion of the name of Dr. P. T. Richardson from the list of executors etc. is not the result of any unkind or unfriendly feelings on my part or a want of confidence in his integrity, but from a conviction that his system and theory of family management etc. does not accord with my views and opinions.

Julien Sidney Devereux.

THE STATE OF TEXAS   ()
COUNTY OF RUSK   ()

BEFORE ME, the undersigned authority, this day personally appeared M. H. Wadsworth and William Howerton to me well known and after being duly sworn on oath says that they saw Julien Sidney Devereux sign the within and foregoing instrument of writing and declared the same to be a codicil to his last will and testament and they signed the same as witnesses at the request of the said Julien Sidney Devereux in his presence and in the presence of each other and that they believe the said Deverux at the time of signing the same was of sound mind and capable of making a will.

Sworn to and subscribed in open court, this the 26th day of May, A. D. 1856.

M. H. Wadsworth
Wm. Howerton
John C. Miller, Chief Justice.

BIBLIOGRAPHY

Manuscripts

Audited Military Claims, Republic of Texas. Archives, Texas State Library, Austin, Texas.

Confederate Muster Rolls. Archives, Texas State Library, Austin, Texas.

Devereux Family Bible. In private possession of Homer E. Davis, Hill City, Georgia.

Devereux Family Bible. In private possession of Willa Allene Robinson, Evergreen, Alabama.

Devereux Family Papers. Archives Collection, University of Texas Library, Austin, Texas.

Election Returns, 1855. Archives, Texas State Library, Austin, Texas.

Muster Rolls of the Veterans of Military Engagements Fought Before and During the Texas Revolution and During the Period of the Republic. Archives, Texas State Library, Austin, Texas.

Probate Records, Rusk County, Texas. County Clerk's Office, Henderson, Texas.

Record of the Devereux Family and Memoirs of John William Devereux. In private possession Colonel Homer Garrison, Jr., Austin, Texas.

Records of the General Land Office. Austin, Texas.

Records of the Post Office Department. Records of Appointments of Postmasters. The National Archives, Washington, D. C.

Richardson, Robert Bruce. Diary. In private possession of Miss Bess Richardson, Henderson, Texas.

Schedule 4, Production of Agriculture in 1850, Census of the United States. Archives, Texas State Library, Austin, Texas.

Starr, James Harper. Papers. Archives Collection, University of Texas Library, Austin, Texas.

Books

Abernethy, Thomas Perkins, **The Formative Period in Alabama, 1815-1828.** Montgomery (The Brown Printing Company), 1922.

Baird, Charles W., **History of the Huguenot Emigration to America.** New York (Dodd, Mead & Company), 1855. 2 vols.

Baird, Henry M., **History of the Rise of the Huguenots of France.** London (Hodder and Stoughton), 1880. 2 vols.

Baird, Henry M., **The Huguenots and the Revocation of the Edict of Nantes.** New York (Charles Scribner's Sons), 1895. 2 vols.

Barker, Eugene C. (ed.), **The Austin Papers.** Washington, D. C. (Annual Report of the American Historical Association for the Years 1919 and 1922), 1924, 1928; Austin (University of Texas Press), 1927. 3 vols.

Barker, Eugene C., **Life of Stephen F. Austin.** Nashville and Dallas (Cokesbury Press), 1926.

Barron, S. B., **The Lone Star Defenders.** New York and Washington (The Neale Publishing Company), 1908.

Bassett, John Spencer (ed.), **Correspondence of Andrew Jackson.** Washington, D. C. (Carnegie Institution of Washington), 1926-1936. 7 vols.

Betts, Edward Chambers, **Early History of Huntsville, Alabama, 1804 to 1870.** Montgomery (The Brown Printing Company), 1916.

Blair, E. L., **Early History of Grimes County.** Austin (n.p.), [c1930].

Brantley, William H., **Three Capitals: A Book About the First Three Capitals of Alabama, St. Stephens, Huntsville, & Cahawba.** Boston (The Merrymount Press), 1947.

Brewer, W., **Alabama: Her History, Resources, War Record and Public Men.** Montgomery (Barrett & Brown), 1872.

[154]

Brock, R. A., Documents, Chiefly Unpublished, Relating to the Huguenot Emigration to Virginia. Richmond (Virginia Historical Society), 1886.

Calendar of Virginia State Papers and Other Manuscripts . . . Preserved in the Capitol at Richmond. Richmond (James E. Goode, Printer), 1875-1893. 11 vols.

Carter, Clarence Edwin (comp. and ed.), The Territorial Papers of the United States. Vol. XVIII, The Territory of Alabama, 1817-1819. Washington (Government Printing Office), 1952. 25 vols.

Carter, Clarence Edwin (comp. and ed.), The Territorial Papers of the United States. Vol. VI, The Territory of Mississippi, 1809-1817. Washington (Government Printing Office), 1938. 25 vols.

Cates, Cliff D., Pioneer History of Wise County. Decatur (Wise County Old Settlers' Association), 1907.

A Century of Population Growth From the First Census of the United States to the Twelfth, 1790-1900. Washington (Government Printing Office), 1909.

The Choir Invisible: An Early History of Montgomery. Montgomery (Montgomery Historical Society), 19('?).

Cook, Anna Maria Green, History of Baldwin County, Georgia. Anderson, South Carolina (Keys-Hearn Printing Company), 1925.

Coulter, E. Merton, Confederate States of America, 1861-1865. Baton Rouge (Louisiana State University Press), 1950.

Daniell, L. E., Personnel of the Texas State Government. Austin (Press of the City Printing Company), 1900.

De Ryee, Wm., and R. E. Moore, The Texas Album, of the Eighth Legislature, 1860. Austin (Minor, Lambert & Perry), 1860.

Diccionario de la Lengua Espanola. Madrid (Real Academia Espanola), 1956.

Du Pont, Henry A., The Story of the Huguenots. Cambridge (The Riverside Press), 1920.

Eaton, Clement, A History of the Old South. New York (Macmillan Company), 1949.

Eckenrode, H. J., The Revolution in Virginia. Boston and New York (Houghton Mifflin Company), 1916.

The Encyclopedia Americana. New York, Chicago, and Washington, D. C. (Americana Corp.), 1957. 30 vols.

Fosdick, Lucian J., The French Blood in America. New York and Chicago (F. H. Revell Company), [c1906].

Gaines, Francis Pendleton, The Southern Plantation, A Study in the Development and the Accuracy of a Tradition. New York (Columbia University Press), 1924.

Gammel, H. P. N., (comp.), Laws of Texas, 1822-1897. Austin (The Gammel Book Company), 1898. 10 vols.

Garrett, William, Reminiscences of Public Men in Alabama. Atlanta (Plantation Publishing Company's Press), 1872.

Giles, Bascom, Abstract of all Original Texas Land Titles Comprising Grants and Locations to August 31, 1941. Austin (General Land Office), 1941. 8 vols.

Gulick, Charles Adams, Jr., and others (eds.), The Papers of Mirabeau Buonaparte Lamar. Austin (A. C. Baldwin and Sons), 1921-1928. 6 vols.

Hamilton, Peter J., Colonial Mobile; An Historical Study. Boston and New York (Houghton Mifflin Company), 1910.

Hodge, F. W., Handbook of American Indians North of Mexico. Washington (Government Printing Office), 1912. 2 vols.

Hollon, W. Eugene, and Ruth Lapham Butler (eds.), William Bollaert's Texas. Norman (University of Oklahoma Press), 1956.

Houghton, Louise Seymour, Handbook of French and Belgian Protestantism. New York (Missionary Education Movement), 1919.

Jones, Charles C., Jr., Biographical Sketches of the Delegates from Georgia to the Continental Congress. Boston and New York (Houghton, Mifflin and Company), 1891.

Journal of the House of Representatives of the State of Texas, Sixth Legislature. Austin (Marshall & Oldham), 1855.

Kane, Harnett T., **Plantation Parade, The Grand Manner in Louisiana.** New York (William Morrow and Company), 1945.

Knight, Lucian Lamar, **Georgia's Landmarks, Memorials and Legends.** Atlanta ('Byrd Printing Company), 1913. 2 vols.

Members of the Legislature of the State of Texas from 1846 to 1939. Austin (n.p.), 1939.

Moore, Albert Burton, **History of Alabama.** University, Alabama (University Supply Store), 1934.

Official Journal of the House of Representatives of the State of Texas at the Adjourned Session, Sixth Legislature. Austin (Marshall & Oldham), 1856.

Paddock, B. B., **A Twentieth Century and Biographical Record of North and West Texas.** Chicago and New York (Lewis Publishing Company), 1906. 2 vols.

Paschal, George W., **Reports of Cases Argued and Decided in the Supreme Court of the State of Texas, during the Conclusion of the Tyler Session, 1860, and the Whole of the Austin Session, 1860.** St. Louis (The Gilbert Book Company), 1882.

Phillips, Ulrich Bonnell, **Life and Labor in the Old South.** Boston (Little, Brown and Company), 1929.

Population of the United States in 1860. Washington (Government Printing Office), 1864.

Ray, Worth S., **Austin Colony Pioneers, Including History of Bastrop, Fayette, Grimes, Montgomery and Washington Counties, Texas and Their Earliest Settlers.** Austin (Privately printed), 1949.

Reynolds, J. A., **Heraldry and You: Modern Heraldic Usage in America.** New York (Thomas Nelson & Sons), 1961.

Riley, B. F., **History of Conecuh County, Alabama.** Columbus, Georgia (Thos. Gilbert), 1881.

Seventh Census of the United States: 1850. Washington (Robert Armstrong, Public Printer), 1853.

Smiles, Samuel, **The Huguenots: Their Settlements, Churches, and Industries, in England and Ireland.** London (John Murray), 1889.

Ward, A. W., G. W. Prothers, and Stanley Leathes (eds.), **The Cambridge Modern History.** Cambridge, England (The University Press), 1902-1912. 13 vols. and atlas.

Watkins, Myrtis, and Pax Watkins, **In Old Rusk County: Being a Sketch of Some of the Early Houses and Pioneer Families.** Henderson (Multigraph), 1940.

Webb, W. P., and H. Bailey Carroll (eds.), **Handbook of Texas.** Austin (Texas State Historical Association), 1952. 2 vols.

White, George, **Historical Recollections of Georgia.** New York (Pudney & Russell, Publishers), 1855.

Winfrey, Dorman H., **A History of Rusk County, Texas.** Waco (Texian Press), 1961.

Yust, Walter (ed.), **Encyclopaedia Britannica.** Chicago, London, Toronto (Encyclopaedia Britannica, Inc.), 1951, 24 vols.

Articles

"Alabama Census Returns, 1820, and An Abstract of Federal Census of Alabama, 1830," **Alabama Historical Quarterly.** Montgomery (Alabama State Department of Archives and History), Vol. VI, Number 3, 1944.

Bonner, James C., "The Georgia Wine Industry on the Eve of the Civil War," **The Georgia Historical Quarterly,** Athens (Georgia Historical Society), Vol. XLI, Number 1, 1957.

Odom, E. Dale, "The Vicksburg, 'Shreveport and Texas: The Fortunes of a Scalawag Railroad," **Southwestern Social Science Quarterly.** Austin (Southwestern Social Science Association and the University of Texas Press), Vol. XLIV, Number 3, 1963.

Redd, John, "Reminiscences of Western Virginia," **Virginia Magazine of History and Biography.** Richmond (Virginia Historical Society), Vol. VI, Number 4, 1899.

"Register of Gubernatorial Appointments Civil and Military Territory of Alabama, February 9, 1818—November 14, 1819," **Alabama Historical Quarterly.** Montgomery (State Department of Archives and History), Vol. VI, Number 2, 1944.

"Virginia State Troops in the Revolution," **Virginia Magazine of History and Geography.** Richmond (Virginia Historical Society), Vol. XXXI, Number 4, 1923.

Weeks, O. Douglas ('ed.), "My Journal of One of My Trips to New York, by John William Devereux of Milledgeville, Georgia," **Georgia Historical Quarterly.** Athens (Georgia Historical Society), Vol. XV, Number 1, 1931.

White, William W., "The Texas Slave Insurrection of 1860," **Southwestern Historical Quarterly.** Austin (Texas State Historical Association), Vol. LII, Number 3, 1949.

Letters

Brannon, Peter A., to D. W., April 27, 1950; May 25, 1956; April 27, 1961; May 9, 1961.

Brantley, W. H. Jr., to D. W., May 5, 1961.

Bryan, Mary Givens, to D. W., May 28, 1956; April 30, 1961.

Buckner, Archie, to D. W., July 28, 1961.

County Clerk, Montgomery County, Texas, to D. W., April 18, 1961; May 6, 1961.

Davis, Homer E., Hill City, Georgia, to D. W., February 22, 1953.

Delalande, Jean, to D. W., November 12, 1958; November 19, 1958.

Department of the Army, Washington, D. C., to D. W., March 22, 1950.

Gandrud, Pauline Jones, to D. W., June 29, 1956.

Hawes, Lilla M., to D. W., September 7, 1956.

Lowry, Mrs. Emmett, to D. W., July 7, 1961.

Owen, Bessie, to D. W., September 2, 1957; February 16, 1959.

Robinson, Willa Allene, Evergreen, Alabama, to D. W., May 15, 1950.

Microfilms and Typescripts

Curlee, Abigail, A Study of Texas Slave Plantations, 1822 to 1865, Ph.D. Dissertation, University of Texas, Austin, Texas, 1932.

Eighth United States Census (1860), Population Schedule (Microfilm), University of Texas Library, Austin, Texas.

Georgia Military Record Book, 1779-1839, W.P.A. Project No. 5993 (1941). Georgia Department of Archives and History, Atlanta, Georgia.

Martin, W. N., A History of Montgomery, M. A. Thesis, Sam Houston State College, Huntsville, Texas, 1950.

Seventh United States Census (1850), Population Schedule (Microfilm), University of Texas Library, Austin, Texas.

Newspapers

Alabama Journal (Montgomery), January 12, 1827.

Dallas Morning News, April 21, 1935.

Evening Picayune (New Orleans), August 20, 1860.

Galveston News, August 16, 1860.

Galveston Tri-Weekly News, June 30, 1865; July 5, 1865.

Henderson Democrat, May 3, 1856.

Henderson Times, April 28, 1863.

Houston Telegraph and Texas Register, May 21, 1845.

State Gazette (Austin), September 1, 1860; September 15, 1860.

Weekly Delta (New Orleans), June 2, 1860.

INDEX

— A —

— B —

— C —

— D —

Devereux, Julien Sidney (son of Julien Sidney Devereux), 96, 118, 119, 125, 127, 128, 136, 137, 143, 146, 147, 151
Devereux, Louisiana, 13, 15; see also Mrs. Louisiana Holcombe
Devereux, Mary Emily (daughter of Julien Sidney and Adaline Rebeccah Bradley Devereux), 20
Devereux, Morgan, 6
Devereux, Nancy, 7
Devereux, Samuel McDowell, 7, 9, 15, 15n
Devereux, Sarah Ann, 50, 54, 76, 85, 91n, 99, 100, 111, 113, 115, 118, 119, 120, 125, 126, 127, 128, 129, 130, 133, 134, 135, 136, 137, 142, 143, 144, 147
Devereux, William Penn (son of Julien Sidney Devereux), 1n, 96, 125, 128, 135, 137, 152
Devereux, Mrs. William Penn (Mary Perkins), 1n
Devereux, Georgia, 15n
Devereux Cathedral, 3n
Dikeman, Cyrus, 37
Dickson, D. C., 108
Dodson, Elijah, 85, 87, 145
Donley, Stockton P., 96
Dougherty, Robert, 29, 35
Dougherty, William, 35
Douglas, Jennie Miller, 137
Doyel, Winchester, 58
Du Pont, H. A., 4
Duval, John C., 2

— E —

Early, Peter, 14
Eastern Texas Railroad, 101
Ector, Mathew Duncan, 94, 95, 107, 108, 110, 112, 113, 116, 120, 122, 123, 133
Edict of Nantes, 3, 4, 5
Eliza Henry Maria (slave), 73

— F —

Federal Road, 17
Few, Elizabeth (Mrs. John William Devereux), 12, 13
Few, Ignatius, 12
Few, Mary, 12
Few, William, 13
Field, D. W., 75
Field, Maxwell W., 43, 50, 52, 69
Flanagan, James Winwright, 94, 95, 98, 108
Flora (slave), 73
Fontaine, Edward, 119
Forest Hill Academy, 97, 100
Fosdick, Lucian J., 4
Fouche, Jonas, 11
Fowler, William, 58
Freeling, W. W., 87

— G —

Gage, David, 94, 95, 97
Galloway, A. P., 87, 152
Galveston, Houston, and Henderson Railroad Company, 101
Galveston, Texas, 35
Garrison, Caleb Jackson, 111, 120, 125, 133, 134, 135, 136
Garrison, Homer, Jr., 1n
Garrison, James Freeborn, 135
Gassiot, F., 41, 42
General Rusk (Steamboat), 101
Goffe, Henry, 49
Gonzales, Romona, league of land, 65
Gourdneck, Texas, 58, 100
Graham, Dr._____, 133
Graham, A. B., 122
Graham, John, 57
Graham, M. D., 122, 123
Granger, Gordon, 135
Green, Miles, 14
Greene, Nathanael, 11
Grigg, Jesse, 13
Grigg, Sally (Mrs. John William Devereux), 13
Grigsby, John P., 148

— H —

Hancock County, Georgia, 13
Haralson, K. L., 109
Harcourt, Mrs. M. A., 91n, 127, 136
Harmony Hill, Texas, 57
Heard, A. C., 52, 53, 59, 70, 73
Henderson, James Pinckney, 57
Henderson, J. R. C., 100
Henderson, Texas, 57, 130
Henderson Democrat, 120
Henderson and Burkeville Railroad 101
Henry, Levice, 62
Henry, Maria (slave), 75
Henry, W. D., 62
Herbert, John, 18
Hines, James R., 32

— N —

Neil, Ray (slave?), 108
Nelson, H. F., 119
New Salem, Texas, 57, 91

Nichols, Ebenezer B., 43
Norton, Judge_____, 85

— O —

Ochiltree, William Beck, 58, 112

Oconee War, 10, 11

— P —

Panic of 1837, 29, 33
Parker, Isaac, 112
Parsons, J. H., 107, 108, 112, 120,
122, 123
Patton, Robert S., 101
Pease, Elisha M., 108, 119

Perkins, Mary, 137
Peyton, Joseph, 89
Pinehill, Texas, 57
Pitner, Thomas R., 122, 123, 148
Poinsett, Joel R., 28
Polk, James K., 49

— R —

Ragsdale, Paul, 23n
Rains, Doctor_____, 88
Ramón, José Domingo, grant of
land, 56
Ramsey, _____ (overseer), 71
Rankin, William M., 37
Reagan, John H., 95
Reagan, William, 73
Redwine, H. D. E., 95
Reed, James B., 60
Renfro, J. B., 73
Rice, William M., 43
Richardson, Peterson T., 75, 87,
146, 147, 149, 151, 153

Richardson, Robert Bruce, 135
Richelieu, Cardinal Armand de, 4
Roberts, Oran M., 94, 95
Robinson, Sr., Julius Gurdon, 30n
Robinson, Willa Allene, 7n, 20n,
30n
Rody (slave), 33
Rosedown, plantation home, 127
Rosencrans, William S., 133
Ross, William M., 147
Runnels, Hardin R., 108
Rusk County, Texas, 56-57, 68, 129
Rusk, Thomas J., 57, 95, 102, 110,
112

— S —

Sabine Navigation Company, 101
Sabine River, 56, 57, 100
Sam (slave), 73
Sanders, L. D., 129
San Jacinto River, 37
Scott (slave), 53 64, 72, 126
Scott, Andrew G., 33, 34, 41, 96, 97
Scott, Antoinette, 33, 33n; see also
Antoinette Devereux
Shackelford, Jr., J., 42, 43
Shortridge, G. D., 28
Shoulder Bone Creek, 10, 11
Silsby, A., 89

Simms, Bartlett, 89
Sinclair, J. J., 137
Smith, Ashbel, 108
Smith, James, 57, 94
Smith, Robert W., 50, 94, 101, 145
Sparta, Georgia, 13
Spinks, J. C., 108
Stamps, Elizabeth A., 137
Starr, James Harper, 83, 95, 147
Stedman, William, 94, 95, 107, 108,
112, 116, 123, 127
Sterne, Adolphus, 83, 95
Stoneum, _____, 53
Stroud, Mark, 70

— T —

Tabby (slave), 64, 72, 126
Tatum, Albert, 57
Taylor, William S., 72
Terrebonne Plantation, 32, 36, 37
Texas Historical Survey Commit-
tee, 140
Thomas, Jett, 15
Thompson, B. F., 78, 94n

Thompson, Wildridge C., 28
Throckmorton, James W., 108
Tolbert, Elijah, 104
Turnball, Daniel, 127
Turner, Larkin, 96
Tutt, Richard B., 57
Tyler, John, 49

— V —

Vaught, James B., 102
Vicksburg, Shreveport and Texas
Railroad, 101
Vinzent, Charles, 62, 75, 84, 85, 86

— W —

Wadsworth, M. H., 153
Walling's Ferry, 101
Watkins, John M., 89
Way, Mrs. Barbara Scott, 41, 41n,
    96, 97
Weeks, Mrs. Oliver Douglas
    (Julien Devereux), 1n

Weeks, Professor Oliver Douglas,
    1n
Wheelis, W. R., 27
Winfield, E. H., 32
Woods, Nancy ('Mrs. Charles
    Devereux), 7
Wornell, Mrs. _____, 75
Wright, James, 9